Machine Learning for Emotion Analysis in Python

Build AI-powered tools for analyzing emotion using natural language processing and machine learning

Allan Ramsay

Tariq Ahmad

BIRMINGHAM—MUMBAI

Machine Learning for Emotion Analysis in Python

Group Product Manager: Gebin George

Publishing Product Manager: Dinesh Chaudhary, Tejashwini R

Book Project Manager: Kirti Pisat

Content Development Editor: Manikandan Kurup

Technical Editor: Rahul Limbachiya

Copy Editor: Safis Editing

Proofreader: Safis Editing

Indexer: Tejal Daruwale Soni

Production Designer: Prafulla Nikalje

DevRel Marketing Coordinator: Vinishka Kalra

First published: September 2023

Production reference: 1310823

Published by Packt Publishing Ltd.
Grosvenor House
11 St Paul's Square
Birmingham
B3 1RB

ISBN 978-1-80324-068-8

www.packtpub.com

Less than a decade ago, I was a software developer immersed in code, seeking an intellectual challenge. Little did I know that I would soon embark on a journey leading me down a path of exploration, growth, and self-discovery. And now, barely a blink of an eye later, here I am writing the Dedication section of my first book.

– Tariq Ahmad

Contributors

About the authors

Allan Ramsay is an emeritus professor of formal linguistics in the School of Computer Science at the University of Manchester, having previously been a professor of artificial intelligence at University College Dublin. He has published over 140 books and research articles on all aspects of natural language processing, from using deep neural nets for identifying accents in spoken Arabic to using higher-order theorem proving to reason about people's intentions when they make jokes and use sarcasm. Much of his research has come from problems posed by Ph.D. students – it is easy to carry out research in areas you are familiar with, but taking on ideas suggested by Ph.D. students broadens your view of the discipline and enriches your understanding of areas you thought you understood.

I am grateful to Tariq Ahmad for suggesting that emotion mining might be an interesting area to investigate. This book is the result of our collaboration in this area!

Tariq Ahmad has been working in the IT industry since 1994. He specializes in .NET and Python and has worked for KPMG and Sybase. He lives in England and currently works for a leading consulting company, helping clients understand and harness the power of NLP by combining his knowledge of NLP algorithms, techniques, and tools with his strong consulting skills to guide clients through the complex landscape of NLP. Prior to this, Tariq was a senior developer for a company that specialized in providing software solutions and services to the public sector.

First and foremost, I am eternally grateful to the Almighty. Thanks also to Professor Ramsay, Packt, my family, friends, and mentors, and all the people who, in one way or another, contributed to the completion of this work.

About the reviewers

Muhammed Sahal is a doctor of pharmacy by education, has been active in the open source realm, and currently serves as a lead machine learning engineer for the community. He has worked on various use cases in healthcare. He is also an incoming candidate for data science at IIT Madras and he believes this will improve the impact he can make.

Anna Astori holds a master's degree in computational linguistics and artificial intelligence from Brandeis University. Over the years, Anna has worked on multiple large-scale machine learning and data science applications for companies such as Amazon and Decathlon. Anna is an AWS Certified Developer and solutions architect. She speaks at conferences and on podcasts, reviews talk proposals for tech conferences, and writes about Python and machine learning for curated publications on Medium. She is currently a co-director of the Women Who Code Boston network.

Sumanas Sarma is the Head of AI at Captur, a Computer Vision AI company. With a foundational 15-year journey in the tech industry, he initially focused on safety-critical systems as a software engineer. This experience was pivotal as he ventured into fintech, grappling with its unique challenges. Seeking a deeper expertise in machine learning, Sumanas pursued an MSc at Queen Mary University of London. Over the past eight years, he has immersed himself in diverse ML domains. He customised large language models (LLMs) for enterprise use in the NLP space, and in Retail AI, he developed models for dynamic pricing, price elasticity, and product recommendations. Today, he steers cutting-edge projects in his pivotal role at Captur.

Table of Contents

3

Labeling Data   75

4

Preprocessing – Stemming, Tagging, and Parsing   99

Part 3: Approaches

Part 4: Case Study

11

Preface

In the modern era, where digital communication has become an integral part of our lives, understanding and analyzing emotions expressed through text has gained tremendous importance. From social media platforms and customer feedback to chatbots and virtual assistants, the ability to decipher emotions from written language has become a valuable skill.

This book is your gateway to exploring this fascinating field, equipping you with the essential knowledge and practical skills to harness the power of Python to unravel the intricate tapestry of human emotions. Whether you are a data scientist, a developer, a researcher, or simply someone intrigued by the intersection of language and emotion, this book will serve as your comprehensive guide.

Throughout the book, we will uncover the underlying theories and techniques behind emotion. At the heart of our exploration lies Python, a versatile and powerful programming language widely used for data analysis and **natural language processing (NLP)**.

In this book, we will gradually build our understanding, starting with the basics of NLP and emotion representation. We will then explore various techniques for feature extraction, sentiment analysis, and emotion classification. You will learn how to preprocess text data, train machine learning models, and evaluate their performance in the context of emotion analysis. Additionally, we will delve into more advanced topics such as handling multi-label data and exploring deep learning approaches, and we will look at a case study involving tweets collected over an extended period, showing how they correlate with real-world events. We will also investigate how robustly models trained on one dataset behave when applied to another.

However, this book is not solely focused on theoretical concepts. There are practical examples aplenty to reinforce your understanding and enable you to apply what you've learned. Python code snippets and real-world datasets will guide you through the implementation of emotion analysis systems from scratch, empowering you to develop your own innovative solutions.

By the end of this book, you will possess a solid foundation in emotion analysis and the ability to leverage Python's extensive ecosystem to build sophisticated emotion-aware applications. You will be able to navigate the nuances of emotions expressed in text, unravel the hidden sentiment behind reviews and comments, and develop insightful solutions.

Whether you are intrigued by the potential of emotion analysis in customer feedback analysis, social media monitoring, or virtual assistant technologies, this book will equip you with the knowledge and skills to unlock the rich world of emotions through Python.

Who this book is for

This book is designed for individuals with a passion for exploring the intersection of language, emotions, and technology. Whether you are a data scientist, a Python developer, a researcher, or a curious enthusiast, this book will cater to your interests and provide you with the necessary knowledge and skills to dive into emotion analysis.

Even if you don't have a data science or programming background, but are simply intrigued by the intricacies of emotions and language, this book will provide you with a comprehensive foundation and practical guidance to explore and apply emotion analysis techniques effectively.

What this book covers

Chapter 1, Foundations, provides an introduction to sentiment and emotion and discusses why they are important. It also provides an introduction to both NLP and machine learning.

Chapter 2, Building and Using a Dataset, provides an overview of datasets. It starts with ready-made data sources and then shows how you can create your own data. The next sections list some of the other free datasets available, describe how datasets can be transformed to fit your task, and demonstrate how even non-English datasets can be used. Finally, this chapter covers evaluation techniques.

Chapter 3, Labeling Data, provides an overview of labeling: why it is important, best practices, and how to label. This chapter will also explain gold tweets, how to assess the suitability of annotators, how to build an annotation system, and whether it is better to buy an annotation tool. Finally, it discusses the results, how to measure their reliability, and why it is a good idea to debrief your annotators at the end of the task.

Chapter 4, Preprocessing – Stemming, Tagging, and Parsing, provides an overview of the tools that are most likely to be useful for sentiment mining and looks at tokenizing, tagging, and parsing.

Chapter 5, Sentiment Lexicons and Vector Space Models, provides an overview of the datasets and metrics that we will be using as we develop the various algorithms in the following chapters. It also considers very simple classifiers based purely on sentiment lexicons. Finally, it looks at ways of calculating how strongly individual words express a sentiment, thus providing a baseline for looking at the performance of more sophisticated algorithms in the later chapters.

Chapter 6, Naïve Bayes, provides an overview of how to prepare datasets for the Python `sklearn` package. It then gives a brief introduction to the Naïve Bayes approach and shows how to implement it. Finally, it considers why the algorithm behaves as it does and what we can do to improve its performance.

Chapter 7, Support Vector Machines, provides an introduction to support vector machines and their use for classification. It also introduces some ways of refining the approach to work with multi-class datasets, and finally, reflects on the results obtained.

Chapter 8, Neural Networks and Deep Neural Networks, provides an overview of single-layer neural nets and their use as classifiers and the extension of this to multi-layer neural nets and their use as classifiers.

Chapter 9, Exploring Transformers, provides an introduction to transformers and also explains the core components. It also covers Hugging Face and existing models, and finally, shows how to use Python to build transformer-based models.

Chapter 10, Multiclassifiers, provides an overview of using confusion matrices to analyze the behavior of classifiers on complex data and how to use neutral as a label to deal with tweets that have no label assigned to them. Finally, it discusses varying thresholds to handle multi-label datasets, and training multiple classifiers to handle multi-label datasets.

Chapter 11, Case Study – The Qatar Blockade, provides a discussion of what happens when one of our classifiers is applied in a real-life situation to real data that has not been carefully curated, that we don't have a Gold Standard for, and that was not the data we trained the classifier on. Finally, it compares the output of a classifier on data collected over an extended period with events in an ongoing news story to see whether changes in the pattern of emotions can be linked to developments in the story and whether it is possible to detect long term changes in public attitudes as well as immediate responses to key events.

To get the most out of this book

To fully benefit from this book, it is recommended that you have a basic understanding of Python programming. A background in NLP or machine learning is not required, as this book covers the fundamental concepts and techniques from scratch. We will gradually introduce and explain NLP and machine learning concepts relevant to emotion analysis, ensuring that readers with diverse backgrounds can follow along and grasp the material. You will need to have the `scipy` and `sklearn` libraries installed, along with the Hugging Face `transformers` and `datasets` packages, `pandas`, `numpy`, and the `google.colab` library for *Chapter 9, Exploring Transformers*.

Software/Hardware used in the book	OS requirements
Python	Windows, macOS X, and Linux (any)
Hugging Face `transformers` and `datasets` packages, `pandas`, and `numpy`	
Google Colab library	
The `sklearn` packages for Naive Bayes, support vector machines, and deep neural nets	

If you are using the digital version of this book, we advise you to type the code yourself or access the code from the book's GitHub repository (a link is available in the next section). Doing so will help you avoid any potential errors related to the copying and pasting of code.

Download the example code files

You can download the example code files for this book from GitHub at `https://github.com/PacktPublishing/Machine-Learning-for-Emotion-Analysis`. If there's an update to the code, it will be updated in the GitHub repository.

We also have other code bundles from our rich catalog of books and videos available at `https://github.com/PacktPublishing/`. Check them out!

> **Important Note**
>
> We make use of a number of datasets for training and evaluating models: some of these allow unrestricted use, but some have conditions or licenses that say you may only use them for non-commercial purposes. The code in the GitHub repository describes where you can obtain these datasets; you must agree to the conditions that are specified for each dataset before downloading and using it with our code examples. We are particularly grateful to Saif Mohammed for permission to use the datasets from the SEMEVAL-2017 and SEMEVAL-2018 competitions for these purposes. If you want to use any of these datasets, please acknowledge the providers, and if you use any of the SEMEVAL data, then please cite the following:
>
> Mohammad, S. M., & Bravo-Marquez, F. (2017). WASSA-2017 Shared Task on Emotion Intensity. *Proceedings of the Workshop on Computational Approaches to Subjectivity, Sentiment and Social Media Analysis (WASSA).*
>
> Mohammad, S. M., Bravo-Marquez, F., Salameh, M., & Kiritchenko, S. (2018). SemEval-2018 Task 1: Affect in Tweets. *Proceedings of International Workshop on Semantic Evaluation (SemEval-2018).*

Conventions used

There are a number of text conventions used throughout this book.

`Code in text`: Indicates code words in text, database table names, folder names, filenames, file extensions, pathnames, dummy URLs, user input, and Twitter handles. Here is an example: "`feedparser` is a Python library that works with feeds in all known formats."

A block of code is set as follows:

```
import pandas as pd

data_file_path = "EI-reg-En-anger-train.txt"
df = pd.read_csv(data_file_path, sep='\t')
```

```
# drop rows where the emotion is not strong
df[df['Intensity Score'] <= 0.2]
```

Any command-line input or output is written as follows:

```
pip install feedparser
```

Bold: Indicates a new term, an important word, or words that you see onscreen. For instance, words in menus or dialog boxes appear in **bold**. Here is an example: "Give your app a name, and make a note of the **API Key**, **API Key Secret**, and **Bearer Token** values."

Tips or important notes
Appear like this.

Get in touch

Feedback from our readers is always welcome.

General feedback: If you have questions about any aspect of this book, email us at customercare@ packtpub.com and mention the book title in the subject of your message.

Errata: Although we have taken every care to ensure the accuracy of our content, mistakes do happen. If you have found a mistake in this book, we would be grateful if you would report this to us. Please visit www.packtpub.com/support/errata and fill in the form.

Piracy: If you come across any illegal copies of our works in any form on the internet, we would be grateful if you would provide us with the location address or website name. Please contact us at copyright@packtpub.com with a link to the material.

If you are interested in becoming an author: If there is a topic that you have expertise in and you are interested in either writing or contributing to a book, please visit authors.packtpub.com.

Share Your Thoughts

Once you've read *Machine Learning for Emotion Analysis in Python*, we'd love to hear your thoughts! Scan the QR code below to go straight to the Amazon review page for this book and share your feedback.

https://packt.link/r/1-803-24068-7

Your review is important to us and the tech community and will help us make sure we're delivering excellent quality content.

Download a free PDF copy of this book

Thanks for purchasing this book!

Do you like to read on the go but are unable to carry your print books everywhere?

Is your eBook purchase not compatible with the device of your choice?

Don't worry, now with every Packt book you get a DRM-free PDF version of that book at no cost.

Read anywhere, any place, on any device. Search, copy, and paste code from your favorite technical books directly into your application.

The perks don't stop there, you can get exclusive access to discounts, newsletters, and great free content in your inbox daily

Follow these simple steps to get the benefits:

1. Scan the QR code or visit the link below

https://packt.link/free-ebook/9781803240688

2. Submit your proof of purchase
3. That's it! We'll send your free PDF and other benefits to your email directly

Part 1: Essentials

The part introduces **natural language processing (NLP)**, **sentiment analysis (SA)**, and **emotion analysis (EA)**. You will learn about the basic concepts behind SA and EA, why and how they are different, and why EA is so challenging. There is also an introduction to some of the tools that will be used. This part will also look at other approaches to multi-emotion classification and discuss emotions from a psychological point of view. Finally, there will be a discussion on why EA is important, its benefits, and usages.

This part has the following chapter:

- *Chapter 1, Foundations*

1

Foundations

Emotions play a key role in our daily lives. Some people define them as the reactions that we as human beings experience as a response to events or situations, some describe them simply as a class of feelings, and others say they describe physiological states and are generated subconsciously. Psychologists describe emotions as "*a complex state of feeling that results in physical and psychological changes that influence thought and behavior.*" So, it appears that although we feel emotions, they are much harder to describe.

Our brains play a crucial role when creating and processing emotions. Historically, it was believed that each emotion was located in a specific part of the brain. However, research has shown that there is no single region of the brain that's responsible for processing emotions – several brain regions are activated when emotions are being processed. Furthermore, different parts of the brain can generate the same emotion and different parts can also contribute to generating an emotion.

The reality may even be that *emotion* and *sentiment* are experiences that result from combined influences of biological, cognitive, and social aspects. Whatever the case, emotions matter because they help us decide what actions to do, how to negotiate tricky situations, and, at a basic level, how to survive. Different emotions rule our everyday lives; for example, we make decisions based on whether we are happy, angry, or sad, and we choose our daily pastimes and routines based on the emotions they facilitate. So, emotions are important, and understanding them may make our lives easier.

In this chapter, you will learn about the main concepts and differences between sentiment analysis and emotion analysis, and also understand why emotion analysis is important in the modern world. By combining this with a basic introduction to **natural language processing (NLP)** and machine learning, we will lay the foundations for successfully using these techniques for emotion analysis.

In this chapter, we'll cover the following topics:

- Emotions
- Sentiment
- Why is emotion analysis important?

- Introduction to natural language processing
- Introduction to machine learning

Emotions

This book is about writing programs that can detect emotions expressed in texts, particularly informal texts. Emotions play a crucial role in our daily lives. They impact how we feel, how we think, and how we behave. Consequently, it stands to reason that they impact the decisions we make. If this is the case, then being able to detect emotions from written text (for example, social media posts) is a useful thing to do because the impact it would have on many practical everyday applications in sectors such as marketing, industry, health, and security would be huge.

However, while it is clear that we all experience emotions and that they play a significant role in our plans and actions, it is much less clear what they *are*. Given that we are about to embark on a detailed study of how to write programs to detect them, it is perhaps worth beginning by investigating the notion of what an emotion is and looking at the various theories that attempt to pin them down. This is a topic that has fascinated philosophers and psychologists from antiquity to the present day, and it is still far from settled. We will briefly look at a number of the most prominent theories and approaches. This overview will not lead us to a definitive view, but before we start trying to identify them in written texts, we should at least become aware of the problems that people still have in pinning them down.

Darwin believed that emotions allowed humans and animals to survive and reproduce. He argued that they evolved, were adaptive, and that all humans, and even other animals, expressed emotion through similar behaviors. He believed that emotions had an evolutionary history that could be traced across cultures and species. Today, psychologists agree that emotions such as fear, surprise, disgust, happiness, and sadness can be regarded as universal regardless of culture.

The James-Lange theory proposes that it is our physical responses that are responsible for emotions. For example, if someone jumps out at you from behind a bush, your heart rate will increase, and it is this increase that causes the individual to feel fear. The facial-feedback theory builds on this idea and suggests that physical activity is responsible for influencing emotion, for example, if you smile, likely, you will automatically feel happier than if you did not smile. However, Cannon-Bard's theory refutes James-Lange, instead suggesting that people experience emotional and physical responses simultaneously. The Schachter-Singer theory is a cognitive theory of emotion that suggests that it is our thoughts that are responsible for emotions, and similarly, cognitive appraisal theory suggests that thinking must come before experiencing an emotion. For instance, the brain might understand a situation as threatening, and hence fear is experienced.

To try to obtain a deeper understanding of emotions, let's look at the three main theories of emotion:

- **Physiological**: Psychologists have the view that emotions are formed when a bodily response is triggered by a stimulus, so as the individual experiences physiological changes, this is also experienced as an emotion

- **Neurological**: Biologists claim that hormones (for example, estrogen, progesterone, and testosterone) that are produced by the body's glands impact the chemistry and circuitry of the brain and these lead to emotional responses

- **Cognitive**: Cognitive scientists believe that thoughts and other mental activities play a crucial role in forming emotions

In all likelihood, all three theories are probably valid to some extent. It has also been postulated that instead of thinking of these as mutually exclusive, it is more likely that they are complementary and that each explains and accounts for a different aspect of what we think of as an emotion.

Although emotions have been studied for many decades, it is probably still true that we still do not fully understand emotions.

Humans can experience a huge number of emotions, but only a handful are considered basic. However, the number of emotions considered in emotion analysis research is not always limited to just these basic emotions. Furthermore, it is not straightforward to demarcate emotions, and hence boundaries are very rarely clearly defined.

We will now consider what are known as the *primary emotions*. These have been described as a reaction to an event or situation, or the immediate strong first reaction experienced when something happens. There has been much research on identifying these primary emotions, but there is still no general agreement, and different models have been suggested by eminent researchers such as Ekman, Plutchik, and Parrot. Some emotions such as anger, fear, joy, and surprise are universally agreed upon. However, the same is not true for other emotions, with disagreements on the emotions that constitute the basic emotions and the number of these emotions. Although there is, again, no consensus on which model is best at covering basic emotions, the models proposed by Ekman and Plutchik are most commonly used. There are two popular approaches: **categorical** and **dimensional**.

Categorical

Ekman is an advocate of the categorical theory, which suggests that emotions arise from separate neural systems. This approach also suggests that there are a limited number of primary, distinct emotions, such as anger, anxiety, joy, and sadness. Ekman suggested that primary emotions must have a distinct facial expression that is recognizable across all cultures. For example, the corners of the lips being turned down demonstrates sadness – and this facial expression is recognized universally as portraying sadness. Similarly, smiling with teeth exposed and the corners of the mouth pointing upwards is universally recognized as joy.

Amazingly, people blind from birth use the same facial expressions when expressing sadness and joy. They have never seen these facial expressions, so it is impossible that these expressions were learned. It is much more likely that these are an integral part of human nature. Using this understanding of distinct, universal facial expressions, Ekman proposed six primary emotions (Ekman, 1993):

- Anger
- Disgust
- Fear
- Joy
- Sadness
- Surprise

Ekman suggested that these *basic* emotions were biologically primitive and have evolved to increase the reproductive fitness of animals and that all other emotions were combinations of these eight primary emotions. Later, Eckman expanded this list to include other emotions that he considered basic, such as embarrassment, excitement, contempt, shame, pride, satisfaction, and amusement.

Another of the most influential works in the area of emotions is Plutchik's psychoevolutionary theory of emotion. Plutchik proposed eight primary emotions (Plutchik, 2001):

- Anger
- Anticipation
- Disgust
- Fear
- Joy
- Sadness
- Surprise
- Trust

From this theory, Plutchik developed a Wheel of Emotions (see *Figure 1.1*). This wheel was developed to help understand the nuances of emotion and how emotions contrast. It has eight sectors representing the eight emotions. Emotions intensify as they move from outside toward the center of the wheel. For example, annoyance increases to anger and then further increases to outright rage. Each sector of the circle has an opposite emotion that is placed directly opposite in the wheel. For example, the opposite of sadness is joy, and the opposite of anger is fear. It also shows how different emotions can be combined.

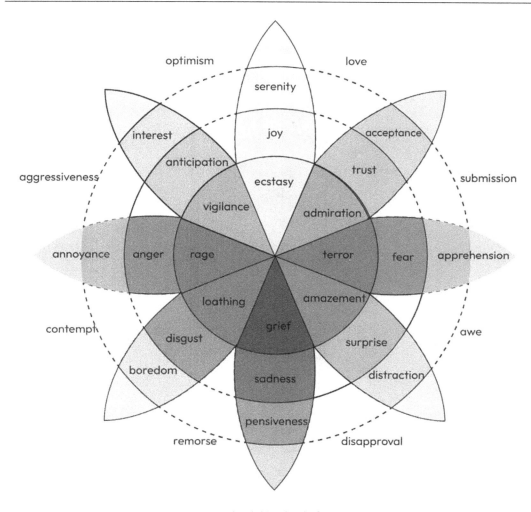

Figure 1.1 – Plutchik's Wheel of Emotions

Although Ekman and Plutchik's theories are the most common, there are other works, but there is little agreement on what the basic emotions are. However, in the area of emotion analysis research, Ekman and Plutchik's models are the most often used classification schemes.

Dimensional

The dimensional approach posits that to understand emotional experiences, the fundamental dimensions of valence (the *goodness* and *badness* of the emotion) and arousal (the *intensity* of the emotion) are vital. This approach suggests that a common and interconnected neurophysiological system is responsible for all affective states. Every emotion can then be defined in terms of these two measures, so the plane can be viewed as a continuous two-dimensional space, with dimensions of valence and arousal, and each point in the place corresponds to a separate emotion state.

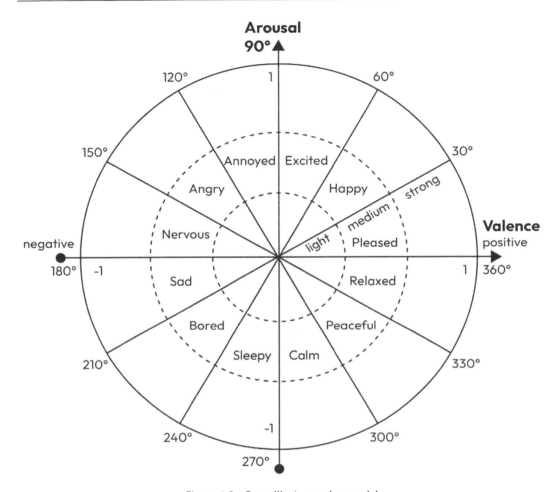

Figure 1.2 – Russell's circumplex model

The most common dimensional model is Russell's circumplex model ((Russell, 1980): see *Figure 1.2*). The model posits that emotions are made up of two core dimensions: valence and arousal. *Figure 1.2* shows that valence ranges from −1 (unpleasant) to 1 (pleasant), and arousal also ranges from −1 (calm) to 1 (excited). Each emotion is then a linear combination of these two dimensions. For example, anger is an unpleasant emotional state (a negative valence) with a high intensity (a positive arousal). Other basic emotions can be seen in *Figure 1.2* with their approximate positions in the two-dimensional space.

Some emotions have similar arousal and valence (for example, grief and rage). Hence, a third dimension (control) has also been suggested that can be used to distinguish between these. Control ranges from *no control* to *full control*. So, the entire range of human emotions can be represented as a set of points in the three-dimensional space using these three dimensions.

The dimensional model has a poorer resolution of emotions; that is, it is harder to distinguish between ambiguous emotions. The categorical model is simpler to understand, but some emotions are not part of the set of basic emotions.

Most emotion analysis research uses a categorical perspective; there seems to be a lack of research using the dimensional approach.

Sentiment

There is a second closely-related term known as **sentiment**. The terms sentiment and emotion seem to be used in an ad hoc manner, with different writers using them almost interchangeably. Given the difficulty we have found in working out what emotions are, and in deciding exactly how many emotions there are, having yet another ill-defined term is not exactly helpful. To try to clarify the situation, note that when people work on sentiment mining, they generally make use of a simple, limited system of classification using *positive*, *negative*, and *neutral* cases. This is a much simpler scheme to process and ascertain, and yields results that are also easier to understand. In some ways, emotion analysis may be regarded as an *upgrade* to sentiment analysis; a more complex solution that analyzes much more than the simple positive and negative markers and instead tries to determine specific emotions (anger, joy, sadness). This may be more useful but also involves much more effort, time, and cost. Emotion and sentiment are, thus, not the same. An emotion is a complex psychological state, whereas a sentiment is a mental attitude that is created through the very existence of the emotion.

For us, sentiment refers exclusively to an expressed opinion that is positive, negative, or neutral. There is some degree of overlap here because, for example, emotions such as joy and love could both be considered positive sentiments. It may be that the terms simply have different granularity – in the same way that ecstasy, joy, and contentment provide a fine-grained classification of a single generic emotion class that we might call happiness, happiness and love are a fine-grained classification of the general notion of feeling positive. Alternatively, it may be that sentiment is the name for one of the axes in the dimensional model – for example, the valence axis in Russell's analysis. Given the range of theories of emotion, it seems best to just avoid having another term for much the same thing. In this book, we will stick to the term emotion; we will take an entirely pragmatic approach by accepting some set of labels from an existing theory such as Plutchik's or Russell's as denoting emotions, without worrying too much about what it is that they denote. We can all agree that *I hate the people who did that and I wish they were all dead* expresses hate and anger, and that it is overall negative, even if we're not sure what hate and anger are or what the scale from negative to positive actually measures.

Now that we know a bit more about what emotion is and how it is categorized and understood, it is essential to understand why emotion analysis is an important topic.

Why emotion analysis is important

The amount of data generated daily from online sources such as social media and blogs is staggering. In 2019, Forbes estimated this to be around 2.5 quintillion bytes of data, though this figure is more than likely even higher now. Due to this, much research has focused on using this data for analysis and for gaining hitherto unknown insights (for example, predicting flu trends and disease outbreaks using Twitter (now known as "X") data).

Similarly, people are also increasingly expressing their opinions online – and many of these opinions are, explicitly or implicitly, highly emotional (for example, *I love summer*). Nowadays, social network platforms such as Facebook, LinkedIn, and Twitter are at the hub of everything we do. Twitter is one of the most popular social network platforms, with more than 300 million users using Twitter actively every month. Twitter is used by people from all walks of life; celebrities, movie stars, politicians, sports stars, and everyday people. Users post short messages, known as **tweets**, and, every day, millions share their opinions about themselves, news, sports, movies, and other topics. Consequently, this makes platforms such as Twitter rich sources of data for public opinion mining and sentiment analysis.

As we have seen, emotions play an important role in human intelligence, decision-making, social interaction, perception, memory, learning, creativity, and much much more.

Emotion analysis is the process of recognizing the emotions that are expressed through texts (for example, social media posts). It is a complex task because user-generated content, such as tweets, is typically understood as follows:

- Written in natural language
- Often unstructured, informal, and misspelled
- Can contain slang and made-up words
- Can contain emojis and emoticons where their usage does not always correspond to the reason for their original creation (for example, using the pizza emoji to express love)

Furthermore, it is also entirely possible to express emotion without using any obvious emotion markers.

One of the big unsolved problems in emotion analysis is detecting emotions such as anticipation, pessimism, and sarcasm. Consider the following tweet:

We lost again. Great.

We humans are fairly knowledgeable when it comes to drilling down to the true meaning implied, and would understand that the user was being sarcastic. We know that a team losing again is not a good thing. Hence, by making use of this understanding, we can easily identify the implied meaning.

The problem is that simply considering each word that has sentiment in isolation will not do a good job. Instead, further rules must be applied to understand the context of the word. These rules will help the analyzer differentiate between sentences that might contain similar words but have completely different meanings. However, even with these rules, analyzers will still make mistakes.

Social media is now viewed as a valuable resource, so organizations are showing an increased interest in social media monitoring to analyze massive, free-form, short, user-generated text from social media sites. Exploiting these allows organizations to gain insights into understanding their customer's opinions, concerns, and needs about their products and services.

Due to its real-time nature, governments are also interested in using social media to identify threats and monitor and analyze public responses to current events.

Emotion analysis has many interesting applications:

- **Marketing**: Lots of Twitter users follow brands (for example, Nike), so there are many marketing opportunities. Twitter can help spread awareness of a brand, generate leads, drive traffic to sites, build a customer base, and more. Some of the biggest marketing campaigns of previous years include `#ShareACoke` by Coca-Cola, `#WantAnR8` by Audi, and `#BeTheFastest` by Virgin Media.

- **Stock markets**: Academics have attempted to use Twitter to anticipate trends in financial markets. In 2013, the Associated Press Twitter account posted a (false) tweet stating that there had been explosions in the White House and that Obama was injured. The post was debunked very quickly but the stock markets still took a nosedive, resulting in hundreds of billions of dollars changing hands.

- **Social studies**: Millions of people regularly interact with the world by tweeting, providing invaluable insights into their feelings, actions, routines, emotions, and behavior. This vast amount of public communication can be used to generate forecasts of various types of events. For example, large-scale data analysis of social media has demonstrated that not only did Brexit supporters have a more powerful, emotional message, but they were also more effective in the use of social media. They routinely outmuscled their rivals and had more vocal and active supporters across nearly all social media platforms. This led to the activation of a greater number of Leave supporters and enabled them to dominate social media platforms – thus influencing many undecided voters.

Gaining an understanding of emotions is also important for organizations to gain insights into public opinion about their products and services. However, it is also important to automate this process so that decisions can be made and actions can be taken in real-time. For example, analysis techniques can automatically analyze and process thousands of reviews about a particular product and extract insights that show whether consumers are satisfied with the product or service. This can be sentiment or emotion, although emotion may be more useful due to it being more granular.

Research has shown that tweets posted by dissatisfied users are shared more often and spread faster and wider than other types of tweets. Therefore, organizations have to provide customer services beyond the old-fashioned agent at the end of the phone line. Due to this, many organizations today also provide social media-based customer support in an attempt to head-off bad reviews and give a good impression. Nowadays, there is so much consumer choice, and it is so much easier for customers to switch to competitors, that it is vitally important for organizations to retain and increase their customer base. Hence, the quicker an organization reacts to a bad post, the better chance they have of retaining the customer. Furthermore, there is no better advertising than word of mouth – such as that generated by happy customers. Emotion analysis is one way to quickly analyze hundreds of tweets, find the ones where customers are unhappy, and use this to drive other processes that attempt to resolve the problem before the customer becomes too unhappy and decides to take their business elsewhere. Emotion analysis not only requires data – it also generates a lot of data. This data can be further analyzed to determine, for example, what the top items on user wishlists are, or what the top user gripes are. These can then be used to drive the next iteration or version of the product or service.

Although sentiment analysis and emotion analysis are not mutually exclusive and can be used in conjunction, the consensus is that sentiment analysis is not adequate for classifying something as complex, multi-layered, and nuanced as emotion. Simply taking the whole range of emotions and considering them as only positive, negative, or neutral runs the considerable risk of missing out on deeper insights and understandings.

Emotion analysis also provides more in-depth insights. Understanding why someone ignored or liked a post needs more than just a sentiment score. Furthermore, gaining *actionable* insights also requires more than just a sentiment score.

Emotion analysis is a sub-field of NLP, so it makes sense to gain a better understanding of that next.

Introduction to NLP

Sentiment mining is about finding the sentiments that are expressed by natural language texts – often quite short texts such as tweets and online reviews, but also larger items such as newspaper articles. There are many other ways of getting computers to do useful things with natural language texts and spoken language: you can write programs that can have conversations (with people or with each other), you can write programs to extract facts and events from articles and stories, you can write programs to translate from one language to another, and so on. These applications all share some basic notions and techniques, but they each lay more emphasis on some topics and less on others. In *Chapter 4, Preprocessing – Stemming, Tagging, and Parsing*, we will look at the things that matter most for sentiment mining, but we will give a brief overview of the main principles of NLP here. As noted, not all of the stages outlined here are needed for every application, but it is nonetheless useful to have a picture of how everything fits together when considering specific subtasks later.

We will start with a couple of basic observations:

- Natural language is *linear*. The fundamental form of language is speech, which is necessarily linear. You make one sound, and then you make another, and then you make another. There may be some variation in the way you make each sound – louder or softer, with a higher pitch or a lower one, quicker or slower – and this may be used to overlay extra information on the basic message, but fundamentally, spoken language is made up of a *sequence* of identifiable units, namely sounds; and since written language is just a way of representing spoken language, it too must be made up of a sequence of identifiable units.

- Natural language is hierarchical. Smaller units are grouped into larger units, which are grouped into larger units, which are grouped into larger units, and so on. Consider the sentence smaller units are grouped into larger units. In the written form of English, for instance, the smallest units are characters; these are grouped into morphemes (meaning-bearing word-parts), as small er unit s are group ed into large er unit s, which are grouped into words (small-er unit-s are group-ed into large-er unit-s), which are grouped into base-level phrases ([small-er unit-s] [are group-ed] [into] [large-er unit-s]), which are grouped into higher-level phrases ([[small-er unit-s] [[are group-ed] [[into] [large-er unit-s]]]]]).

These two properties hold for all natural languages. All natural languages were spoken before they were written (some widely spoken languages have no universally accepted written form!), and hence are fundamentally linear. But they all express complex hierarchical relations, and hence to understand them, you have to be able to find the ways that smaller units are grouped into larger ones.

What the bottom-level units are like, and how they are grouped, differs from language to language. The sounds of a language are made by moving your articulators (tongue, teeth, lips, vocal cords, and various other things) around while trying to expel air from your lungs. The sound that you get by closing and then opening your lips with your vocal cords tensed (/b/, as in the English word *bat*) is different from the sound you get by doing the same things with your lips while your vocal cords are relaxed (/p/, as in *pat*). Different languages use different combinations – Arabic doesn't use /p/ and English doesn't use the sound you get by closing the exit from the chamber containing the vocal cords (a **glottal stop**): the combinations that are used in a particular language are called its **phonemes**. Speakers of a language that don't use a particular combination find it hard to distinguish words that use it from ones that use a very similar combination, and very hard to produce that combination when they learn a language that does.

To make matters worse, the relationship between the bottom-level units in spoken language and written language can vary from language to language. The phonemes of a language can be represented in the written form of that language in a wide variety of ways. The written form may make use of **graphemes**, which are combinations of ways of making a shape out of strokes and marks (so, A𝐴𝒜𝐀A𝓗are all written by producing two near-vertical more-or-less-straight lines joined at the top with a cross-piece about half-way up), just as phonemes are combinations of ways of making a sound; a single phoneme may be represented by one grapheme (the short vowel /a/ from *pat* is represented in English by the character *a*) or by a combination of graphemes (the sound /sh/ from *should* is represented by the pair of graphemes *s* and *h*); a sound may have no representation in the written form (Arabic text omits short vowels and some other distinctions between phonemes); or there may simply be no connection between the written form and the way it is pronounced (written Chinese, Japanese kanji symbols). Given that we are going to be largely looking at text, we can at least partly ignore the wide variety of ways that written and spoken language are related, but we will still have to be aware that different languages combine the basic elements of the written forms in completely different ways to make up words.

The bottom-level units of a language, then, are either identifiable sounds or identifiable marks. These are combined into groups that carry meaning – **morphemes**. A morpheme can carry quite a lot of meaning; for example, *cat* (made out of the graphemes *c*, *a*, and *t*) denotes a small mammal with pointy ears and an inscrutable outlook on life, whereas *s* just says that you've got more than one item of the kind you are thinking about, so *cats* denotes a group of several small mammals with pointy ears and an opaque view of the world. Morphemes of the first kind are sometimes called **lexemes**, with a single lexeme combining with one or more other morphemes to express a concept (so, the French lexeme *noir* (*black*) might combine with *e* (feminine) and *s* (plural) to make *noires* – several black female things). Morphemes that add information to a lexeme, such as about how many things were involved or when an event happened, are called **inflectional** morphemes, whereas ones that radically change their meaning (for example an *incomplete* solution to a problem is *not* complete) are called **derivational** morphemes, since they derive a new concept from the original. Again, most languages make use of inflectional and derivational morphemes to enrich the basic set of lexemes, but exactly how this works varies from language to language. We will revisit this at some length in *Chapter 5* , *Sentiment Lexicons and Vector Space Models* since finding the core lexemes can be significant when we are trying to assign emotions to texts.

A lexeme plus a suitable set of morphemes is often referred to as a **word**. Words are typically grouped into larger tree-like structures, with the way that they are grouped carrying a substantial part of the message conveyed by the text. In the sentence *John believes that Mary expects Peter to marry Susan*, for instance, *Peter to marry Susan* is a group that describes a particular kind of event, *Mary expects [Peter to marry Susan]* is a group that describes Mary's attitude to this event, and *John believes [that Mary expected [Peter to marry Susan]]* is a group that describes John's view of Mary's expectation.

Yet again, different languages carry out this kind of grouping in different ways, and there are numerous ways of approaching the task of analyzing the grouping in particular cases. This is not the place for a review of all the grammatical theories that have ever been proposed to analyze the ways that words get grouped together or of all the algorithms that have ever been proposed for applying those theories to specific cases (**parsers**), but there are a few general observations that are worth making.

Phrase structure grammar versus dependency grammar

In some languages, groups are mainly formed by merging adjacent groups. The previous sentence, for instance, can be analyzed if we group it as follows:

In some languages groups are mainly formed by merging adjacent groups

In [some languages]$_{np}$ groups are mainly formed by merging [adjacent groups]$_{np}$

[In [some languages]]$_{pp}$ groups are mainly formed by [merging [adjacent groups]]$_{vp}$

[In [some languages]]$_{pp}$ groups are mainly formed [by [merging [adjacent groups]]]$_{pp}$

[In [some languages]]$_{pp}$ groups are mainly [formed [by [merging [adjacent groups]]]]$_{vp}$

[In [some languages]]$_{pp}$ groups are [mainly [formed [by [merging [adjacent groups]]]]]$_{vp}$

[In [some languages]]$_{pp}$ groups [are [mainly [formed [by [merging [adjacent groups]]]]]]$_{vp}$

[In [some languages]]$_{pp}$ [groups [are [mainly [formed [by [merging [adjacent groups]]]]]]]$_{s}$

[[In [some languages]][groups [are [mainly [formed [by [merging [adjacent groups]]]]]]]]$_{s}$

This tends to work well for languages where word order is largely fixed – no languages have completely fixed word order (for example, the preceding sentence could be rewritten as *Groups are mainly formed by merging adjacent groups in some languages* with very little change in meaning), but some languages allow more freedom than others. For languages such as English, analyzing the relationships between words in terms of adjacent phrases, such as using a **phrase structure grammar**, works quite well.

For languages where words and phrases are allowed to move around fairly freely, it can be more convenient to record pairwise relationships between words. The following tree describes the same sentence using a **dependency grammar** – that is, by assigning a parent word to every word (apart from the full stop, which we are taking to be the root of the tree):

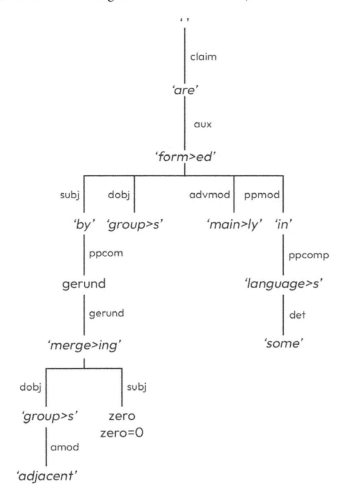

Figure 1.3 – Analysis of "In some languages, groups are mainly formed by merging adjacent groups" using a rule-based dependency parser

There are many variations of phrase structure grammar and many variations of dependency grammar. Roughly speaking, dependency grammar provides an easier handle on languages where words can move around very freely, while phrase structure grammar makes it easier to deal with *invisible* items such as the subject of *merging* in the preceding example. The difference between the two is, in any case, less clear than it might seem from the preceding figure: a dependency tree can easily be transformed into a phrase structure tree by treating each subtree as a phrase, and a phrase structure tree can be transformed into a dependency tree if you can specify which item in a phrase is its **head** – for example, in the preceding phrase structure tree, the head of a group labeled as **nn** is its noun and the head of a group labeled as **np** is the head of **nn**.

Rule-based parsers versus data-driven parsers

As well as having a theory of how to describe the structure of a piece of text, you need a program that applies that theory to specific texts – a **parser**. There are two ways to approach the development of a parser:

- **Rule-based**: You can try to devise a set of rules that describe the way that a particular language works (a **grammar**), and then implement a program that tries to apply these rules to the texts you want analyzed. Devising such rules is difficult and time-consuming, and programs that try to apply them tend to be slow and fail if the target text does not obey the rules.

- **Data-driven**: You can somehow produce a set of analyses of a large number of texts (a **treebank**), and then implement a program that extracts patterns from these analyses. Producing a treebank is difficult and time-consuming – you need hundreds of thousands of examples, and the trees all have to be consistently annotated, which means that if this is to be done by people, then they have to be given consistent guidelines that cover every example they will see (which is, in effect, a grammar) (and if it is not done by people then you must already have an automated way of doing it, that is, a parser!).

Both approaches have advantages and disadvantages: when considering whether to use a dependency grammar or a phrase structure grammar and then when considering whether to follow a rule-based approach or a data-driven one, there are several criteria to be considered. Since *no* existing system optimizes all of these, you should think about which ones matter most for your application and then decide which way to go:

- **Speed**: The first criterion to consider is the speed at which the parser runs. Some parsers can become very slow when faced with long sentences. The worst-case complexity of the standard **chart-parsing** algorithm for rule-based approaches is $O(N^3)$, where N is the length of the sentence, which means that for long sentences, the algorithm can take a *very* long time. Some other algorithms have much better complexity than this (the MALT (Nivre et al., 2006) and MST (McDonald et al., 2005) parsers, for instance, are linear in the length of the sentence), while others have much worse. If two parsers are equally good according to all the other criteria, then the faster one will be preferable, but there will be situations where one (or more) of the other criteria is more important.

- **Robustness**: Some parsers, particularly rule-based ones, can fail to produce any analysis at all for some sentences. This will happen if the input is ungrammatical, but it will also happen if the rules are not a complete description of the language. A parser that fails to produce a perfectly grammatical input sentence is less useful than one that can analyze every grammatically correct sentence of the target language. It is less clear that parsers that will do something with every input sentence are necessarily more useful than ones that will reject some sentences as being ungrammatical. In some applications, detecting ungrammaticality is a crucial part of the task (for example, in language learning programs), but in any case, assigning an analysis to an ungrammatical sentence cannot be either right or wrong, and hence any program that makes use of such an analysis cannot be sure that it is doing the right thing.

- **Accuracy**: A parser that assigns the *right* analysis to every input text will generally be more useful than one that does not. This does, of course, beg the question of how to decide what the right analysis is. For data-driven parsers, it is impossible to say what the right analysis of a sentence that does not appear in the treebank is. For rule-based parsers, any analysis that is returned will be right in the sense that it obeys the rules. So, if an analysis looks odd, you have to work out how the rules led to it and revise them accordingly.

There is a trade-off between accuracy and robustness. A parser that fails to return any analysis at all in complex cases will produce fewer wrong analyses than one that tries to find some way of interpreting every input text: the one that simply rejects some sentences will have lower recall but may have higher precision, and that can be a good thing. It may be better to have a system that says *Sorry, I didn't quite understand what you just said* than one that goes ahead with whatever it is supposed to be doing based on an incorrect interpretation.

- **Sensitivity and consistency**: Sometimes, sentences that look superficially similar have different underlying structures. Consider the following examples:

1. a) I want to see the queen

    b) I went to see the queen

1(a) is the answer to *What do you want?* and 2(b) is the answer to *Why did you go?* If the structures that are assigned to these two sentences do not reflect the different roles for *to see the queen*, then it will be impossible to make this distinction:

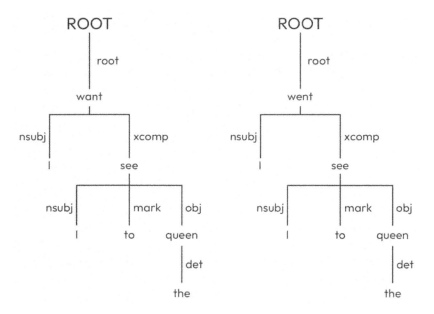

Figure 1.4 – Trees for 1(a) and 1(b) from the Stanford dependency parser (Dozat et al., 2017)

2.   a) One of my best friends is watching old movies
      b) One of my favorite pastimes is watching old movies

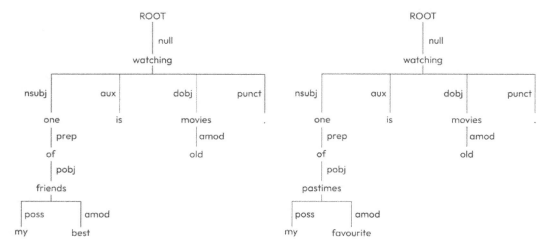

Figure 1.5 – Trees for 2(a) and 2(b) from the Stanford dependency parser

The **Stanford dependency parser** (**SDP**) trees both say that the subject (*One of my best friends*, *One of my favorite pastimes*) is carrying out the action of watching old movies – it is sitting in its most comfortable armchair with the curtains drawn and the TV on. The first of these makes sense, but the second doesn't: pastimes don't watch old movies. What we need is an equational analysis that says that *One of my favorite pastimes* and *watching old movies* are the same thing, as in *Figure 1.6*:

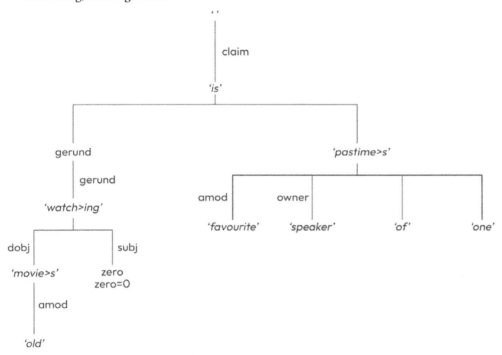

Figure 1.6 – Equational analysis of "One of my favorite pastimes is watching old movies"

Spotting that 2(b) requires an analysis like this, where my favorite pastime is the predication in an equational use of *be* rather than the agent of a watching-old-movies event, requires more detail about the words in question than is usually embodied in a treebank.

It can also happen that sentences that look superficially different have very similar underlying structures:

3.   a) Few great tenors are poor

     b) Most great tenors are rich

This time, the SDP assigns quite different structures to the two sentences:

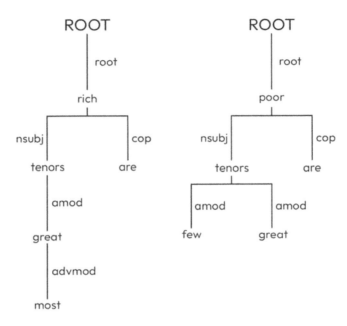

Figure 1.7 – Trees for 3(a) and 3(b) from the SDP

The analysis of 3(a) assigns *most* as a modifier of *great*, whereas the analysis of 3(b) assigns *few* as a modifier of *tenors*. *Most* can indeed be used for modifying adjectives, as in *He is the most annoying person I know*, but in 3(a), it is acting as something more like a determiner, just as *few* is in 3(b).

4.   a) There are great tenors who are rich
       b) Are there great tenors who are rich?

It is clear that 4(a) and 4(b) should have almost identical analyses – 4(b) is just 4(a) turned into a question. Again, this can cause problems for treebank-based parsers:

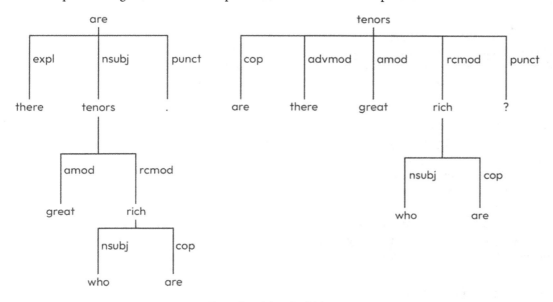

Figure 1.8 – Trees for 4(a) and 4(b) from MALTParser

The analysis in *Figure 1.8* for 4(a) makes *are* the head of the tree, with *there, great tenors who are rich*, and as daughters, whereas 4(b) is given *tenors* as its head and *are, there, great, who are rich*, and *?* as daughters. It would be difficult, given these analyses, to see that 4(a) is the answer to 4(b)!

Treebank-based parsers frequently fail to cope with issues of the kind raised by the examples given here. The problem is that the treebanks on which they are trained tend not to include detailed information about the words that appear in them – that *went* is an intransitive verb and *want* requires a sentential complement, that friends are human and can therefore watch old movies while pastimes are events, and can therefore be equated with the activity of watching something, or that *most* can be used in a wide variety of ways.

It is not possible to say that all treebank-based parsers suffer from these problems, but several very widely used ones (the SDP, the version of MALT distributed with the NLTK, the EasyCCG parser (Lewis & Steedman, 2014), spaCy (Kitaev & Klein, 2018)) do. Some of these issues are fairly widespread (the failure to distinguish 1(a) and 1(b)), and some arise because of specific properties of either the treebank or the parsing algorithm. Most of the pre-trained models for parsers such as MALT and SPACY are trained on the well-known Wall Street Journal corpus, and since this treebank does not distinguish between sentences such as 1(a) and 1(b), it is impossible for parsers trained on it to do so. All the parsers listed previously assign different structures to 3(a) and 3(b), which may be a characteristic of the treebank or it may be some property of the training algorithms. It is worth evaluating the output of any such parser to check that it does give distinct analyses for obvious cases such as 1(a) and 1(b) and does give parallel analyses for obvious cases such as 4(a) and 4(b).

So, when choosing a parser, you have to weigh up a range of factors. Do you care if it sometimes makes mistakes? Do you want it to assign different trees to texts whose underlying representations are different (this isn't quite the same as accuracy because it could happen that what the parser produces isn't wrong, it just doesn't contain all the information you need, as in 1(a) and 1(b))? Do you want it to always produce a tree, even for texts that don't conform to any of the rules of normal language (should it produce a parse for *#anxious don't know why .... #worry* 😶 *slowly going #mad hahahahahahahahaha*)? Does it matter if it takes 10 or 20 seconds to parse some sentences? Whatever you do, *do not trust what anyone says about a parser*: try it for yourself, on the data that you are intending to use it on, and check that its output matches your needs.

Semantics (the study of meaning)

As we've seen, finding words, assigning them to categories, and finding the relationships between them is quite hard work. There would be no point in doing this work unless you had some application in mind that could make use of it. The key here is that the choice of words and the relationships between them are what allow language to carry messages, to have meaning. That's why language is important; because it carries messages. Almost all application programs that do anything with natural language are concerned with the message carried by the input text, so almost all such programs have to identify the words that are present and the way they are arranged.

The study of how language encodes messages is known as semantics. As just noted, the message is encoded by the words that are present (**lexical semantics**) and the way they are arranged (**compositional semantics**). They are both crucial: you can't understand the difference between *John loves Mary* and *John hates Mary* if you don't know what *loves* and *hates* mean, and you can't understand the difference between *John loves Mary* and *Mary loves John* if you don't know how being the subject or object of a verb encodes the relationship between the things denoted by *John* and *Mary* and the event denoted by *loves*.

The key test for a theory of semantics is the ability to carry out inference between sets of natural language texts. If you can't do the inferences in 1–7 (where P1, …, Pn |- Q means that Q can be inferred from the premises P1, …, Pn), then you cannot be said to understand English:

1. John hates Mary |- John dislikes Mary

2. (a) John and Mary are divorced |- John and Mary are not married

3. (b) John and Mary are divorced |- John and Mary used to be married

4. I saw a man with a big nose |- I saw a man

5. Every woman distrusts John, Mary is a woman |- Mary distrusts John

6. I saw more than three pigeons |- I saw at least four birds

7. I doubt that she saw anyone |- I do not believe she saw a fat man

These are very simple inferences. If someone said that the conclusions didn't follow from the premises, you would have to say that they just don't understand English properly. They involve a range of different kinds of knowledge – simple entailment relationships between words (*hates* entails *dislikes* (1)); more complex relationships between words (getting divorced means canceling an existing marriage (2), so if John and Mary are divorced, then they are not now married but at one time they were); the fact that *a man with a big nose* is something that is a man and has a big nose plus the fact that *A and B* entails *A* (3); an understanding of how quantifiers work ((4) and (5)); combinations of all of these (6) – but they are all inferences that anyone who understands English would agree with.

Some of this information can be fairly straightforwardly extracted from corpora. There is a great deal of work, for instance, on calculating the similarity between pairs of words, though extending that to cover entailments between words has proved more difficult. Some of it is much more difficult to find using data-driven methods – the relationships between *more than* and *at least*, for instance, cannot easily be found in corpora, and the complex concepts that lie behind the word *divorce* would also be difficult to extract unsupervised from a corpus.

Furthermore, some of it can be applied by using tree-matching algorithms of various kinds, from simple algorithms that just compute whether one tree is a subtree of another to more complex approaches that pay attention to polarity (that *doubt* flicks a switch that turns the direction of the matching algorithm round – *I know she loves him* |- *I know she likes him*, *I doubt she likes him* |- *I doubt she loves him*) and to the relationships between quantifiers (*the* |- *some, more than N* |- *at least N-1*) (Alabbas & Ramsay, 2013) (MacCartney & Manning, 2014). Some of it requires more complex strategies, in particular examples with multiple premises (4), but all but the very simplest (for example, just treating a sentence as a bag of words) require accurate, or at least consistent, trees.

Exactly how much of this machinery you need depends on your ultimate application. Fortunately for us, sentiment mining can be done reasonably effectively with fairly shallow approaches, but it should not be forgotten that there is a great deal more to understanding a text than simply knowing lexical relationships such as similarity or subsumption between words.

Before wrapping up this chapter, we will spend some time learning about machine learning, looking at various machine learning models, and then working our way through a sample project using Python.

Introduction to machine learning

Before discussing machine learning, it makes sense to properly understand the term artificial intelligence. Broadly speaking, artificial intelligence is a branch of computer science and is the idea that machines can be made to think and act just like us humans, without explicit programming instructions.

There is a common misconception that artificial intelligence is a *new thing*. The term is widely considered to have been coined in 1956 by assistant Professor of Mathematics John McCarthy at the Dartmouth Summer Research Project on Artificial Intelligence. We are now in an AI boom – but it was not always so; artificial intelligence has a somewhat chequered history. Following on from the 1956 conference, funding flowed generously and rapid progress was made as researchers developed systems that could play chess and solve mathematical problems. Optimism was high, but progress stalled because promises made earlier about artificial intelligence were not able to be fulfilled, and hence the funding dried up; this cycle was repeated in the 1980s. The current boom we are experiencing is due to the timely advances and emergence of three key technologies:

- **Big data**: Giving us the amounts of data required to be able to do artificial intelligence
- **High-speed high-capacity storage devices**: Giving us the ability to store the data
- **GPUs**: Giving us the ability to process the data

Nowadays, AI is everywhere. Here are some examples of AI:

- Chatbots (for example, customer service chatbots)
- Amazon Alexa, Apple's Siri, and other smart assistants
- Autonomous vehicles
- Spam filters
- Recommendation engines

According to experts, there are four types of AI:

- **Reactive**: This is the simplest type and involves machines programmed to always respond in the same predictable manner. They cannot learn.

- **Limited memory**: This is the most common type of AI in use today. It combines pre-programmed information with historical data to perform tasks.

- **Theory of mind**: This is a technology we may see in the future. The idea here is that a machine with a theory of mind AI will understand emotions, and then alter its own behavior accordingly as it interacts with humans.

- **Self-aware**: This is the most advanced type of AI. Machines that are self-aware of their own emotions, and the emotions of those around them, will have a level of intelligence like human beings and will be able to make assumptions, inferences, and deductions. This is certainly one for the future as the technology for this doesn't exist just yet.

Machine learning is one way to exploit AI. Writing software programs to cater to all situations, occurrences, and eventualities is time-consuming, requires effort, and, in some cases, is not even possible. Consider the task of recognizing pictures of people. We humans can handle this task easily, but the same is not true for computers. Even more difficult is programming a computer to do this task. Machine learning tackles this problem by getting the machine to program itself by learning through experiences.

There is no universally agreed-upon definition of machine learning that everyone subscribes to. Some attempts include the following:

- A branch of computer science that focuses on the use of data and algorithms to imitate the way that humans learn

- The capability of machines to imitate intelligent human behavior

- A subset of AI that allows machines to learn from data without being programmed explicitly

Machine learning needs data – and sometimes lots and lots of it.

Lack of data is a significant weak spot in AI. Without a reasonable amount of data, machines cannot perform and generate sensible results. Indeed, in some ways, this is just like how we humans operate – we look and learn and then apply that knowledge in new, unknown situations.

And, if we think about it, everyone has data. From the smallest sole trader to the largest organization, everyone will have sales data, purchase data, customer data, and more. The format of this data may differ between different organizations, but it is all useful data that can be used in machine learning. This data can be collected and processed and can be used to build machine learning models. Typically, this data is split into the following sets:

- **Training set**: This is always the largest of the datasets (typically 80%) and is the data that is used to train the machine learning models.

- **Development set**: This dataset (10%) is used to tweak and try new parameters to find the ones that work the best for the model.

- **Test set**: This is used to test (validate) the model (10%). The model has already seen the training data, so it cannot be used to test the model, hence this dataset is required. This dataset also allows you to determine whether the model is working well or requires more training.

It is good practice to have both development and test datasets. The process of building models involves finding the best set of parameters that give the best results. These parameters are determined by making use of the development set. Without the development set, we would be reduced to using the same datasets for training, testing, and evaluation. This is undesirable, but it can also present further problems unless handled carefully. For example, the datasets should be constructed such that the original dataset class proportions are preserved across the test and training sets. Furthermore, as a general point, training data should be checked for the following:

- It is relevant to the problem

- It is large enough such that all use cases of the model are covered

- It is unbiased and contains no imbalance toward any particular category

Modern toolkits such as `sklearn` (Pedregosa et al., 2011) provide ready-made functions that will easily split your dataset for you:

```
res = train_test_split(data, labels,
    train_size=0.8,
    test_size=0.2,
    random_state=42,
    stratify=labels)
```

However, there are times when the data scientist will not have enough data available to be able to warrant splitting it multiple ways – for example, there is no data relevant to the problem, or the process to collect the data is too difficult, expensive, or time-consuming. This is known as **data scarcity** and it can be responsible for poor model performance. In such cases, various solutions may help alleviate the problem:

- **Augmentation**: For example, taking an image and performing processing (for example, rotation, scaling, and modifying the colors) so that new instances are slightly different

- **Synthetic data**: Data that is artificially generated using computer programs

To evaluate models where data is scarce, a technique known as k-fold cross-validation is used. This is discussed more fully in *Chapter 2*, briefly the dataset is split into a number (k) of groups; then, in turn, each group is taken as the test dataset with the remaining groups as the training dataset, and the model is fit and evaluated. This is repeated for each group, hence each member of the original dataset is used in the test dataset exactly once and in a training dataset k-1 times. Finally, the model accuracy is calculated by using the results from the individual evaluations.

This poses an interesting question about how much data is needed. There are no hard-and-fast rules but, generally speaking, the more the better. However, regardless of the amount of data, there are typically other issues that need to be addressed:

- Missing values

- Inconsistencies

- Duplicate values

- Ambiguity

- Inaccuracies

Machine learning is important. It has many real-world applications that can allow businesses and individuals to save time, money, and effort by, for example, automating business processes. Consider a customer service center where staff are required to take calls, answer queries, and help customers. In such a scenario, machine learning can be used to handle some of the more simple repetitive tasks, hence relieving burden from staff and getting things done more quickly and efficiently.

Machine learning has dramatically altered the traditional ways of doing things over the past few years. However, in many aspects, it still lags far behind human levels of performance. Often, the best solutions are hybrid human-in-the-loop solutions where humans are needed to perform final verification of the outcome.

There are several types of machine learning:

- Supervised learning

- Unsupervised learning

- Semi-supervised learning

- Reinforcement learning

Supervised learning models must be trained with **labeled** data. Hence, both the inputs and the outputs of the model are specified. For example, a machine learning model could be trained with human-labeled images of apples and other fruits, labeled as *apple* and *non-apple*. This would allow the machine to learn the best way to identify pictures of apples. Supervised machine learning is the most common type of machine learning used today. In some ways, this matches how we humans function; we look and learn from experiences and then apply that knowledge in unknown, new situations to work out an answer. Technically speaking, there are two main types of supervised learning problems:

- **Classification**: Problems that involve predicting labels (for example, *apple*)

- **Regression**: Problems that involve predicting a numerical value (for example, a house price)

Both of these types of problems can have any number of inputs of any type. These problems are known as **supervised** from the idea that the output is supplied by a teacher that shows the system what to do.

Unsupervised learning is a type of machine learning that, opposite to supervised learning, involves training algorithms on data that is **unlabeled**. Unsupervised algorithms examine datasets looking for meaningful patterns or trends that would not otherwise be apparent – that is, the target is for the algorithm to find the structure in the data on its own. For example, unsupervised machine learning algorithms can examine sales data and pinpoint the different types of products being purchased. However, the problem with this is that although these models can perform more complex tasks than their supervised counterparts, they are also much more unpredictable. Some use cases that adopt this approach are as follows:

- **Dimensionality reduction**: The process of reducing the number of inputs into a model by identifying the key (*principal*) components that capture the majority of the data without losing key information.

- **Association rules**: The process of finding associations between different inputs in the input dataset by discovering the probabilities of the co-occurrence of items. For example, when people buy ice cream, they also typically buy sunglasses.

- **Clustering**: Finds hidden patterns in a dataset based on similarities or differences and groups the data into clusters or groups. Unsupervised learning can be used to perform clustering when the exact details of the clusters are unknown.

Semi-supervised learning is, unsurprisingly, a combination of supervised and unsupervised learning. A small amount of labeled data and a large amount of unlabeled data is used. This has the benefits of both unsupervised and supervised learning but at the same time avoids the challenges of requiring large amounts of labeled data. Consequently, models can be trained to label data without requiring huge amounts of labeled training data.

Reinforcement learning is about learning the best behavior so that the maximum reward is achieved. This behavior is learned by interacting with the environment and observing how it responds. In other words, the sequence of actions that maximize the reward must be independently discovered via a trial-and-error process. In this way, the model can learn the actions that result in success in an unseen environment.

Briefly, here are the typical steps that are followed in a machine learning project:

1. **Data collection**: Data can come from a database, Excel, or text file – essentially it can come from anywhere.

2. **Data preparation**: The quality of the data used is crucial. Hence, time must be spent fixing issues such as missing data and duplicates. Initial **exploratory data analysis** (**EDA**) is performed on the data to discover patterns, spot anomalies, and test theories about the data by using visual techniques.

3. **Model training**: An appropriate algorithm and model is chosen to represent the data. The data is split into training data for developing the model and test data for testing the model.

4. **Evaluation:** To test the accuracy, the test data is used.

5. **Improve performance:** Here, a different model may be chosen, or other inputs may be used.

Let's start with the technical requirements.

Technical requirements

This book describes a series of experiments with machine learning algorithms – some standard algorithms, some developed especially for this book. These algorithms, along with various worked examples, are available as Python programs at `https://github.com/PacktPublishing/Machine-Learning-for-Emotion-Analysis/tree/main`, split into directories corresponding to the chapters in which the specific algorithms will be discussed.

One of the reasons why we implemented these programs in Python is that there is a huge amount of useful material to build upon. In particular, there are good -quality, efficient implementations of several standard machine learning algorithms, and using these helps us be confident that where an algorithm doesn't work as well as expected on some dataset, it is because the algorithm isn't very well suited to that dataset, rather than that we just haven't implemented it very well. Some of the programs in the repository use very particular libraries, but there are several packages that we will use throughout this book. These are listed here. If you are going to use the code in the repository – which we hope you will because looking at what actual programs do is one of the best ways of learning – you will need to install these libraries. Most of them can be installed very easily, either by using the built-in package installer `pip` or by following the directions on the relevant website:

- **pandas:** This is one of the most commonly used libraries and is used primarily for cleaning and preparing data, as well as analyzing tabular data. It provides tools to explore, clean, manipulate, and analyze all types of structured data. Typically, machine learning libraries and projects use `pandas` structures as inputs. You can install it by typing the following command in the command prompt:

  ```
  pip install pandas
  ```

- Or you can go to `https://pandas.pydata.org/docs/getting_started/install.html` for other options.

- **NumPy:** This is used primarily for its support of *N*-dimensional arrays. It has functions for linear algebra and matrices and is also used by other libraries. Python provides several collection classes that can be used to represent arrays, notably as lists, but they are computationally slow to work with – NumPy provides objects that are up to 50 times faster than Python lists. To install it, run the following command in the command prompt:

  ```
  pip install numpy
  ```

  Alternatively, you can refer to the documentation for more options: `https://numpy.org/install/`.

- **SciPy:** This provides a range of scientific functions built on top of NumPy, including ways of representing sparse arrays (arrays where most elements are 0) that can be manipulated thousands of times faster than standard NumPy arrays if the vast majority of elements are 0. You can install it using the following command:

```
pip install scipy
```

You can also refer to the SciPy documentation for more details: https://scipy.org/install/.

- **scikit-learn (Pedregosa et al., 2011):** This is used to build machine learning models as it has functions for building supervised and unsupervised machine learning models, analysis, and dimensionality reduction. A large part of this book is about investigating how well various standard machine learning algorithms work on particular datasets, and it is useful to have reliable good-quality implementations of the most widely used algorithms so that we are not distracted by issues due to the way we have implemented them.

scikit-learn is also known as `sklearn` – when you want to import it into a program, you should refer to it as sklearn. You can install it as follows:

```
pip install scikit-learn
```

Refer to the documentation for more information: https://scikit-learn.org/stable/install.html.

The `sklearn` implementations of the various algorithms generally make the internal representations of the data available to other programs. This can be particularly valuable when you are trying to understand the behavior of some algorithm on a given dataset and is something we will use extensively as we carry out our experiments.

- **TensorFlow:** This is a popular library for building neural networks as well as performing other tasks. It uses *tensors* (multi-dimensional arrays) to perform operations. It is built to take advantage of parallelism, so it is used to train neural networks in a highly efficient manner. Again, it makes sense to reuse a reliable good-quality implementation when testing neural network models on our data so that we know that any poor performances arise because of problems with the algorithm rather than with our implementation of it. As ever, you can just install it using `pip`:

```
pip install tensorflow
```

For more information, refer to the TensorFlow documentation: https://www.tensorflow.org/install.

You will not benefit from its use of parallelism unless you have a GPU or other hardware accelerator built into your machine, and training complex models is likely to be intolerably slow. We will consider how to use remote facilities such as Google Colab to obtain better performance in *Chapter 9, Exploring Transformers*. For now, just be aware that running `tensorflow` on a standard computer without any kind of hardware accelerator probably won't do anything within a reasonable period.

- **Keras:** This is also used for building neural networks. It is built on top of TensorFlow. It creates computational graphs to represent machine learning algorithms, so it is slow compared to other libraries. Keras comes as part of TensorFlow, so there is no need to install anything beyond TensorFlow itself.

- **Matplotlib:** This is an interactive library for plotting graphs, charts, plots, and visualizing data. It comes with a wide range of plots that help data scientists understand trends and patterns. Matplotlib is extremely powerful and allows users to create almost any visualization imaginable. Use the following command to install `matplotlib`:

  ```
  pip install matplotlib
  ```

  Refer to the documentation for more information: `https://matplotlib.org/stable/users/installing/index.html`.

  Matplotlib may install NumPy if you do not have it already installed, but it is more sensible to install them separately (NumPy first).

- **Seaborn:** This is built on the top of Matplotlib, and is another library for creating visualizations. It is useful for making attractive plots and helps users explore and understand data. Seaborn makes it easy for users to switch between different visualizations. You can easily install Seaborn by running the following command:

  ```
  pip install seaborn
  ```

  For more installation options, please refer to `https://seaborn.pydata.org/installing.html`.

We will use these libraries throughout this book, so we advise you to install them now, before trying out any of the programs and examples that we'll discuss as we go along. You only have to install them once so that they will be available whenever you need them. We will specify any other libraries that the examples depend on as we go along, but from now on, we will assume that you have at least these ones.

A sample project

The best way to learn is by doing! In this section, we will discover how to complete a small machine learning project in Python. Completing, and understanding, this project will allow you to become familiar with machine learning concepts and techniques.

Typically, the first step in developing any Python program is to import the modules that are going to be needed using the `import` statement:

```
import sklearn
import pandas as pd
```

> **Note**
>
> Other imports are needed for this exercise; these can be found in the GitHub repository.

The next step is to load the data that is needed to build the model. Like most tutorials, we will use the famous Iris dataset. The Iris dataset contains data on the length and width of sepals and petals. We will use `pandas` to load the dataset. The dataset can be downloaded from the internet and read from your local filesystem, as follows:

```
df = pd.read_csv("c:\iris.csv")
```

Alternatively, `pandas` can read it directly from a URL:

```
df = pd.read_csv("https://gist.githubusercontent.com/
netj/8836201/raw/6f9306ad21398ea43cba4f7d537619d0e07d5ae3/iris.
csv")
```

The `read_csv` command returns a DataFrame. It is probably the most commonly used `pandas` object and is simply a two-dimensional data structure with rows and columns, just like a spreadsheet.

Since we will be using `sklearn`, it is interesting to see that `sklearn` also makes it easy to access the dataset:

```
from sklearn import datasets

iris = datasets.load_iris()
df = iris.data
```

We can now check that the dataset has been successfully loaded by using the `describe` function:

```
df.describe()
```

The `describe` function returns a descriptive summary of a DataFrame reporting values such as the mean, count, and standard deviation:

```
      sepal.length sepal.width petal.length petal.width
count 150.000000   150.000000  150.000000   150.000000
mean  5.843333     3.057333    3.758000     1.199333
std   0.828066     0.435866    1.765298     0.762238
min   4.300000     2.000000    1.000000     0.100000
25%   5.100000     2.800000    1.600000     0.300000
50%   5.800000     3.000000    4.350000     1.300000
75%   6.400000     3.300000    5.100000     1.800000
max   7.900000     4.400000    6.900000     2.500000
```

This function is useful to check that the data has been loaded correctly but also to provide a first glance at some interesting attributes of the data.

Some other useful commands tell us more about the DataFrame:

- This shows the first five elements in the DataFrame:

  ```
  df.head(5)
  ```

- This shows the last five elements in the DataFrame:

  ```
  df.tail(5)
  ```

- This describes the columns of the DataFrame:

  ```
  df.columns
  ```

- This describes the number of rows and columns in the DataFrame:

  ```
  df.shape
  ```

It is usually a good idea to use these functions to check that the dataset has been successfully and correctly loaded into the DataFrame and that everything looks as it should.

It is also important to ensure that the dataset is balanced – that is, there are relatively equal numbers of each class.

The majority of machine learning algorithms have been developed with the assumption that there are equal numbers of instances of each class. Consequently, imbalanced datasets present a big problem for machine learning models as this results in models with poor predictive performance.

In the Iris example, this means that we have to check that we have equal numbers of each type of flower. This can be verified by running the following command:

```
df['variety'].value_counts()
```

This prints the following output:

```
Setosa 50
Versicolor 50
Virginica 50
Name: variety, dtype: int64
```

We can see that there are 50 examples of each variety. The next step is to create some visualizations. Although we used the `describe` function to get an idea of the statistical properties of the dataset, it is much easier to observe these in a visual form as opposed to in a table.

Box plots (see *Figure 1.9*) plot the distribution of data based on the sample minimum, the lower quartile, the median, the upper quartile, and the sample maximum. This helps us analyze the data to establish any outliers and the data variation to better understand each attribute:

```
import matplotlib.pyplot as plt

attributes = df[['sepal.length', 'sepal.width',
    'petal.length', 'petal.width']]
attributes.boxplot()
plt.show()
```

This outputs the following plot:

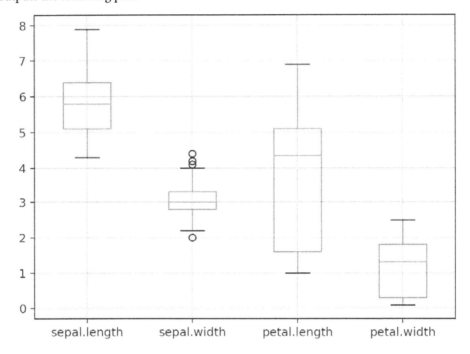

Figure 1.9 – Box plot

Heatmaps are useful for understanding the relationships between attributes. Heatmaps are an important tool for data scientists to explore and visualize data. They represent the data in a two-dimensional format and allow the data to be summarized visually as a colored graph. Although we can use matplotlib to create heatmaps, it is much easier in seaborn and requires significantly fewer lines of code – something we like!

```
import seaborn as sns

sns.heatmap(iris.corr(), annot=True)
plt.show()
```

This outputs the following heatmap:

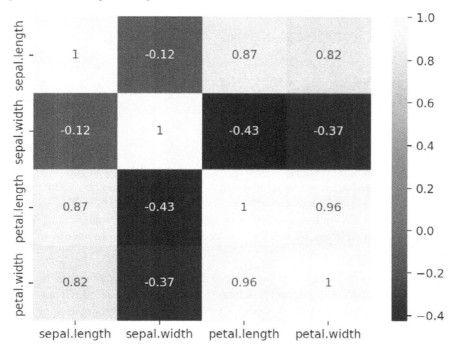

Figure 1.10 – Heatmap

The squares in the heatmap represent the correlation (a measure that shows how much two variables are related) between the variables. The correlation values range from -1 to +1:

- The closer the value is to 1, the more positively correlated they are – that is, as one increases, so does the other

- Conversely, the closer the value is to -1, the more negatively correlated they are – that is, as one variable decreases, the other will increase

- Values close to 0 indicate that there is no linear trend between the variables

In *Figure 1.10*, the diagonals are all 1. This is because, in those squares, the two variables are the same and hence the correlation is to itself. For the remainder, the scale shows that the lighter the color (toward the top of the scale), the higher the correlation. For example, the petal length and petal width are highly correlated, whereas petal length and sepal width are not. Finally, it can also be seen that the plot is symmetrical on both sides of the diagonal. This is because the same set of variables are paired in the squares that are the same.

We can now build a model using the data and estimate the accuracy of the model on data that it has not seen previously. Let's start by separating the data and the labels from each other by using Python:

```
data = df.iloc[:, 0:4]
labels = df.iloc[:, 4]
```

Before we can train a machine learning model, it is necessary to split the data and labels into testing and training data. As discussed previously, we can use the train_test_split function from sklearn:

```
from sklearn.model_selection import train_test_split
X_train,X_test,y_train,y_test = train_test_split(data,
    labels, test_size=0.2)
```

The capital X and lowercase y are a nod to math notation, where it is common practice to write matrix variable names in uppercase and vector variable names using lowercase letters. This has no special Python function and these conventions can be ignored if desired. For now, note that X refers to data, and y refers to the associated labels. Hence, X_train can be understood to refer to an object that contains the training data.

Before we can begin to work on the machine learning model, we must *normalize* the data. Normalization is a scaling technique that updates the numeric columns to use a common scale. This helps improve the performance, reliability, and accuracy of the model. The two most common normalization techniques are min-max scaling and standardization scaling:

- **Min-max scaling:** This method uses the minimum and maximum values for scaling and rescales the values so that they end up in the range 0 to 1 or -1 to 1. It is most useful when the features are of different scales. It is typically used when the feature distribution is unknown, such as in k-NN or neural network models.

- **Standardization scaling:** This method uses the mean and the standard deviation to rescale values so that they have a mean of 0 and a variance of 1. The resultant scaled values are not confined to a specific range. It is typically used when the feature distribution is normal.

It is uncommon to come across datasets that perfectly follow a certain specific distribution. Typically, every dataset will need to be standardized. For the Iris dataset, we will use sklearn's StandardScaler to scale the data by making the mean of the data 0 and the standard deviation 1:

```
from sklearn.preprocessing import StandardScaler
from sklearn.model_selection import cross_val_score
scaler = StandardScaler()
scaler.fit(X_train)
X_train = scaler.transform(X_train)
X_test = scaler.transform(X_test)
```

Now that the data is ready, `sklearn` makes it easy for us to test and compare various machine learning models. A brief explanation of each model has been provided but don't worry – we explain these models in more detail later in later chapters.

Logistic regression

Logistic regression is one of the most popular machine learning techniques. It is used to predict a categorical dependent variable using a set of independent variables and makes use of a *sigmoid* function. The sigmoid is a mathematical function that has values from 0 to 1 and asymptotes both values. This makes it useful for binary classification with 0 and 1 as potential output values:

```
from sklearn.linear_model import LogisticRegression
lr = LogisticRegression()
lr.fit(X_train, y_train)
score = lr.score(X_train, y_train)
print(f"Training data accuracy {score}")
score = lr.score(X_test, y_test)
print(f"Testing data accuracy {score}")

Training data accuracy 0.9666666666666667
Testing data accuracy 0.9666666666666667
```

> **Note**
>
> There is also a technique called linear regression but, as its name suggests, this is used for regression problems, whereas the current Iris problem is a classification problem.

Support vector machines (SVMs)

Support vector machine (SVM) is one of the best "out-of-the-box" classification techniques. SVM constructs a hyperplane that can then be used for classification. It works by calculating the distance between two observations and then determining a hyperplane that maximizes the distance between the closest members of separate classes. The linear **support vector classifier** (SVC) method (as used in the following example) applies a linear kernel function to perform classification:

```
from sklearn.svm import SVC
svm = SVC(random_state=0, gamma='auto', C=1.0)
svm.fit(X_train, y_train)
score = svm.score(X_train, y_train)
print(f"Training data accuracy {score}")
score = svm.score(X_test, y_test)
print(f"Testing data accuracy {score}")

data accuracy 0.9666666666666667
Testing data accuracy 0.9666666666666667
```

The following parameters are used:

- `random_state`: This controls the random number generation that is used to shuffle the data. In this example, a value hasn't been set, hence a randomly initialized state is used. This means that results will vary between runs.

- `gamma`: This controls how much influence a single data point has on the decision boundary. Low values mean "far" and high values mean "close." In this example, gamma is set to "auto," hence allowing it to automatically define its own value based on the characteristics of the dataset.

- `C`: This controls the trade-off between maximizing the distance between classes and correctly classifying the data.

K-nearest neighbors (k-NN)

k-NN is another widely used classification technique. k-NN classifies objects based on the closest training examples in the feature space. It is a simple algorithm that stores all available cases and classifies new cases by a majority vote of its *k* neighbors. The case being assigned to the class is the most common among its k-NNs measured by a distance function:

```
from sklearn.neighbors import KNeighborsClassifier
knn = KNeighborsClassifier(n_neighbors = 5)
knn.fit(X_train,y_train)
score = knn.score(X_train, y_train)
print(f"Training data accuracy {score}")
score = knn.score(X_test, y_test)
print(f"Testing data accuracy {score}")
```

```
Training data accuracy 0.9583333333333334
Testing data accuracy 0.9333333333333333
```

Decision trees

Decision trees attempt to create a tree-like model that predicts the value of a variable by learning simple decision rules that are inferred from the data features. Decision trees classify examples by sorting down the tree from the root to a leaf node, with the leaf node providing the classification for our example:

```
from sklearn import tree
dt = tree.DecisionTreeClassifier()
dt.fit(X_train, y_train)
score = dt.score(X_train, y_train)
print(f"Training data accuracy {score}")
score = dt.score(X_test, y_test)
print(f"Testing data accuracy {score}")
```

```
Training data accuracy 1.0
Testing data accuracy 0.9333333333333333
```

Random forest

Random forest builds decision trees using different samples and then takes the majority vote as the answer. In other words, random forest builds multiple decision trees and then merges them to get a more accurate prediction. Due to its simplicity, it is also one of the most commonly used algorithms:

```
from sklearn.ensemble import RandomForestClassifier
rf = RandomForestClassifier()
rf.fit(X_train, y_train)
score = rf.score(X_train, y_train)
print(f"Training data accuracy {score}")
score = rf.score(X_test, y_test)
print(f"Testing data accuracy {score}")
```

```
Training data accuracy 1.0
Testing data accuracy 0.9666666666666667
```

Neural networks

Neural networks (also referred to as deep learning) are algorithms that are inspired by how the human brain works, and are designed to recognize numerical patterns. Neural networks consist of input and output *layers* and (optionally) hidden layers. These layers contain units (*neurons*) that transform the inputs into something useful for the output layer. These neurons are connected and work together. We will look at these in more detail later in this book.

Making predictions

Once we have chosen and fit a machine learning model, it can easily be used to make predictions on new, unseen data – that is, take the final model and one or more data instances and then predict the classes for each of the data instances. The model is needed because the result classes are not known for the new data. The class for the unseen data can be predicted using scikit-learn's `predict()` function.

First, the unseen data must be transformed into a pandas DataFrame, along with the column names:

```
df_predict = pd.DataFrame([[5.9, 3.0, 5.1, 1.8]],
    columns = ['sepal.length', 'sepal.width',
    'petal.length', 'petal.width'])
```

This DataFrame can then be passed to scikit-learn's `predict()` function to predict the class value:

```
print (dt.predict(df_predict))
```

```
['Virginica']
```

A sample text classification problem

Given that this is a book on emotion classification and emotions are generally expressed in written form, it makes sense to take a look at how a text classification problem is tackled.

We have all received spam emails. These are typically emails that are sent to huge numbers of email addresses, usually for marketing or phishing purposes. Often, these emails are sent by bots. They are of no interest to the recipients and have not been requested by them. Consequently, email servers will often automatically detect and remove these messages by looking for recognizable phrases and patterns, and sometimes placing them into special folders labeled *Junk* or *Spam*.

In this example, we will build a spam detector and use the machine learning abilities of scikit-learn to train the spam detector to detect and classify text as spam and non-spam. There are many labeled datasets available online (for example, from Kaggle); we chose to use the dataset from https://www.kaggle.com/datasets/uciml/sms-spam-collection-dataset?resource=download.

The dataset contains SMS messages that have been collected for spam research. It contains 5,574 SMS messages in English that are labeled as spam or non-spam (ham). The file contains one message per line, and each line has two columns; the label and the message text.

We have seen some of the basic `pandas` commands already, so let's load the file and split it into training and test sets, as we did previously:

```python
import pandas as pd
from sklearn.feature_extraction.text import CountVectorizer
from sklearn.model_selection import train_test_split
from sklearn.neighbors import KNeighborsClassifier

spam = pd.read_csv("spam.csv", encoding_errors="ignore")
labels = spam["v1"]
data = spam["v2"]
X_train,X_test,y_train,y_test = train_test_split(data,
    labels, test_size = 0.2)
```

> **Note**
>
> The file may have an encoding error; for now, we will ignore this as it is not relevant to the task at hand.

A handy function called `CountVectorizer` is available in `sklearn`. This can be used to transform text into a vector of term-token counts. It is also able to preprocess the text data before generating the vector representations, hence it is an extremely useful function. `CountVectorizer` converts the raw text into a numerical vector representation, which makes it easy to use the text as inputs in machine learning tasks:

```python
count_vectorizer = CountVectorizer()
X_train_features = count_vectorizer.fit_transform(X_train)
```

Essentially, it assigns a number, randomly, to each word and then counts the number of occurrences of each. For example, consider the following sentence:

The quick brown fox jumps over the lazy dog.

This would be converted as follows:

word	the	quick	brown	fox	jumps	over	lazy	dog
index	0	1	2	3	4	5	6	7
count	2	1	1	1	1	1	1	1

Notice that there are eight unique words, hence eight columns. Each column represents a unique word in the vocabulary. Each count row represents the item or row in the dataset. The values in the cells are the word counts. Armed with this knowledge about the types and counts of common words that appear in spam, the model will be able to classify text as spam or non-spam.

We will use the simple k-NN model introduced earlier:

```
knn = KNeighborsClassifier(n_neighbors = 5)
```

The `fit()` function, as we have seen earlier, trains the model with the vectorized counts from the training data and the training labels. It compares its predictions against the real answers in `y_train` and then tunes its hyperparameters until it achieves the best possible accuracy. Note how here, since this is a classification task, the labels must also be passed to the `fit()` function. The Iris example earlier was a regression task; there were no labels, so we did not pass them into the `fit()` function:

```
knn.fit(X_train_features, y_train)
```

We now have a model that we can use on the test data to test for accuracy:

```
X_test_features = count_vectorizer.transform(X_test)
score = knn.score(X_test_features, y_test)
print(f"Training data accuracy {score}")
Training data accuracy 0.9255605381165919
```

Note how this time, we use `transform()` instead of `fit_transform()`. The difference is subtle but important. The `fit_transform()` function does `fit()`, followed by `transform()` – that is, it calculates the initial parameters, uses these calculated values to modify the training data, and generates a term-count matrix. This is needed when a model is being trained. The `transform()` method, on the other hand, only generates and returns the term-count matrix. The `score()` function then scores the prediction of the test data term-count matrix against the actual labels in test data labels, `y_test`, and even using a simplistic model we can classify spam with high accuracy and obtain reasonable results.

Summary

In this chapter, we started by examining emotion and sentiment, and their origins. Emotion is not the same as sentiment; emotion is more fine-grained and is much harder to quantify and work with. Hence, we learned about the three main theories of emotion, with psychologists, neurologists, and cognitive scientists each having slightly different views as to how emotions are formed. We explored the approaches of Ekman and Plutchik, and how the categorical and dimensional models are laid out.

We also examined the reasons why emotion analysis is important but difficult due to the nuances and difficulty of working with content written in natural language, particularly the kind of informal language we are concerned with in this book. We looked at the basic issues in NLP and will return to the most relevant aspects of NLP in *Chapter 4, Preprocessing – Stemming, Tagging, and Parsing*. Finally, we introduced machine learning and worked through some sample projects.

In the next chapter, we will explore where to find suitable data, the steps needed to make it fit for purpose, and how to construct a dataset suitable for emotion analysis.

References

To learn more about the topics that were covered in this chapter, take a look at the following resources:

- Alabbas, M., & Ramsay, A. M. (2013). *Natural language inference for Arabic using extendedtree edit distance with subtrees.* Journal of Artificial Intelligence Research, 48, 1–22.

- Dozat, T., Qi, P., & Manning, C. D. (2017). *Stanford's Graph-based Neural Dependency Parser at the CoNLL 2017 Shared Task.* Proceedings of the CoNLL 2017 Shared Task: Multilingual Parsing from Raw Text to Universal Dependencies, 20–30. https://doi.org/10.18653/v1/K17-3002.

- Ekman, P. (1993). *Facial expression and emotion. American Psychologist, 48(4)*, 384.

- Kitaev, N., & Klein, D. (2018). *Constituency Parsing with a Self-Attentive Encoder.* Proceedings of the 56th Annual Meeting of the Association for Computational Linguistics (Volume 1: Long Papers), 2,676–2,686. https://doi.org/10.18653/v1/P18-1249.

- Lewis, M., & Steedman, M. (2014). *A* CCG Parsing with a Supertag-factored Model.* Proceedings of the 2014 Conference on Empirical Methods in Natural Language Processing (EMNLP), 990–1,000. https://doi.org/10.3115/v1/D14-1107.

- MacCartney, B., & Manning, C. D. (2014). *Natural logic and natural language inference.* In Computing Meaning (pp. 129–147). Springer.

- McDonald, R., Pereira, F., Ribarov, K., & Hajič, J. (2005). *Non-Projective Dependency Parsing using Spanning Tree Algorithms.* Proceedings of Human Language Technology Conference and Conference on Empirical Methods in Natural Language Processing, 523–530. https://aclanthology.org/H05-1066.

- Nivre, J., Hall, J., & Nilsson, J. (2006). MaltParser: *A data-driven parser-generator for dependency parsing.* Proceedings of the International Conference on Language Resources and Evaluation (LREC), 6, 2,216–2,219.

- Pedregosa, F., Varoquaux, G., Gramfort, A., Michel, V., Thirion, B., Grisel, O., Blondel, M., Prettenhofer, P., Weiss, R., Dubourg, V., Vanderplas, J., Passos, A., Cournapeau, D., Brucher, M., Perrot, M., & Duchesnay, E. (2011). *Scikit-learn: Machine Learning in Python.* Journal of Machine Learning Research, 12, 2,825–2,830.

- Plutchik, R. (2001). *The Nature of Emotions: Human emotions have deep evolutionary roots, a fact that may explain their complexity and provide tools for clinical practice. American Scientist,* 89(4), 344–350.

- Russell, J. A. (1980). *A circumplex model of affect.* Journal of Personality and Social Psychology, 39(6), 1,161–1,178. https://doi.org/10.1037/h0077714.

Part 2: Building and Using a Dataset

The process of collecting data (e.g., tweets and news articles) is described in this part, followed by the preprocessing steps that are required to get good results to create a corpus.

This part has the following chapters:

- *Chapter 2, Building and Using a Dataset*
- *Chapter 3, Labeling Data*
- *Chapter 4, Preprocessing – Stemming, Tagging, and Parsing*

2
Building and Using a Dataset

The data collection and curation process is one of the most important stages in model building. It is also one of the most time-consuming. Typically, data can come from many sources; for example, customer records, transaction data, or stock lists. Nowadays, with the timely conjunction of big data, fast, high-capacity SSDs (to store big data), and GPUs (to process big data), it is easier for individuals to collect, store, and process data.

In this chapter, you will learn about finding and accessing pre-existing, ready-made data sources that can be used to train your model. We will also look at ways to create your own datasets, transforming datasets so that they are useful for your problem, and we will also see how non-English datasets can be utilized.

In the remainder of this book, we will be using a selection of the datasets listed in this chapter to train and test a range of classifiers. When we do this, we will want to assess how well the classifiers work on each of the datasets—one of the major lessons of this book is that different classifiers work well with different datasets, and to see how well a classifier works with a given dataset, we will need ways of measuring performance. We will therefore end this chapter by looking at metrics for assessing the performance of a classifier on a dataset.

In this chapter, we'll cover the following topics:

- Ready-made data sources
- Creating your own dataset
- Other data sources
- Transforming data
- Non-English datasets
- Evaluation

Ready-made data sources

There are lots of places where ready-made data is available and usually freely downloadable. These are typically referred to as **public data sources** and are usually made available by companies, institutions, and organizations that are happy to either share their data (perhaps for publicity, or to entice others to share) or to act as a repository for others to make their data easily searchable and accessible. Clearly, these will only be useful to you if your need matches the data source, but if it does, it can be a great starting point or even a supplement to your own data. The good news is that these data sources usually cover a wide range of domains, so it's likely you'll find something useful.

We'll now discuss some of these public data sources (in no particular order):

- **Kaggle**: Founded in 2010, Kaggle is a part of Google and, according to *Wikipedia*, is an "online community of data scientists and machine learning practitioners ". Kaggle has many features, but it is best known for its competitions in which anyone (for example, individuals and organizations) can publish a competition (typically a data science task) for participants to enter and compete to win prizes (sometimes in the form of cash!). However, Kaggle also allows users to find and publish datasets. Users can upload their datasets to Kaggle and also download datasets published by others.

  Everything on Kaggle is completely free, including datasets, and although the datasets are open source (open and free for download, modification, and reuse), for some datasets, it will be necessary to refer to the license to ascertain the purposes for which the dataset can be used. For example, some datasets may not be used for academic publications or commercial purposes. Users are also allowed to upload code to process the dataset, post comments against the dataset, and upvote the dataset so that others know that it is a reliable and useful dataset. There are also various other **Activity Overview** metrics, such as when the dataset was downloaded, how many times the dataset was downloaded, and how many times it was viewed. Since there are so many datasets (approximately 170,000 at the time of writing) these metrics can help you decide whether a dataset is worth downloading or not.

  URL: `https://www.kaggle.com/datasets`

- **Hugging Face**: The Hugging Face Hub is a community-driven collection of datasets that span a variety of domains and tasks—for example, **natural language processing** (**NLP**), **computer vision** (**CV**), and audio. Each dataset is a Git repository that has the scripts required to download the data and generate splits for training, evaluation, and testing. There are approximately 10,000 datasets that can be filtered by the following criteria:

  - Task categories (text classification, QA, text generation, etc.)

  - Tasks (language modeling, multi-class classification, language inference, etc.)

  - Language (English, French, German, etc.)

  - Multilinguality (monolingual, multilingual, translation, etc.)

- Size (10-100K, 1K-10K, 100K-1M, etc.)

- License (CC by 4.0, MIT, others, etc.)

Each dataset page includes a view of the first 100 rows of the dataset and also has a handy feature that allows you to copy the code to load a dataset. Some datasets also contain a loading script, which also allows you to easily load the dataset. Where the dataset does not include this loading script, the data is usually stored directly in the repository, in CSV, JSON, or Parquet format.

URL: `https://huggingface.co/datasets`

- **TensorFlow Datasets**: TensorFlow Datasets offers a set of datasets that are suitable for use not just with TensorFlow but also with other Python **machine learning** (ML) frameworks. Each dataset is presented as a class to allow the building of efficient data input pipelines and user-friendly input processes.

URL: `https://www.tensorflow.org/datasets`

- **Papers With Code**: This is a site that contains, as the name suggests, research papers along with their code implementations. At the time of writing, there are around 7,000 ML datasets available to freely download. These can be searched by using the following filters:

- Modality (text, images, video, audio, etc.)

- Task (QA, object detection, image classification, text classification, etc.)

- Language (English, Chinese, German, French, etc.)

According to its *About* page, all datasets are licensed under the CC BY-SA license, allowing anyone to use the datasets as long as the creator(s) are acknowledged. Usefully, each dataset lists papers that utilize the dataset, associated benchmarks, code, and similar datasets, and explains how the dataset can be loaded from within popular frameworks such as TensorFlow.

Papers With Code also encourages users to share their datasets with the community. The process is relatively simple and involves registering, uploading the dataset, and providing links and information (e.g. description, modality, task, language, etc.) about the dataset.

> **Note**
> Papers With Code's *About* page states that although the core team is based at Meta AI Research no data is shared with any Meta Platforms product.

URL: `https://paperswithcode.com/datasets`

- **IEEE DataPort**: IEEE DataPort is an online data repository that was created, and is owned by, the **Institute of Electrical and Electronics Engineers** (**IEEE**), a professional association for electronic engineering, electrical engineering, and associated disciplines. At the time of writing, there are around 6,000 datasets available. These can be searched by using either free-text search terms (for example, title, author, or **digital object identifier** (**DOI**)) or filters, such as the following:

- Category (**artificial intelligence** (**AI**), CV, ML, etc.)
- Type (Standard, Open Access)

Open Access datasets allow free access to all users, whereas accessing Standard datasets requires an IEEE paid subscription. IEEE DataPort also offers three options (Standard, Open Access, and Competition) for users to upload their datasets. Standard and Competition are free to upload and access; however, Open Access requires the purchase of an Open Access credit.

URL: `https://ieee-dataport.org/datasets`

- **Google Dataset Search**: Google Dataset Search is a search engine for datasets that features a simple keyword search engine (similar to the Google search page we all know and love) that allows users to find datasets that are themselves hosted in repositories (e.g. Kaggle) across the web. Results can then be filtered by the following criteria:

  - Last updated (past month, year)
  - Download format (text, tabular, document, image, etc.)
  - Usage rights (commercial use allowed/not allowed)
  - Topic (architecture and urban planning, computing, engineering, etc.)
  - Free or paid

The website states that the search engine only came out of beta in 2020, hence there may be more features added later. Being part of the Google ecosystem, it also allows users to easily bookmark datasets to return to later. As one would expect with Google, there is data available on a vast range of topics, from mobile apps to fast food and everything in between.

URL: `https://datasetsearch.research.google.com`

- **BigQuery public datasets**: BigQuery is a **Google Cloud Platform** (**GCP**) product that was built to provide serverless, cost-effective, highly scalable data warehouse capabilities. Hence, BigQuery is used to host and access public datasets, making them publicly available for users to integrate into their applications via projects. Although the datasets are free, users must pay for the queries that are performed on the data. However, at the time of writing, the first 1 TB per month is free. There are many ways to access BigQuery public datasets: by using the Google Cloud console, by using the BigQuery REST API, or through Google Analytics Hub.

URL: `https://cloud.google.com/bigquery/public-data`

- **Google Public Data Explorer**: Google Public Data Explorer is a web-based tool that makes it easy to explore and visualize datasets as line graphs, bar graphs, plots, or on maps. It provides data from about 135 organizations and academic institutions such as The World Bank, The **World Trade Organization** (**WTO**), Eurostat, and the US Census Bureau. Users are also able to upload, visualize, and share their own data by making use of Google's **Dataset Publishing Language** (**DSPL**) data format. Where the system really shines is when the charts are animated over time, making it easy even for non-scientists to understand the impact and gain insights.

URL: `https://www.google.com/publicdata/directory`

- **UCI Machine Learning Repository**: The **University of California Irvine (UCI)** Machine Learning Repository was created as an FTP archive in 1987 by graduate students at UCI. It is a free (registration not required) collection of approximately 600 datasets that are available for the ML community. The main website is rudimentary and outdated with a Google-powered search and no filtering capabilities, but (at the time of writing) a new version is in beta testing and offers the ability to search using the following filters:

  - Characteristics (text, tabular, sequential, time-series, image, etc.)

  - Subject area (business, computer science, engineering, law, etc.)

  - Associated tasks (classification, regression, clustering, etc.)

  - Number of attributes (fewer than 10, 10-100, more than 100)

  - Number of instances (fewer than 10, 10-100, more than 100)

  - Attribute types (numerical, categorical, mixed)

  The datasets in the repository are donated by different authors and organizations, hence each dataset has individual license requirements. The site states that to use the datasets, citation information should be used, and usage policies and licenses should be checked.

  URL: `https://archive.ics.uci.edu`

- **Registry of Open Data on AWS**: The Registry of Open Data on AWS (short for Amazon Web Services) is a centralized repository that makes it easy to find publicly available datasets. These datasets are not provided by Amazon, as they are owned by government organizations, researchers, businesses, and individuals. The registry can be used to discover and share datasets. There are approximately 330 datasets available, and these are accessed via the AWS Data Exchange service (an online marketplace offering thousands of datasets). Being Amazon, much of this infrastructure is tied to the core AWS services; for example, datasets can be used with AWS resources and easily integrated into AWS cloud-based applications. As an example, it only takes minutes to provision an Amazon **Elastic Compute Cloud (EC2)** instance and start working with the data.

  URL: `https://registry.opendata.aws`

- **US Government open data**: Launched in 2009, *Data.gov* is managed and hosted by the US General Services Administration and was created and launched by the US Government to provide access to federal, state, and local datasets. There are approximately 320,000 datasets that are made available in open, machine-readable formats, while continuing to maintain privacy and security, and can be searched by keyword or filtered by the following criteria:

  - Location

  - Topic (local government, climate, energy, etc.)

  - Topic category (health, flooding water, etc.)

- Dataset type (geospatial)
- Format (CSV, HTML, XML, etc.)
- Organization type (federal, state, local, etc.)
- Organization (NASA, state, department, etc.)
- Publisher
- Bureau

The datasets are made available for free and without restriction, although they do advise that non-federal data available may have a different licensing method.

URL: `https://data.gov`

- **data.gov.uk**: Similarly, the *data.gov.uk* site allows users to find public sector, non-personal data published by the UK central government, UK local authorities, and UK public bodies. The datasets are typically hosted on AWS. There are approximately 52,000 datasets that can be filtered by the following criteria:

  - Publisher (council)
  - Topic (business and economy, crime and justice, education, etc.)
  - Format (CSV, HTML, XLS, etc.)

  The datasets are free (registration required), and licensing appears to be a mix, with some being **Open Government License (OGL)**, which permits anyone to copy, distribute, or exploit the data, and others requiring **Freedom of Information (FOI)** requests for the dataset.

  URL: `https://ukdataservice.ac.uk`

- **Microsoft Azure Open Datasets**: This is a curated repository of datasets that can be used to train models. However, there are only about 50 datasets, covering areas such as transport, health, and labor, as well as some common datasets. There are no charges for using most of the datasets.

  URL: `https://azure.microsoft.com/en-us/products/open-datasets/`

- **Microsoft Research Open Data**: This is another collection of free datasets from Microsoft and contains datasets useful for areas such as NLP and CV. Again, there are only about 100 datasets, which can be searched by text or can be filtered by the following criteria:

  - Category (computer science, math, physics, etc.)
  - Format (CSV, DOCX, JPG, etc.)
  - License (Creative Commons, legacy Microsoft Research Data License Agreement, etc.)

  URL: `https://msropendata.com`

The preceding list is intended as an indicative, non-exhaustive guide for those who are unsure where to go to get data and provides examples of repositories from a number of organizations. There are also "repositories of repositories" where lists of dataset repositories are maintained, and these are good places to start searching for data. These include sites such as the DataCite Commons Repository Finder (`https://repositoryfinder.datacite.org`) and the Registry of Research Data Repositories `https://re3data.org/`, which offers researchers an overview of existing repositories for research data.

It should also be noted that some of the most common popular datasets are also easily available from within Python packages such as TensorFlow, **scikit-learn (sklearn)**, and the **Natural Language Toolkit (NLTK)**.

In this section, we saw how we can access ready-made data sources. However, sometimes these are inadequate, so let us next see how we can create our own data sources.

Creating your own dataset

Although we have seen several sources where datasets can be obtained, sometimes it is necessary to build your own datasets either using your own data or using data from other sources. This may be because the available datasets are not adequate for our problem, and this approach also brings some additional benefits, as follows:

- Creating your own dataset can eliminate the challenges associated with third-party datasets that often have licensing terms or usage restrictions.
- There are no fees to pay (although building the dataset will incur costs).
- If the dataset is being created using your own data, there are no ownership issues. If not, then it is your responsibility to consider ownership issues, and appropriate steps should be taken.
- You have complete ownership and flexibility in how you use the data.
- A fuller understanding of the data is gained as part of building the dataset.

Creating your own dataset also comes with increased responsibility; in other words, if there are any errors, issues, or biases, there will be only one person to blame!

Clearly, many types of data can be collected—for example, financial data, data from **Internet of Things (IoT)** devices, and data from databases. However, since the purpose of this book is the emotional analysis of text, we will demonstrate some ways to collect textual data to build datasets.

Data from PDF files

The **Portable Document Format (PDF)** format is one of the most popular and widely used digital file formats and is used to present and exchange documents. Many organizations use the PDF format to publish documentation, release notes, and other document types because files can be read anywhere, on any device, as long as (free) tools such as Adobe Acrobat Reader are installed. Consequently, this makes PDF files a good place to look for data. Luckily for us, Python has a number of libraries to help us extract text from PDF files, as listed here:

- PyPDF4

- PDFMiner

- PDFplumber

There are many others, but these seem to be the most popular. For this example, due to our previous experiences, we will use PyPDF4.

Firstly, we need to ensure that the PyPDF4 module is installed. Here's the command we run to achieve this:

```
pip install PyPDF4
```

Then, we need to import the package and set up a variable that contains the name of the file we wish to process. For this example, a sample PDF was downloaded from `https://www.jbc.org/article/S0021-9258(19)52451-6/pdf`:

```
import PyPDF4
file_name = "PIIS0021925819524516.pdf"
```

Next, we need to set up some objects that will actually allow us to read the PDF file, as follows:

```
file = open(file_name,'rb')
pdf_reader = PyPDF4.PdfFileReader(file)
```

PyPDF4 can also extract metadata (data about the file) from the PDF. Here's how to do that:

```
metadata = pdf_reader.getDocumentInfo()
print (f"Title: {metadata.title}")
print (f"Author: {metadata.author}")
print (f"Subject: {metadata.subject}")
```

The output shows the title, author, and subject of the document (there are also other fields available):

```
Title: PROTEIN MEASUREMENT WITH THE FOLIN PHENOL REAGENT
Author: Oliver H. Lowry
Subject: Journal of Biological Chemistry, 193 (1951) 265-275.
doi:10.1016/S0021-9258(19)52451-6
```

We can also get a count of the number of pages in the document by executing the following code:

```
pages = pdf_reader.numPages
print(f"Pages: {pages}")
```

The output shows the number of pages in the document:

```
Pages: 11
```

We can now iterate through each page, extract the text, and write it to a database or a file, like so:

```
page = 0
while page < pages:
    pdf_page = pdf_reader.getPage(page)
    print(pdf_page.extractText())
    page+=1
    # write to a database here
```

That's it! We have extracted the text from a PDF file and can use it to build a dataset and ultimately use it to train a model (after cleaning and preprocessing). Of course, in reality, we would wrap this into a function and iterate a folder of files to create a proper dataset, so let's do that.

First, we need to import the appropriate libraries and set up a folder where the PDF files are, as follows:

```
import PyPDF4
from pathlib import Path

folder = "./"
```

Now, we can refactor the code we had originally and reengineer it in the form of some handy reusable functions:

```
def print_metadata(pdf_reader):
    # print the meta data
    metadata = pdf_reader.getDocumentInfo()
    print (f"Title: {metadata.title}")
    print (f"Author: {metadata.author}")
    print (f"Subject: {metadata.subject}")


def save_content(pdf_reader):
    # print number of pages in pdf file
    pages = pdf_reader.numPages
    print(f"Pages: {pages}")

    # get content for each page
    page = 0
    while page < pages:
        pdf_page = pdf_reader.getPage(page)
        print(pdf_page.extractText())
        page+=1
        # write each page to a database here
```

Note how, in `save_content`, there is a placeholder where you would normally write the extracted content to a database.

And finally, here's the main code where we iterate the folder and, for each PDF file, extract the content:

```
pathlist = Path(folder).rglob('*.pdf')
for file_name in pathlist:
    file_name = str(file_name)

    pdf_file = open(file_name,'rb')
    pdf_reader = PyPDF4.PdfFileReader(pdf_file)
    print (f"File name: {file_name}")
    print_metadata(pdf_reader)
    save_content(pdf_reader)

    pdf_file.close()
```

As we have seen, extracting text from PDF files is pretty straightforward. Let's now see how we can get data from the internet.

Data from web scraping

Nowadays, there is so much publicly available data on the web in the form of (for example) news, blogs, and social media that it makes sense to gather ("harvest") and make use of this. The process of extracting data from a website is known as **web scraping**, and although this can be done manually, that would not be an efficient use of time and resources, especially when there are plenty of tools to help automate the process. The steps to do this are something like this:

1. Identify a root URL (a starting point).
2. Download the page content.
3. Process/clean/format the downloaded text.
4. Save the cleaned text.

Although there are no hard and fast rules, there are some rules of etiquette that will stop your program from getting blocked and some rules that will make scraping easier that should be followed:

- Add a delay between each scrape request so the site does not get overloaded
- Scrape during non-peak hours

Do note here that it is important that data is only scraped from sources that allow it, as unauthorized scraping can infringe terms of service and intellectual property rights and may even have legal ramifications. It is also a sensible idea to examine the metadata as it may provide guidance on whether the data is sensitive or private, data provenance, permissions, and restrictions on use. Being respectful of source permissions and data sensitivity are important considerations in responsible and ethical web scraping.

Let's begin!

Firstly, we need to ensure that the Beautiful Soup module is installed. We can do that using the following code:

```
pip install beautifulsoup4
```

> **Note**
>
> To prevent any unforeseen errors, please ensure that the following versions are installed:
>
> Beautiful Soup 4.11.2
>
> lxml 4.9.3

We then import the required libraries:

```
import bs4 as bs
import re
import time
from urllib.request import urlopen
```

We also need a URL to start scraping from. Here's an example:

```
ROOT_URL = "https://en.wikipedia.org/wiki/Emotion"
```

We now need to separate interesting, relevant content from the non-useful elements of a web page, such as the menu, header, and footer. Every website has its own set of design styles and conventions and will display its content in its own unique manner. For the website we chose, we found that looking for three consecutive <p> tags homed in on the content part of the page. It's very likely that this logic will be different for the website you are scraping from. To find these <p> tags, we define a **regular expression (regex)**, as follows:

```
p = re.compile(r'((<p[^>]*>(.(?!</p>))*.</p>\s*){3,})',
    re.DOTALL)
```

We now need to request the HTML for the website and extract the paragraphs using the regex. This text can then be cleaned (for example, any inline HTML removed) and saved to a database:

```
def get_url_content(url):
    with urlopen(url) as url:
        raw_html = url.read().decode('utf-8')
        for match in p.finditer(raw_html):
            paragraph = match.group(1)
            # clean up, extract HTML and save to database
```

However, we can go one step further. By extracting the hyperlinks from this page, we can get our program to keep scraping deeper into the website. This is where the previous commentary on best practices should be applied:

```python
def get_url_content(url):
    with urlopen(url) as url:
        raw_html = url.read().decode('utf-8')
        # clean up, extract HTML and save to database
        for match in p.finditer(raw_html):
            paragraph = match.group(1)
            soup = bs.BeautifulSoup(paragraph,'lxml')
            for link in soup.findAll('a'):
                new_url = (link.get('href'))
                # add a delay between each scrape
                time.sleep(1)
                get_url_content(new_url)
```

Finally, we need some code to start the scrape:

```python
raw_html = get_url_content(ROOT_URL)
```

To prevent the program from ending up in a loop, a list of visited URLs should be maintained and checked before scraping each URL—we have left this as an exercise for the reader.

> **Note**
>
> If you get a `<urlopen error [SSL: CERTIFICATE_VERIFY_FAILED] certificate verify failed: unable to get local issuer certificate (_ssl.c:997)>` error, you can use this link to resolve it: `https://stackoverflow.com/a/70495761/5457712`.

Data from RSS feeds

RSS (short for **Really Simple Syndication**) is a relatively old technology. Once upon a time, it was used to collate all the latest news into a web browser. Nowadays, it is not as popular as it once was but is still used by many to stay up to date. Most news providers provide RSS feeds on their websites.

An RSS feed is typically an **Extensible Markup Language** (**XML**) document that includes a URL to a web page (that can be scraped, as we have seen), full or summarized text, and metadata such as the publication date and the author's name.

Let's see how we can create a dataset of news headlines.

As usual, firstly we need to ensure that the module we need is installed. `feedparser` is a Python library that works with feeds in all known formats. You can install it using the following command:

```
pip install feedparser
```

Then, we import it, like so:

```
import feedparser
```

We also need a feed URL to work with. Here's an example:

```
RSS_URL = "http://feeds.bbci.co.uk/news/rss.xml"
```

Then, it is a simple matter of downloading the feed and extracting the relevant parts. For news headlines, we envisage that the summary contains more information, so it should be saved to a database:

```
def process_feed(rss_url):
    feed = feedparser.parse(rss_url)
    # attributes of the feed
    print (feed['feed']['title'])
    print (feed['feed']['link'])
    print (feed.feed.subtitle)

    for post in feed.entries:
        print (post.link)
        print (post.title)
        # save to database
        print (post.summary)
```

Finally, we need some code to start the process:

```
process_feed(RSS_URL)
```

The output shows the URL, title, and summary from each element in the feed:

```
BBC News - Home
https://www.bbc.co.uk/news/
BBC News - Home
https://www.bbc.co.uk/news/world-asia-63155169?at_medium=RSS&at_
campaign=KARANGA
Thailand: Many children among dead in nursery attack
An ex-police officer killed at least 37 people at a childcare centre
before killing himself and his family.
https://www.bbc.co.uk/news/world-asia-63158837?at_medium=RSS&at_
campaign=KARANGA
Thailand nursery attack: Witnesses describe shocking attack
There was terror and confusion as sleeping children were attacked by
the former policeman.
https://www.bbc.co.uk/news/science-environment-63163824?at_
medium=RSS&at_campaign=KARANGA
UK defies climate warnings with new oil and gas licences
More than 100 licences are expected to be granted for new fossil fuel
exploration in the North Sea.
```

Let us next take a look at how a more robust technology, APIs, can be used to download data.

Data from APIs

X (formerly Twitter) is a fantastic place to obtain text data; it offers an easy-to-use API. It is free to start off with, and there are many Python libraries available that can be used to call the API.

> **Note**
> At the time of writing, the free X (Twitter) API is in a state of flux, and it may no longer be possible to use the `tweepy` API.

Given that, later on in this book, we work with tweets, it is sensible at this point to learn how to extract tweets from Twitter. For this, we need a package called `tweepy`. Use the following command to install `tweepy`:

```
pip install tweepy
```

Next, we need to sign up for an account and generate some keys, so proceed as follows:

1. Go to `https://developer.twitter.com/en` and sign up for an account.
2. Go to `https://developer.twitter.com/en/portal/projects-and-apps`.
3. Click **Create App** in the **Standalone Apps** section.
4. Give your app a name, and make a note of the **API Key**, **API Key Secret**, and **Bearer Token** values.
5. Click **App Settings** and then click the **Keys and Tokens** tab.
6. On this page, click **Generate** in the **Access Token and Secret** section and again make a note of these values.

We are now ready to use these keys to get some tweets from Twitter! Let's run the following code:

```
import tweepy
import time

BEARER_TOKEN = "YOUR_KEY_HERE"
ACCESS_TOKEN = "YOUR_KEY_HERE"
ACCESS_TOKEN_SECRET = "YOUR_KEY_HERE"
CONSUMER_KEY = "YOUR_KEY_HERE"
CONSUMER_SECRET ="YOUR_KEY_HERE"
```

> **Note**
> You must replace the YOUR_KEY_HERE token with your own keys.

We then create a class with a subclassed special method called on_tweet that is triggered when a tweet is received from this stream. The code is actually pretty simple and looks like this:

```
client = tweepy.Client(BEARER_TOKEN, CONSUMER_KEY,
    CONSUMER_SECRET, ACCESS_TOKEN, ACCESS_TOKEN_SECRET)
auth = tweepy.OAuth1UserHandler(CONSUMER_KEY,
    CONSUMER_SECRET, ACCESS_TOKEN, ACCESS_TOKEN_SECRET)
api = tweepy.API(auth)

class TwitterStream(tweepy.StreamingClient):

    def on_tweet(self, tweet):
        print(tweet.text)
        time.sleep(0.2)
        # save to database

stream = TwitterStream(bearer_token=BEARER_TOKEN)
```

Tweepy insists that "rules" are added to filter the stream, so let's add a rule that states we are only interested in tweets that contain the #lfc hashtag:

```
stream.add_rules(tweepy.StreamRule("#lfc"))
print(stream.get_rules())
stream.filter()

Response(data=[StreamRule(value='#lfc', tag=None,
    id='1579970831714844672')], includes={}, errors=[],
    meta={'sent': '2022-10-12T23:02:31.158Z',
    'result_count': 1})
RT @TTTLLLKK: Rangers Fans after losing 1 - 7 (SEVEN) to Liverpool.
Sad Song 🎵 #LFC #RFC https://t.co/CvTVEGRBU1
Too bad Liverpool aren't in the Scottish league. Strong enough to
definitely finish in the Top 4. #afc #lfc
RT @LFCphoto: VAR GOAL CHECK
#LFC #RANLIV #UCL #Elliott @MoSalah https://t.co/7A7MUzW0Pa
Nah we getting cooked on Sunday https://t.co/bUhQcFICUg
RT @LFCphoto: #LFC #RANLIV #UCL https://t.co/6DrbZ2b9NT
```

> **Note**
>
> See here for more about Tweepy rules: `https://developer.twitter.com/en/docs/twitter-api/tweets/filtered-stream/integrate/build-a-rule`.
>
> Heavy use of the X (Twitter) API may need a paid package.

Other data sources

We have listed some of the commonly used sources of data in the previous section. However, there are probably many thousands of other free datasets available. You just need to know where to look. The following is a list of some of the interesting ones that we came across as part of our work on emotion analysis. There are probably many more available all over the internet:

- Dr. Saif Mohammad is a Senior Research Scientist at the **National Research Council (NRC)** Canada. He has published many papers and has been heavily involved with *SemEval*, as one of the organizers, for many years. He has also published many different, free-for-research purposes datasets that have been used primarily for competition purposes. Many of these are listed on his website at `http://saifmohammad.com/WebPages/SentimentEmotionLabeledData.html`, although some are better described on the associated competition page, as presented here:

  - The **Emotion Intensity (EmoInt)** dataset has four datasets for four emotions (`http://saifmohammad.com/WebPages/EmotionIntensity-SharedTask.html`).

  - The **Workshop on Computational Approaches to Subjectivity, Sentiment and Social Media Analysis (WASSA)** dataset is a total of 3,960 English tweets, each labeled with an emotion of anger, fear, joy, and sadness. Each tweet also has a real-valued score between 0 and 1, indicating the degree or intensity of the emotion felt by the speaker (`https://wt-public.emm4u.eu/wassa2017/`).

  - *SemEval* (Mohammad et al., 2018) is an annual competition in which teams of researchers from all over the world work on tasks where they develop systems to categorize datasets. The exact task varies from year to year. It has been running intermittently since 1998, but since 2012, it has become an annual event. A number of datasets have come about from this competition, as follows:

    - **2018 Task E-c**: A dataset containing tweets classified as "neutral or no emotion" or as 1, or more, of 11 given emotions that best represent the mental state of the tweeter.

    - **2018 Task EI-reg**: A dataset containing tweets labeled for emotion (anger, fear, joy, sadness), and for intensity, a real-valued score between 0 and 1, with a score of 1 indicating that the highest amount of emotion was inferred and a score of 0 indicating the lowest amount of emotion was inferred. The authors note that these scores have no inherent meaning; they are only used as a mechanism to convey that the instances with higher scores correspond to a greater degree of emotion than instances with lower scores.

- **2018 Task EI-oc:** A dataset containing tweets labeled for emotion (anger, fear, joy, sadness) and one of four ordinal classes of the intensity of emotion that best represented the mental state of the tweeter.

  These datasets are all available from `https://competitions.codalab.org/competitions/17751`.

- Across the competition years, there also seem to be plenty of datasets labeled for sentiment, as follows:

  - `https://alt.qcri.org/semeval2014/task9/`

  - `https://alt.qcri.org/semeval2015/task10/index.php?id=data-and-tools`

  - `https://alt.qcri.org/semeval2017/task4/`

- The Hashtag Emotion Corpus dataset contains tweets with emotion word hashtags (`http://saifmohammad.com/WebDocs/Jan9-2012-tweets-clean.txt.zip`).

- The **International Survey On Emotion Antecedents And Reactions (ISEAR)** dataset contains reports of situations in which student respondents had experienced emotions (joy, fear, anger, sadness, disgust, shame, and guilt) (`https://www.unige.ch/cisa/research/materials-and-online-research/research-material/`).

- A popular dataset labeled for sentiment (negative, neutral, positive) (`https://data.mendeley.com/datasets/z9zw7nt5h2`).

- A dataset labeled for six emotions (anger, fear, joy, love, sadness, surprise) (`https://github.com/dair-ai/emotion_dataset`).

- **Contextualized Affect Representations for Emotion Recognition (CARER)** is an emotion dataset collected through noisy labels, annotated for six emotions (anger, fear, joy, love, sadness, and surprise) (`https://paperswithcode.com/dataset/emotion`).

> **Note**
> It is vitally important to consider data privacy and ethical concerns when using these datasets.

We have seen how to access ready-made data sources and how to create your own data source. However, there may be occasions where these are good but not quite what we are looking for. Let's see how we can tackle that problem.

Transforming data

Although we have seen that there are many sentiment and emotion datasets available, it is rare that a dataset meets all the exact requirements. However, there are ways to tackle this problem.

We have seen some datasets labeled for sentiment, some for emotion, and also others labeled for more exotic things such as valence that do not seem to fit into what we are looking for: the emotion analysis problem. However, in certain circumstances, it is still possible to repurpose and use these. For example, if a dataset contains emotions, we can transform this into a sentiment dataset simply by assuming that the "anger" emotion is a negative sentiment and the "joy" emotion is a positive sentiment. A degree of subjectivity and manual analysis of the individual dataset is then required to determine which emotions would constitute a good substitute for the neutral sentiment. In our experience, this is typically not straightforward.

Data transformation is the name given to the process of applying changes to a dataset to make that dataset more useful for your purpose. This could include adding data, removing data, or any process that makes that data more useful. Let us consider some examples from the *Other data sources* section and see how we can repurpose them.

The EI-reg dataset, as described previously, contains tweets that were annotated for emotion (anger, fear, joy, sadness) and for intensity with a score between 0 and 1. We can sensibly guess that scores around and under 0.5 are not going to be indicative of highly emotive tweets and hence tweets with scores under 0.5 can be removed and the remaining tweets used to create a reduced, but potentially more useful dataset.

The EI-oc dataset also contained tweets that were annotated for emotion (anger, fear, joy, sadness) and one of four ordinal classes of the intensity of emotion that best represented the mental state of the tweeter, as follows:

- *0*: No emotion can be inferred
- *1*: Low amount of emotion can be inferred
- *2*: Moderate amount of emotion can be inferred
- *3*: High amount of emotion can be inferred

Again, we can sensibly guess that by removing tweets with scores lower than 3, we will get a dataset much better tuned to our needs.

These are relatively straightforward ideas of how datasets can be repurposed to extract data that is strongly emotive to create new datasets. However, any good dataset needs to be balanced, so let us now return to the problem of creating neutral tweets and see how this may be done. The following example assumes that the dataset is already downloaded and available; you can download it from here: http://www.saifmohammad.com/WebDocs/AIT-2018/AIT2018-DATA/EI-reg/English/EI-reg-En-train.zip.

> **Note**
> You may get an **EI-reg-En-train.zip can't be downloaded securely** error. In that case, simply click the **Keep** option.

The code is shown here:

```
import pandas as pd

data_file_path = "EI-reg-En-anger-train.txt"

df = pd.read_csv(data_file_path, sep='\t')

# drop rows where the emotion is not strong
df[df['Intensity Score'] <= 0.2]
```

A quick eyeball scan of the results shows tweets such as the following:

ID	Tweet	Affect Dimension	Intensity Score
2017-En-40665	i love the word fret so much and im in heaven	anger	0.127
2017-En-11066	I don't like pineapple I only eat them on pizza, they lose the sting when they get cooked.	anger	0.192
2017-En-41007	hate to see y'all frown but I'd rather see him smiling 🍃	anger	0.188

Figure 2.1 – Sample anger tweets with intensity scores < 0.2

We can see that there are tweets that, although they are low in anger intensity, are high in some other emotion and hence not neutral, and so we need some way to remove these. Clearly, it is the words themselves that tell us whether the tweet is neutral or not (for example, "love" or "hate"). There are plenty of lists of emotion words freely available on the internet; downloading one (https://www.ndapandas.org/wp-content/uploads/archive/Documents/News/FeelingsWordList.pdf) and printing the results shows the following output:

```
Abused
Admired
Afraid
.
.
.
Lonely
```

```
Loved
Mad
.
.
.
```

It is then a trivial matter, as a first pass, to remove tweets that contain any of these words. However, we can see that while tweet 2017-En-40665 says "love," the emotion words list says "Loved." This is problematic because this will prevent the tweet from being flagged as non-neutral. To address this, we simply have to stem or lemmatize (see *Chapter 5, Sentiment Lexicons and Vector Space Models* for further details) both the tweet and the emotion words list, as follows:

```python
stemmer = PorterStemmer()
def stem(sentence):
    res = (" ".join([stemmer.stem(i) for i in
        sentence.split()]))
    return res


# create some new columns
emotion_words['word_stemmed'] = emotion_words['word']
df['Tweet_stemmed'] = df['Tweet']


# stem the tweets and the emotions words list
df['Tweet_stemmed'] = df['Tweet_stemmed'].apply(stem)
emotion_words['word_stemmed'] = emotion_words[
    'word_stemmed'].apply(stem)


# remove tweets that contain an emotion word
res = []
dropped = []
for _, t_row in df.iterrows():
    tweet = t_row["Tweet_stemmed"]
    add = True
    for _, e_row in emotion_words.iterrows():
        emotion_word = e_row["word_stemmed"]
        if emotion_word in tweet:
            add = False
            break
    if add:
        res.append(t_row["Tweet"])
    else:
        dropped.append(t_row["Tweet"])
```

When we look at the results, here's what we see:

```
@Kristiann1125 lol wow i was gonna say really?! haha have you seen
chris or nah? you dont even snap me anymore dude!
And Republicans, you, namely Graham, Flake, Sasse and others are not
safe from my wrath, hence that Hillary Hiney-Kissing ad I saw about
you
@leepg \n\nLike a rabid dog I pulled out the backs of my cupboards
looking for a bakewell..Found a french fancie &amp; a mini batternburg
#Winner!
```

These are the tweets that were dropped:

```
@xandraaa5 @amayaallyn6 shut up hashtags are cool #offended
it makes me so fucking irate jesus. nobody is calling ppl who like
hajime abusive stop with the strawmen lmao
Lol Adam the Bull with his fake outrage...
```

We can see by and large this simplistic method has done a reasonable job. However, there are still cases that have slipped through—for example, where the hashtag contained an emotion word:

```
Ever put your fist through your laptops screen? If so its time for a
new one lmao #rage #anger #hp
```

It is easy to update the code to catch this. We'll leave that as an exercise for you, but the results must be examined carefully to catch edge cases such as this.

So far, we have looked solely at English datasets. However, there are many non-English datasets available. These may be useful when the dataset you need either does not exist or does exist but perhaps does not have enough data in it, or is imbalanced, and hence needs to be augmented. This is where we can turn to non-English datasets.

Non-English datasets

Often, finding a dataset to train your model is the most challenging part of the project. There may be occasions where a dataset is available but it is in a different language—this is where translation can be used to make that dataset useful for your task. There are a number of different ways to translate a dataset, as listed here:

- Ask someone you know, who knows the language
- Employ a specialist translation company
- Use an online translation service (e.g. Google Translate) either through the GUI or via an API

Clearly, the first two are the preferred options; however, they come with an associated cost in terms of effort, time, and money. The third option is also a good option, especially if there is a lot of data that needs translating. However, this option should be used with care because (as we will see) translation services have nuances, and each can produce different results.

There are lots of different translation services available (e.g. Google, Bing, Yandex, etc.) and lots of Python packages to utilize these (e.g. TextBlob, Googletrans, translate-api, etc.). We will use **translate-api** because it is easy to install, supports lots of translation services, and lets you start translating with only a few lines of code. Consider the following tweet:

توتر فز قلبي

First, we need to install the package, like so:

```
pip install translators
```

The code itself is deceptively simple:

```
import translators as ts

phrase = 'توتر فز قلبي'

FROM_LANG = 'ar'
TO_LANG = 'en'

text = ts.translate_text(phrase, translator='google',
    from_language=FROM_LANG , to_language=TO_LANG)
print (res)
```

This will produce the following output:

```
Twitter win my heart
```

Let's see what happens when we try one of the other translation providers:

```
ts.baidu
text = ts.translate_text(phrase, translator='bing',
    from_language=FROM_LANG ,
    to_language=TO_LANG)print (res)
```

The output is as follows:

```
Tension broke my heart
```

We can see that the results are not the same! This is why it is generally a good idea to get translation service results verified by a native speaker.

It can be seen, however, that the preceding code can easily be used to translate a complete dataset into English, thus generating new data for our model.

Evaluation

Once we have chosen a dataset, we will want to use it to train a classifier and see how well that classifier works. Assume that we have a dataset stored in the `dataset` variable and a classifier stored in `classifier`. The first thing we have to do is to split the dataset into two parts—one, stored in `training`, to be used for training the classifier, and one, stored in `testing`, for testing it. There are two obvious constraints on the way we do this split, as outlined here:

- `training` and `testing` must be disjoint. **This is essential**. If they are not, then there is a trivial classifier that will get everything 100% correct—namely, just remember all the examples you have seen. Even ignoring this trivial case, classifiers will generally perform better on datasets that they have been trained on than on unseen cases, but when a classifier is deployed in the field, the vast majority of cases will be unknown to it, so testing should always be done on unseen data.

- The way that data is collected can often introduce bias. To take a simple example, tweets are often collected in chronological order—that is, tweets that were written on the same day will often occur together in the dataset. But if everyone was very happy about some topic on days 1 to 90 of the collection process and very unhappy about it on days 91 to 100, then there would be lots of happy tweets at the start of the dataset and lots of unhappy ones at the end. If we chose the first 90 days of the dataset for training and the final day for testing, our classifier would probably overstate the likelihood that a tweet in the test set is happy.

  Therefore, it makes sense to randomize the data before splitting it into training and testing sections. However, if we do this, we should make sure that we always randomize it in the same way; otherwise, we will be unable to compare different classifiers on the same data since the randomization will mean that they are being trained and tested on different datasets.

There is a third issue to be considered. If we do not have all that much data, we will want to use as much of it as possible for training—in general, the more training data we have, the better our classifier will perform, so we do not want to waste too much of the data on testing. On the other hand, if we do not have much data for testing, then our tests cannot be relied on to give reliable results.

The solution is to use **cross-fold validation** (sometimes called **X-fold validation**). We construct a series of **folds**, where each fold splits the data into N-T points for training and T points for testing (N is the size of the whole dataset, while T is the number of points we want to use for testing). If we do this N/T times, using a different set for testing in each fold, we will eventually use all the data points for testing.

How big should T be? If we use very small sections for testing, we will have as much data as we can for training for each fold, but we will have to do a lot of rounds of training and testing. If we use large sections for testing, then we will have less data for training for each fold, but we will not have to do as many rounds. Suppose we have a dataset with 1000K data points. If we split it into two folds, using 500K points for training and 500K for testing, we will have quite substantial training sets (the scores for most of the classifiers we will be looking at in the remainder of the book flatten out well before we have 500K training points) and we will use all the data for testing (half of it in the first fold and the other half in the second), and we will only have to do two rounds of training and testing. If, on the other hand, we just have 1,000 data points, splitting it into two folds, each of which has 500 points for training and 500 for testing, will give us very small training sets. It would be better to split it into 10 folds, each with 900 points for training and 100 for testing, or even into 100 folds, each with 990 points for training and 10 for testing, or even 1,000 folds, each with 999 points for training and 1 for testing. Whichever we choose, we will use every point for testing exactly once, but if we use small test sets, we will maximize the size of the training set at the cost of carrying out more rounds of training and testing.

The following makeSplits function will divide a dataset into f folds, each with $N*(1-1/f)$ points for training and N/f for testing, and apply a classifier to each:

```
def makeSplits(dataset, classifier, f):
    scores = []
    N = len(dataset)/f
    # Randomize the dataset, but *make sure that you always shuffle
    # it the same way*
    random.seed(0)
    random.shuffle(pruned)
    for i in range(f):
        # test is everything from i*N to (i+1)*N,
        # train is everything else
        test = dataset[i*N:(i+1)*N]
        train, = dataset[:i*N]+dataset[(i+1)*N:]
        clsf = classifier.train(training)
        score = clsf.test(test)
        scores.append(score)
    return scores
```

In the remainder of this book, we use 10 folds for datasets with fewer than 20K data points and 5 folds for datasets with more than 20K data points. If we have 20K data points, using 5 folds will give us 16K points for training in each fold, which is typically enough to get a reasonable model, so since we will *always* eventually use every data point for testing, no matter how many or how few folds we use, this seems like a reasonable compromise.

In the preceding definition of makeSplits, classifier.train(training) trained the classifier and clsf.test(test) returned a score. For both of these tasks, we need to know which class each point in the dataset ought to belong to—we need a set of **Gold Standard** values. Without a set of Gold Standard values, the training phase does not know what it is supposed to be learning and the testing phase does not know whether the classifier is returning the right results. We will therefore assume that each data point has a Gold Standard label: how can we use these labels to assess the performance of a classifier?

Consider a classifier that is required to assign each data point to one of a set C1, C2, …, Cn of classes, and let `tweet.GS` and `tweet.predicted` be the Gold Standard value and the label assigned by the classifier. There are three possibilities: `tweet.GS` and `tweet.predicted` are the same, they are different, and the classifier simply fails to assign a value to `tweet.predicted`. If the classifier always assigns a value, then it is easy enough to calculate its accuracy since this is just the proportion of all cases that the classifier gets right:

```
def accuracy(dataset):
    return sum(x.GS==x.predicted for x in
        dataset)/len(dataset)
```

However, most classifiers allow for the third option—that is, in some cases, they can simply not provide an answer. This is a sensible thing to allow: if you ask a person whether one of their friends is happy or not, they might say yes, they might say no, but they might perfectly reasonably say they don't know. If you don't have any evidence that tells you whether something belongs to a given class, the only sensible thing to do is to say that you don't know.

This holds true for ML algorithms just as much as it does for people. It is always better for a classifier to say it is uncertain than for it to say the wrong thing. This does, however, make the task of comparing two classifiers less straightforward. Is a classifier that says "I don't know" in 95% of cases but gets the remaining 5% right better or is it worse than one that never admits it is uncertain but only gets 85% of cases right?

There is no single answer to this question. Suppose that giving a wrong answer would be disastrous— for example, if you thought someone might have taken some poison but the only known antidote is lethal for people who have not taken it. In that case, the classifier that frequently says it doesn't know but is always right when it does say something is better than the one that always makes a decision but is quite often wrong. If, on the other hand, giving the wrong answer won't really matter—for example, if you are considering giving someone statins because you think they might be prone to heart problems, then the one that always makes a decision but is sometimes wrong will be better. If you are likely to have heart problems, then taking statins is a good idea, and doing so when you don't need to is unlikely to lead to problems. Therefore, we have to be able to combine scores flexibly to allow for different situations.

We start by defining four useful parameters, as follows:

- **True positives (TP)**: The number of times that the classifier predicts that a tweet belongs to class C and the Gold Standard says that it does belong to C.

- **False positives (FP)**: The number of times that the classifier predicts that a tweet belongs to C and the Gold Standard says that it does not belong to C.

- **False negatives (FN)**: The number of times that the classifier makes no prediction but the Gold Standard says it does belong to some class (so it is not right, but it is not really wrong).

- **True negatives** (TN): The number of times that the classifier makes no prediction and the Gold Standard also says that the item in question does not belong to any of the available classes. In cases where each item belongs to exactly one class, this group is always empty, and it is typically not used in the assessment of classifiers.

Given these parameters, we can provide a number of metrics, as follows:

- **Precision**: How often the classifier is right when it makes a prediction—$TP/(TP + FP)$.

- **Recall**: How many of the cases where it should make a prediction it makes the right one—$TP/(TP + FN)$.

- **F-measure**: As noted previously, sometimes precision matters more (diagnosing a poison when the antidote is potentially lethal), while sometimes recall matters more (prescribing statins to someone who may have heart problems). F-measure, defined as $(P \times R)/(a \times P + (1 - a) \times R)$ for some a between 0 and 1, allows us to balance these two: we choose a to be greater than 0.5 if precision matters more than recall and less than 0.5 if recall matters more than precision. Setting a equal to 0.5 provides a midway point, usually called F1-measure.

- **Macro F1** and **micro F1**: When a task involves several classes, there are two ways of calculating F1. You can take all the cases where the classifier makes a decision and use these to calculate P and R, and thence F1, or you can calculate F1 for each class and then take the average over all classes. The first of these is called micro F1 and the second is macro F1. If one class contains many more cases than the others, then micro F1 can be misleading. Suppose that 99% of people with symptoms of poisoning actually have indigestion. Then, a classifier that classifies all cases of people with symptoms of poisoning actually having indigestion will have overall scores of P = 0.99 and R = 0.99, for a micro F1 score of 0.99. But that means that no one will ever get treated with the antidote: the individual P and R scores would be 0.99 and 1 for indigestion and 0.0, 0.0 for poisoning, for individual F1 scores of 0.99 and 0, averaging out at 0.495. In general, micro F1 gives more weight to the majority classes and provides an overestimate of the scores for the minority cases.

- The **Jaccard measure** provides an alternative way of combining TP, FP, and FN, using $TP/(TP + FP + FN)$. Given that simple F1 is easily shown to be the same as $TP/(TP + 0.5 \times (FP + FN))$ it is clear that the Jaccard measure and simple F1 will always provide the same ranking, with the Jaccard score always less than F1 (unless they are both 1). There is thus very little to choose between macro F1 and the Jaccard measure, but since some authors use one when comparing classifiers and others the other, we will give macro F1, micro F1, and Jaccard in all tables where we compare classifiers.

A number of the datasets we will be looking at allow tweets to have arbitrary numbers of labels. Many tweets express no emotions at all, so we need to allow for cases where the Gold Standard does not assign anything, and quite a few express multiple emotions. We will refer to datasets of this kind as **multi-label datasets**. This must be distinguished from datasets where there are several classes (**multi-class datasets**) and the task is to assign each tweet to exactly one of the options. As we will see, multi-label datasets are significantly harder to work with than single-label multi-class datasets. As far as metrics are concerned, true negatives (which are not used in any of the metrics given previously) become more significant for multi-label tasks, particularly for tasks where the Gold Standard may assign no labels at all to a tweet. We will look in detail at multi-label tasks in *Chapter 10, Multiclassifiers*. For now, we will just note that training and testing should be carried out using multiple folds to make sure that every data point gets used exactly once for testing, with smaller test sets (and hence more folds) for small datasets, and that macro F1 and Jaccard scores are the most useful metrics for comparing classifiers.

Summary

There is no doubt that finding suitable data can be a challenge, but there are ways and means to mitigate that. For example, there are plenty of repositories with comprehensive search features that allow you to find relevant datasets.

In this chapter, we started by looking at public data sources and went through some of the most popular ones. We saw that many datasets are free, but access to some required a subscription to the repository. Even with the existence of these repositories, there is still sometimes a need to "roll your own" dataset, so we looked at the benefit of doing that and some ways in which we might collect our own data and create our own datasets. We then discussed some niche places to find datasets specific to the emotion analysis problem—for example, from competition websites. Datasets often contain sensitive information about individuals, such as their personal beliefs, behaviors, and mental health status, hence we noted that it is crucial to consider data privacy and ethics concerns when using datasets. We also looked at how we could take datasets that were similar to what we required and how to transform them into something more useful. Finally, we looked at how we could take a non-English dataset and transform it into our target language, and also the problems of doing so.

We also considered issues that arise when we are trying to evaluate classifiers, introducing the notion of cross-fold validation and looking at a number of metrics that can be used for assessing classifiers. We noted that splitting the data into a large number of folds, each with a small set for testing, is important when you have a fairly small dataset. Doing, for instance, 10-fold cross-validation is not necessarily more rigorous than using 5 folds: if we have a lot of data, then using a few folds, each with a large amount of test data, is a perfectly reasonable thing to do. We also considered the merits of the various metrics that are most commonly used and decided that since different authors use different metrics it makes sense to report all of them since that makes it possible to compare the scores for a given classifier with scores published elsewhere.

In the next chapter, we will look at labeling, key considerations, and some good practices that can improve the effectiveness and accuracy of the process. We will also explore techniques to improve outcomes and look at a simple architecture and UI for the data labeling task.

References

To learn more about the topics that were covered in this chapter, take a look at the following resources:

- Mohammad, S. M., Bravo-Marquez, F., Salameh, M., and Kiritchenko, S. (2018). *SemEval-2018 Task 1: Affect in Tweets*. Proceedings of International Workshop on Semantic Evaluation (SemEval-2018).

3

Labeling Data

Artificial Intelligence (AI) models are only as good as the data they are trained with. Hence good, high-quality data is vitally important.

AI algorithms generally start in a basic, simplified, form. In supervised learning, accurately labeling (also known as annotating) data is a vitally important step to train an algorithm, improve its predictions, and ensure that what it learns is right. Numerous studies, reports, and surveys show that data scientists spend anywhere between 50-80% of their time doing data preparation and preprocessing (see *Figure 3.1*) – and data labeling is usually a huge part of this.

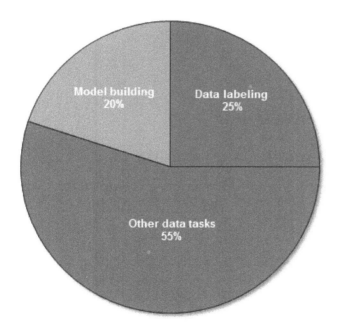

Figure 3.1 – Distribution of time allocated to machine learning tasks

In this chapter, you will learn why it is important to ensure that data is labeled correctly; how this can be achieved; how to assess whether it has indeed been achieved; and in particular, how to identify annotators who have not carried out the task to the required standard.

In this chapter, we will cover the following topics:

- Why labeling must be high quality
- The labeling process
- Best practices
- How to label data
- Determining what the best labeling option is for you
- Gold tweets
- Competency tasks
- Annotation
- Deciding whether to buy or build an annotation solution
- Results from the example scenario
- Inter-annotator reliability
- Krippendorff's alpha
- Debriefing after annotation

Before we investigate in depth how to do labeling, let us think about why maximum effort must be put into ensuring that labels are high quality.

Why labeling must be high quality

The process of labeling data is the process of preparing a dataset such that algorithms can learn to recognize patterns that repeat in the data. The idea is that once the algorithm has seen enough data labeled in a certain way, it should be able to identify such patterns in data that it has not seen previously (known as unlabeled data).

Remember, data labeling facilitates the algorithms that power AI to build accurate models. With more and more businesses getting interested in AI to help gain insights and make predictions, it is no surprise that data labeling is a huge market worth billions. It is no exaggeration to say that without data labeling, it is impossible to build AI models.

Nowadays, **Explainable AI (XAI)** is more important than ever. Stakeholders want to know why a model came to the decision that it did. In turn, this also helps build confidence in the model. Part of this is the data labeling stage, hence it is vital to ensure that this process is subject to the same rigorous checks and balances as other parts of the process; even minor errors can have significant consequences upstream that can be problematic for model accuracy.

It is also important to understand that data labeling is not a one-off process. Instead, it is a continuous process of building and refinement.

The labeling process

The process of data labeling usually begins by getting humans to use their domain expertise or knowledge, intelligence, sense, and perception to make a decision about data that is unlabeled.

Generally, labeled data consists of data that is unlabeled along with a tag, label, or name corresponding to some feature found in the data. In **natural language processing** (**NLP**), annotators (also known as labelers) will mentally identify important aspects of the text and use these to create labels. For example, to ascertain the emotion of a text, annotators would perhaps combine an approach that looked for key indicators of emotion (e.g., *happy*, *amazed*) with an understanding of the context and an exploration of the emotional undertones of the words themselves.

Other types of data labeling include images and audio. When labeling a dataset containing images, each image might be labeled as a fruit (e.g., `apple`, `banana`, `pear`), or the labeling process may be as simple as asking the annotator to tag images as `true` if they contain an apple, or `false` otherwise. When annotators are required to consider audio (e.g., speech or other sounds), the annotation process can be quite complex, since the labels may have to be attached to segments of the input or otherwise time-stamped, which may require sophisticated annotation tools.

Although data labeling can be performed by anyone with suitable training, there are specialists who are experts in the art of data labeling, ensuring that labeling is standardized, robust, and accurate.

When labeling data, it is a good idea to consider the following:

- The goal is high-quality data labels. This may entail navigating problems such as poorly trained or poorly equipped personnel, inadequate methods and processes, or unclear instructions being provided.

- For most AI problems that involve training a model from scratch, non-trivial amounts of training data are required. Furthermore, this may not be a one-time process. Consequently, keeping scaling in mind when putting together processes, training, and other requirements is essential. This then allows the labeling capacity to be increased with minimal effort, in a streamlined way, and with minimum disruption.

- Cost may also be a factor as labeling can end up being a costly process, and to make things worse, this may not always be apparent. For example, paying highly-qualified staff to preprocess or clean data using laborious, tedious, and repetitive processes is clearly not an efficient use of resources. It might be beneficial to employ data labeling specialists under such circumstances.

- **Quality assurance** (**QA**) must also be considered. The quality and accuracy of labeling are directly proportional to the accuracy and care taken when labeling. There are various algorithms and techniques that can be used to obtain a measure of annotation accuracy. For example, when multiple annotators are used, Fleiss' kappa is a statistical measure that can be used to determine the level of agreement between the annotators.

Typically, the data labeling process consists of the following steps:

1. **Collection**: Data is collected (e.g., tweets, images, files, etc.), and although there is no perfect amount needed, typically, this is a large amount as it guarantees to cover the distribution of data better and give better results. Note that for fine-tuning the model, smaller amounts may be sufficient.

2. **Tagging**: This involves humans identifying objects or aspects of the data, typically using a data labeling tool.

3. **QA**: There is little point in laboriously labeling data if it is not accurate and does not inform the model as intended. Consequently, QA processes must be in place to assess the accuracy of the labeled data. Without these, it is likely the model will not perform adequately.

Before we finish this section, a word on what to do if there isn't enough data. There are a number of methods that can help here:

- **Augmentation**: This involves creating new data based on the existing data. For example, for images, techniques such as horizontal and vertical shifting/flipping, random rotation, and random zoom can be used to generate *new* images with different resolutions that are cropped, rotated, or zoomed. As an added benefit, this also exposes the model to this sort of image and helps it to become more robust.

- **Synthesis**: This involves creating new instances using techniques such as **Synthetic Minority Oversampling TEchnique (SMOTE)** or **generative adversarial networks (GANs)** and is typically used when there are not enough examples of a minority class for a model to be able to learn the decision boundary. SMOTE works by selecting examples that are near to each other in the feature space, drawing a line between these, and then creating new samples at points along the line. GANs are deep learning models that generate data that impersonates the real data by using a method in which two neural networks work against each other: a generator, to generate the synthetic data, and a discriminator, which attempts to distinguish between real and synthetic data. Both these techniques are risky since they rely on assumptions about the data that may not be true, and hence they should only be used when very little data is available. Furthermore, any biases present in GAN datasets will also be inherited by the model when it generates data.

- **Regularization**: This involves penalizing data points that are somehow deemed less important, hence giving more weight to the more important data points.

It is important to note that even with these methods, it is always preferable to use well-curated data that covers all cases and is well-distributed.

Next, let's look at some best practices that can make the process run more smoothly and with fewer errors.

Best practices

Data labeling is a tedious, but necessary, process. The last thing you want to do is have to repeat the process due to some misunderstanding. That is why following good practice can improve the effectiveness and accuracy of the process. The following are some of the things you can do to ensure that your data is labeled efficiently and correctly:

- **Use the right software**: You could just use a spreadsheet, but why not make things easier for yourself? There are lots of commercial products available that will speed up the process. If you have the right programming skills, it's also worth considering fashioning your own solution. It doesn't need to be commercial -grade – just good enough to do the job. Some of the things you should consider are as follows (we talk about these in depth later in this chapter):

  - Provide logins for annotators, so they can log back in later and carry on where they left off. Labeling is a tedious, mundane task. Logins allow users to log off, take a break, and come back (e.g., the next day) refreshed.

  - Annotators are typically paid to do the task. It is a good idea to intersperse **gold standard** data points throughout the task to check that the annotator isn't just randomly selecting an option. If an annotator provides labels that fail to match the gold standard points, it is likely that they are not paying proper attention to the task. In that case, it may be worth looking in more detail at a larger sample of their annotations and, if necessary, eliminating their contributions.

  - If your annotators are volunteers, they may get fed up long before the end. In a dataset of 200 items (for example), what you don't want is that 5 annotators (for example) all label data items from 1-100, and no one managed to get to 101-200. To mitigate this probability, you should develop your solution so that annotators work on different parts of the dataset. This also helps in the learning process because the models won't learn anything from seeing the same example numerous times.

- **Measure model performance**: Research has shown that beyond a certain point, throwing more data at a model yields little benefit. Labeling is a time-consuming and costly exercise, hence it makes sense to know when to stop, or at least consider how to extract further improvements from the model.

- **Organize**: Sometimes, you might even want multiple annotators working on the same data. It stands to reason that the more annotators you have, the quicker you can get the job done. However, you should organize the task so that different sections of the dataset are labeled but there should also be some overlap so that annotator agreement can be measured.

- **Provide clear instructions**: Producing a document or a web page or some other written means of getting your instructions across to your annotators in a clear, consistent way will help in improving the accuracy of labeling.

- **Measure agreement**: Ideally, to ensure high-quality labeling, there should be a sensible level of agreement between annotators. This can be ascertained by making use of one of the inter-annotator reliability metrics.

Following these practices will ensure a streamlined, error-free process that provides good-quality labeled data.

Where multiple annotators consistently disagree on the label, it is very likely that the data point is not suitable for training and should be discarded from the dataset. Furthermore, not all data points gathered need to be labeled if the requirement is high-quality labels. For example, a noisy or blurry image might lead different annotators to see the image differently.

Now that we have seen some best practices, we are ready to think about how to actually do the labeling.

Labeling the data

There are many ways to get data labeled, each with its own pros and cons:

- **Internal (in-house) labeling**: This is when experts from within an organization are used to label data. These are usually people who are domain experts and hence are very familiar with the process and requirements. Consequently, this leads to better quality control and high-quality labeling. Furthermore, as the data doesn't need to leave the building, there are fewer associated security risks. However, internal labeling is not always possible (e.g., the company size is small or there is a lot of data to label). Furthermore, domain experts are expensive people so asking them to spend inordinate amounts of time on menial annotation tasks is probably not the best use of resources!

- **External (outsourced) labeling**: As the name suggests, this is when the job is outsourced to companies that specialize in data labeling. These companies are experts at data labeling, and consequently, the process is much smoother, quicker, and often, much cheaper as well. However, the danger here is that although they may be experts at data labeling, they likely will not be experts in the specific domain, and this increases the risk of error. Furthermore, there are also increased security risks as data will have to be made available to them.

- **Crowdsourcing**: This is the process of turning to a group of people, sourced online, to help with any task. Typically, these people are freelancers and can be paid or unpaid. Many of the world's biggest companies (e.g., McDonald's) have used crowdsourcing for tasks such as research, logo design, and more. It is a good option for organizations that are unable to implement internal labeling and cannot find a suitable external labeling partner. One of the most popular ways to approach crowdsourcing is by using Amazon's **Mechanical Turk** (**MTurk**). **MTurk** is a crowdsourcing marketplace that makes it easier for individuals and businesses to connect and hence allows businesses to outsource tasks to a workforce that then performs these tasks virtually. This workforce can work in collaboration with an in-house team or even alone. It is an extremely efficient way to get the job done but does suffer from the fact that quality is not guaranteed, there are associated data security risks, and there is a bigger associated management overhead.

Clearly, internal labeling is the go-to option, if it is viable. The problem here is that some companies just don't have the resources to do this. Consequently, any of the other options can be considered but each has its pros and cons – for example, crowdsourcing requires much more quality control than the other methods. All things considered, it is probably sensible to either crowdsource (and put up with the extra management that will be required) or employ an external labeling service, which, in any case, is not as expensive as you might think.

The next sections consider and describe how, for a previous task, we manually labeled a dataset by sourcing annotators, building a UI, and including checks and balances to ensure that the labeling was fit for purpose and as accurate as possible.

Gold tweets

It is a sensible idea to intersperse a number of special tweets within the dataset that is to be labeled. These should be a mixture of different types of tweets. These tweets, referred to as **gold tweets**, were annotated internally beforehand (by the authors) and were interspersed within the dataset. They are important as they can be used as a mechanism to avoid malicious or incompetent annotations. For example, if an annotator's gold tweet results are below some threshold (e.g., 70%), it can be assumed that they either didn't understand the task, or were demotivated to utilize the deeper thinking required on such tasks, and hence their annotations should probably be discarded. Essentially, this is a mechanism that avoids malicious annotations. Furthermore, to ensure that the results are valid, a metric such as Fleiss' kappa or Krippendorff's alpha (we will explain these later in this chapter) should be used to ensure that there are no problems with rater agreement.

Let's next look at another way we can determine whether an individual is of the required level to undertake our annotation task.

The competency task

When opting for internal, external, or crowdsource approaches, it is always a good idea to implement some initial competency tasks, or tests, to assess the suitability of the annotators. For example, if you are asking an annotator to label Arabic tweets, not only must they understand Arabic but they must also be familiar with the nuances of the language and the intricacies of the language used on X (formerly known as Twitter).

Furthermore, the labeling exercise should be manageable for the annotators, and the level of annotator attention kept high, hence the dataset should be constructed with (for example) a mixture of challenging and easy tasks.

We will now describe a robust scenario for labeling. In this example, the objective is to label tweets; however, the ideas and methodologies can be adapted for any type of data (e.g., images). Consider the following scenario. The task is to label 1,000 Arabic tweets, hence a request for native Arabic speakers is placed on a crowdsourcing website to examine 1,000 tweets and classify them for emotion.

> **Note**
>
> Although the task itself was to label Arabic tweets, for ease of reading, the screenshots presented in this section have been translated into English.

The task itself could be done using Excel, an off-the-shelf software solution, or even a custom solution developed in-house. A payment of $100 is offered to annotators, but it is made clear that this payment will only be made after the annotations are completed. Each of the annotators is asked to perform the same task: namely, annotate 1,000 tweets for the same number of emotions.

> **Multi-class or multi-label?**
>
> The terms *multi-class* classification and *multi-label* classification describe two different problems.
>
> When instances can only be labeled with one from three or more classes, this is known as multi-class classification. For example, when classifying images of fruits into [Apple, Banana, Orange], each image can belong to one, and only one, category.
>
> However, where multiple labels can be predicted for each instance, this is known as multi-label classification. For example, when labeling a text with one of [Education, Politics, Religion, Sports], the text might be about all of these or none of these.
>
> The scenario presented in this chapter addresses the problem of multi-label classification.

One tweet at a time was presented to the annotators and two questions were asked. The first was a single-answer multiple- choice question:

Q1. Which of the following options best describes the emotional state of the tweeter?

- anger (including annoyance, rage)
- anticipation (including interest, vigilance)
- disgust (including disinterest, dislike, loathing)
- fear (including apprehension, anxiety, terror)
- joy (including serenity, ecstasy)
- love (including affection)
- optimism (including hopefulness, confidence)
- pessimism (including cynicism, no confidence)
- sadness (including pensiveness, grief)
- surprise (including distraction, amazement)
- trust (including acceptance, liking, admiration)
- neutral or no emotion

The second question was a checkbox question, where more than one answer could be selected:

Q2. In addition to your response to Q1, which of the following options further describe the emotional state of the tweeter?

This question included the same choices as Q1, but *neutral or no emotion* was replaced with *none of the above*.

In this scenario, it is not unusual to receive a huge number of responses. How are you to decide whom to select for the task? It is a good idea to gauge the competence levels of the applicants who expressed an interest by asking them to complete a short, online, emotion classification exercise consisting of a small number of tweets that are representative of the overall task, and ideally sourced from the same dataset as the task tweets. To perform the test fairly and consistently, applicants should be provided with clear instructions, as seen in *Figure 3.2*.

Instructions

1. Review the examples on the next page and ensure you understand why the emotions apply.

2. Use your unique username (supplied to you) to login.

3. Read each tweet story fully.

4. Ponder over the emotions the **tweeter** was feeling.

5. Select **ONE** primary emotion from the red headings.

6. Select **as many** secondary emotions as neccessary from the green headings.

7. It is the emotions of the **tweeter** we are interested in, **NOT** your emotions.

8. Click "Submit" to move on to the next tweet story.

NOTE: These tweets were automatically gathered, therefore there may be offensive tweets.

Apologies in advance.

 (Click next to continue to the examples.)

Figure 3.2 – Instructions for tweet annotators (source: Classification of tweets using multiple thresholds with self-correction and weighted conditional probabilities, Ahmad and Ramsay, 2020)

It is also sensible to provide the annotators with examples, as seen in *Figure 3.3*.

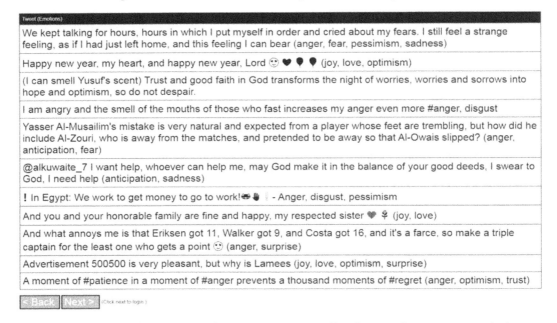

Figure 3.3 – Example annotations for annotators (source: Classification of tweets using multiple thresholds with self-correction and weighted conditional probabilities, Ahmad and Ramsay, 2020)

In this scenario, applicants are asked to examine each tweet and select one primary emotion and as many secondary emotions as appropriate (we'll explain why we use this setup shortly). It is important to understand that the annotators do not possess the same domain knowledge as you; consequently, the instructions need to be clear, concise, unambiguous, and easily understood. The instructions should clearly describe what you want the annotators to do and contain ample examples. For example, in the emotion annotation task, it is a good idea to include the different variations of an emotion (e.g., for anger: annoyance and rage). It is also usually a good idea to conduct an iterative review of the instructions to ensure that any issues are identified before publication. Although instructions can be published in any format (Word, PDF, etc.), HTML is a good choice because it allows changes to be made without having the overhead of having to redistribute copies of the instructions. However, it is a good idea to use version numbering and source code management (e.g., Git). Indeed, it may also be sensible to link instruction versions with versions of your build.

Instructions are also required because labeling tweets is generally a subjective task, open to the labeler's understanding, experiences, background, and interpretation of the text with no single point of truth. Indeed, the same annotator may give different answers if asked to reannotate the tweet in the future. The following tweet is an example where there is no, one, definitive answer:

This is good airline service but comes with high tariff. They do not provide good service. Best part of this airline is they are always available.

In this situation, the instructions need to provide clear guidance as to how to understand the item, and how to label it.

The job of the annotator is not easy. The annotator has to reflect, understand, and then select the label, or labels, that will ultimately form the inputs to the machine learning model. On the face of it, this is not a difficult task, with no specific training or knowledge required, and it can be tackled increasingly as an independent resource working from home. However, having to do the same thing repeatedly, while at the same time maintaining a level of accuracy and consistency, is not straightforward. However, there is no magic wand that can be waved, and the expertise of the annotators is as important as any other part of the solution. Some of the skills that an annotator is expected to have include the following:

- **Concentration**: An annotator should have the ability to concentrate on what's on the screen for long periods of time, without becoming side-tracked, and without making mistakes

- **Paying attention to detail**: Getting annotations wrong repeatedly could end up in a biased or an underperforming model, which could have other consequences

- **Working alone**: Annotating can involve long periods of working alone, which might be feasible for some, but not for others

- **Understanding the language**: Things such as sarcasm and humor can be hard to detect, hence these require a proper level of understanding of the language and an advanced level of cognitive process

In summary, the annotator will have to achieve a consistent level of commitment, concentration, and care in order to do a good job. However, it must also be understood that it is impossible to entirely remove human error, no matter how good the procedures and instructions are. It should also be noted that the task is intrinsically subjective, and two annotators can sometimes assign different labels to the same tweet without either of them being wrong.

Figure 3.4 – Tweet annotation page

Both the tweets and the emotion answers were sourced from the complete dataset that we wish to label. Since these tweets are carefully selected specifically for the purpose of the test, the answers are clear, well-defined, and known. Hence it is relatively straightforward to select whatever number of annotators is required, and who scored the highest.

Having selected the annotators to move forward with, it is now time to move on to the task of labeling the proper dataset itself.

The annotation task

The same annotation platform as used for the competence task can also be repurposed for the annotation task. However, in the competency task, the tweets were presented in sequence, whereas in the annotation task, some clever logic is used. Without going into too much detail, it is a good idea to use a database such as Access or MySQL. This allows questions to be partitioned, answers to be tracked, and the results to be analyzed. This also enables the ability to determine how much of the dataset has been labeled, which tweets have been labeled, and, importantly, the distribution of those answers (we'll explain why this is important shortly).

A schema describes how data will be organized and connected and includes tables, relationships, and other elements. *Figure 3.5* shows a simple sample database schema.

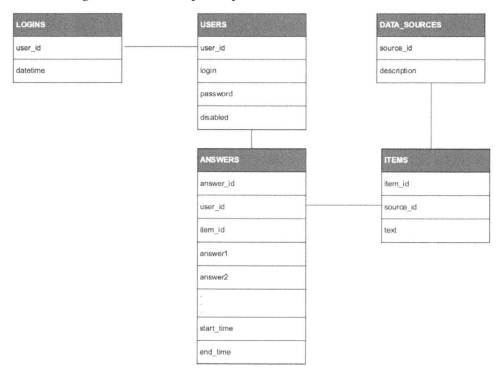

Figure 3.5 – Database schema diagram

The USERS table contains a record for each person who will be labeling. Note that the disabled column can be used to bar access to the system – for example, if a user has failed the competency test. Note also the LOGINS table. This simply logs the date and time each time a user successfully logs in to the system. This can be used to obtain useful information such as the time the user did the labeling, and how many sittings were required to do the labeling. In turn, this could be useful to pinpoint why (for example) they didn't do a good job. For example, if the LOGINS table showed that they were logging in daily late in the evening when people are generally tired, this might be a reason for a poor labeling score (this is entirely speculative, of course, as in today's modern world, many people prefer working in the afternoons or evenings).

The DATA_SOURCES table can be used to group tweets by function (e.g., Competency, Live, and Test). The ITEMS table then contains items that require labeling with a foreign key back to the data source they belong to. Finally, the ANSWERS table is self-explanatory, linking each item to a user and the answers that were supplied.

> **Note**
>
> For the purposes of labeling 11 emotions, we simply created 11 columns – one for each emotion. However, for a truly generic, customizable solution, the labels should be stored in a separate table and another table used to link them to the items. Furthermore, the number and type of answer expected (single, multiple, etc.) should also be configurable.

Although there was payment involved, respondents were free to annotate as many tweets as they wished. However, the ideal scenario was that even if each of the participants only did some of the task, the overall labeled dataset would be distributed across the dataset. In other words, if each of the 5 annotators only labeled 200 tweets each, the totality should be across the whole dataset (see *Figure 3.6*).

Annotator 1	Annotator 2	Annotator 3	Annotator 4	Annotator 5
Tweets 1-200	Tweets 201-400	Tweets 401-600	Tweets 601-800	Tweets 801-1000

Figure 3.6 – Distributed tweet labeling

We can ensure this by making use of some clever programming. Each tweet in the database has a unique ID (item_id). This is also stored in the ANSWERS table when an answer is submitted, along with the users ID. In this way, we can keep track of which questions have been answered and by whom. Recall that each question has to be answered by every annotator. It is then a simple task to fashion some SQL, as follows, that finds the question that has been answered the least (i.e., has the least number of rows in the ANSWERS table):

```
select count(answers.item_id) as 'count', items.item_id
from items
left outer join
```

```
answers
on items.item_id = answers.item_id
group by (items.item_id)
order by count(answers.item_id) asc , items.item_id asc limit 1
```

This is done at the beginning when the web page is loading and the system is deciding which question to display. Although there are situations where this might be useful, this mechanism does not guarantee that each annotator will see every tweet; however, it does ensure that by the time every annotator reaches the end of the dataset, every item in the dataset will have been annotated. Clearly, this is not what is required as it is unhelpful in obtaining measurements on annotator agreement. A more useful modification to this technique would be to look for the next tweet that needs to be annotated by the user. This then allows users to log off and carry on where they left off when they next log in:

```
select min(items.item_id) as 'item_id'
from items
where items.item_id NOT IN
(
    select answers.item_id
    from answers
    where answers.user_id = [USERS_ID]
)
```

Validation mechanisms were added to the web page to prevent *lazy* annotation, so that it was not possible to move to the next tweet until an answer had been selected for *Q1* and at least one answer was selected for *Q2*. In conjunction with the *neutral* and *none* options, the idea was that, in theory, this would prevent users from simply clicking the **Submit** button without considering the tweet (i.e., even if the user didn't think any of the emotions applied, they were still required to register that fact). These options forced the user to proactively indicate that there were no emotions in the tweet, the idea being that if they were forced to select an option to proceed to the next tweet, then they may as well select something relevant as opposed to choosing at random. Users were also given four weeks to complete the task, hence there was no requirement to rush to complete the task. To facilitate this, the system allowed them to stop and come back later to resume from where they left off.

The same interface as the one used for the competency task was used to annotate 1,000 tweets. One tweet was displayed at a time, as can be seen in *Figure 3.4*. Following the guidelines from Mohammad and Kiritchenko, the annotator was asked to answer two questions. The first was a single-answer multiple- choice question that asked the user to select one option that best describes the emotional state of the tweeter from the emotions. The second was a checkbox question, where multiple answers could be selected.

Earlier, we described how the applicants were asked to examine each tweet and select one primary emotion and as many secondary emotions as appropriate. This is the technique described by Mohammad and Kiritchenko, reasoning that they wanted to include all emotions, however subtle, that applied in the answer, not just the primary emotion. They argue that one of the criticisms of natural language annotation is that only the instances with high agreement are kept, and low agreement instances are discarded. The high agreement instances typically tend to be simple examples of the emotion class, and hence are easier to model. However, in the real world, there are hugely more complex and complicated examples and usages of language to elicit emotion. If the model has been trained largely on high agreement instances, it then performs sub-optimally when it has to process instances that it has not seen during training.

Given the amalgamated results from *Q1* and *Q2*, a primary emotion was established by a majority vote. Where there was a tie, all tied emotions were deemed as primary emotions. The aggregated responses from *Q1* and *Q2* were used to obtain a full set of labels for a tweet.

Two criteria were applied to these aggregated responses:

- If at least half of the annotators indicated that a certain emotion applied, then that label was chosen

- If no emotion was indicated by at least half of the annotators and more than half of the responses indicated that the tweet was neutral, then the tweet was marked as neutral

A typical trend is that the highest-scoring secondary emotions are primary emotions such as anger and fear. These usually correspond well with the highest-scoring primary emotions. In general, the highest-scoring primary emotions are also the highest-scoring secondary emotions, and the lowest-scoring primary emotions are the lowest-scoring secondary emotions. However, there may be anomalies in emotions such as trust, where it may be a high-ranking primary emotion but a low-ranking secondary emotion, indicating that in the presence of other emotions, the usefulness of such emotions is limited.

Clearly, there are some obvious limitations to this method. The participants were self-selected, and no information was available regarding the conditions (e.g., whether the participant completed the survey under strict conditions conducive to clear thinking) under which the exercise was completed. It is also possible that some annotators perhaps did not fully understand the instructions, but declined to say so. Hence, even after the competency test, it is likely that there may still be invalid annotations. Annotating tweets in this manner is clearly a monotonous, time-consuming activity. However, the annotators were paid, hence they should be highly motivated to annotate to a high standard. Furthermore, a key advantage of datasets constructed as this one was, is that the tweets were not gathered by making use of emotion-bearing keywords; hence the dataset should be more representative of the types of tweets seen on X (formerly known as Twitter).

Buy or build?

For this section, you will need the following prerequisites:

- Software development tools such as VS Code

- Database tools such as MySQL Workbench or SQL Server

- Access to a web browser

- A version control system such as Git or GitHub

There is certainly a debate around whether you should develop your own interface, or buy a ready-made one off the shelf. Naturally, being programmers at heart, our initial inclination is always to go for the former! However, this may not always be possible with company size, work priorities, and cost among the factors having to be considered. Clearly, for certain situations, it is preferable to use one of the ready-made tools. Here are some examples:

Tool	Data Type
Amazon SageMaker Ground Truth	Text, image, and video
Label Studio	Text, image, video, audio, and more
Sloth	Image and video
Dataturk	Text, image, and video
Superannotate	Image
Audio-annotator	Audio

Building an annotation interface is not a straightforward task; it requires a number of different features, but with a little planning, it can be a smooth process. The following are some of the features that should be considered:

- The option to view any associated metadata of the item (e.g., for images, the dimensions or the date and time it was taken), as well as the item itself
- A mobile-friendly interface because not everyone will access it from a desktop or a laptop
- Administrator login to access stats and view current progress
- Standard reports, and the ability to create custom reports
- The ability to easily add new sets of items for labeling
- The ability to finalize item sets so that no more annotations are allowed
- The ability to add gold tweets
- The ability to import items for labeling
- The ability to export results so they can be shared

Typically, the data that requires labeling will be collected on a different platform and also processed via machine learning algorithms on a different platform. Consequently, the data will need to be imported and exported from the labeling platform in an appropriate format. Ideally, these processes should be part of an automated pipeline, so that manual bottlenecks are not created. It is important to note that these non-labeling processes will remain the same, regardless of whether an in-house or an external solution is used. There is also a possibility, if an external solution is used, that carefully-crafted interfaces that work well in a pipeline may suddenly stop working and require altering if the external supplier changes the way their solution interfaces with the outside world. Furthermore, although many external solutions are feature-rich, there may be something niche that isn't available, and although it can be requested, there is no guarantee when it will be implemented, if at all. As a final benefit to convince you of the merits of developing an in-house solution, if the necessary engineers and time are available, bugs can also be fixed, tested, and deployed quicker.

It may still be unclear whether to choose from the abundance of annotation tools available or to embark on building a solution from scratch. We'll, therefore, finalize this discussion with a summary table to help you decide which route to take:

Situation	Decision
If this is a one-off task, and very unlikely to be repeated again	Buy
If you need a quick turnaround	Buy
If cost is not a concern	Buy
If you have tight security requirements that dictate, for example, that the data should not leave the premises	Build/Buy
If you know that this is a process that will be repeated often and especially if costs adding up are a concern	Build/Buy
If you have a niche requirement that may be useful to others, and hence your platform could be sold as a SaaS model, for example	Build
If your requirements are niche or bespoke and unlikely to be catered for by one of the commercial solutions	Build

Results

Figure 3.7 shows the overall results screen. This can be used to get an update on the current status of the labeling and how many each annotator has done, and can also be used to access the detailed analysis screen. These details were enough for our work, but this screen could be further enhanced with useful information such as the following:

- How many times the annotator logged in
- Average response time
- When the annotator last logged in

Clearly, analyzing such information can lead to further insights that may ultimately lead to better annotation and, hence, a better-performing model.

Results

User	Questions answered
Muhammed Hassan Test Analysis	1028
Yazan Ashqar Test Analysis	1006
Omar Youssef Test Analysis	1003
Yassine Ceifeddine Test Analysis	1002
Nourhan Wageeh Test Analysis	1000
Test Account Test Analysis	5
Tariq Test Analysis	1
Fateh Singh Test Analysis	0
Jaila Yousri Test Analysis	0

Figure 3.7 – Labeling status screen

Figure 3.8 shows the results summary screen for an individual annotator.

Results for Test Account

Question	Actual answersUser answers	%Correct
#Jizan Al-Sarkhi reference.. O Sistani, many sources prove the weakness of Al-Zuhri's condition. {NEWLINE} #Jizan The Sarkhi Referee . Al-Bukhari and the correct response to the Nawasib Takfiris. {NEWLINE} #Jizan The Sarkhi Reference.. Where is Sistani's asceticism?!! {NEWLINE} #Jizan Al-Sarkhi. Because of Al-Sistani and ISIS, people deserted and went to western countries and left Islam.	A A D F J L O P S S T 0 1 0 0 0 0 0 0 0 0 0	0 (0/1)
Urgent investigations into the incidents of the two Muslim students in California Saddam Hussein, the continuation of the demonstrations against the American president, Trump, demonstrations that spread America.. {NEWLINE} Broadcast of self-development. Send a subscription on WhatsApp 0502047778.	A A D F J L O P S S T 0 1 0 0 0 0 0 0 0 0 0	0 (0/1)
#Urgent... the head of the #Clinton campaign, commenting on #Trump's progress in the election results: We haven't given up yet, and we can wait a little while {NEWLINE} - Via @NabdApp {NEWLINE} #Urgent.. Turkish Prime Minister Yildirim calls on #Trump to extradite Fethullah Gulen to #Turkey	A A D F J L O P S S T 0 0 1 1 1 0 0 0 0 0 0	0 (0/1)
#Urgent... the head of the #Clinton campaign, commenting on #Trump's progress in the election results: We haven't given up yet, and we can wait a little while {NEWLINE} - Via @NabdApp {NEWLINE} #Urgent..Turkish Prime Minister Yildirim calls on #Trump to extradite Fethullah Gulen to #Turkey	A A D F J L O P S S T 0 0 1 1 1 0 0 0 0 0 0	0 (0/1)
A top view of the ancient university of #Istanbul #Turkey_Post {NEWLINE} Former Turkish Interior Minister: PKK and ISIS cooperate in northern #Iraq #Turkey_Post {NEWLINE} Former Turkish Interior Minister: Menemeh #Gulen and ISIS cooperate in northern #Iraq #Turkey_Post	A A D F J L O P S S T 1 1 1 0 0 0 0 0 0 0 0	0 (0/1)

OVERALL 0%

Figure 3.8 – Labeling results

Each tweet is listed along with the selections made for the tweet and how many the annotator got correct. This allows administrators to examine, in detail, each tweet and the answers that the annotator supplied. When this screen is used to display the competency results (where the actual answers are known), the **Actual answersUser answers** column shows the actual answers and the responses, so that quick comparisons can be made, and the final **%Correct** column shows how many the annotator got correct.

Having collected the labeling results, it is a good idea to understand whether the answers are reliable. We look at this in the next section.

Inter-annotator reliability

Inter-annotator reliability is the widely used term to describe "*the extent to which independent coders evaluate the characteristic of a message, or artefact, and reach the same conclusion*" (Tinsley and D. J. Weiss). It is an important metric because it determines whether the data can be considered valid and is an indication of the trustworthiness of the data. Without this reliability, any content analysis is useless. From a practical point of view, establishing a high level of reliability also has the benefit of allowing the work to be divided among multiple annotators. Measuring reliability is actually measuring reproducibility, that is, "the *likelihood that different coders who receive the same training and textual guidance will assign the same value to the same piece of content*" (Joyce).

There are many ways to measure reliability – two of the most common are Fleiss' kappa and Krippendorff's alpha:

- **Fleiss' kappa:** This is a statistical measure for assessing the reliability of agreement between a fixed number of raters when assigning categorical ratings to a number of items or classifying items (i.e., it is a measurement of agreement). It can be interpreted as expressing the extent to which the observed amount of agreement among raters exceeds what would be expected if all raters made their ratings completely randomly. Many kappas only work when assessing the agreement between two raters. However, Fleiss' kappa does not suffer from this limitation as it measures the overall agreement between all the raters. The measure calculates the degree of agreement in classification over that which would be expected by chance. Perfect agreement would equate to a kappa of 1 and chance agreement would equate to 0. There is no generally agreed-upon measure of significance, although guidelines have been given; the commonly cited scale as described can be seen in *Table 3.1*. Fleiss' kappa can only be used with binary (yes/no) or nominal-scale (gender, nationality, etc.) ratings.

Kappa	Strength of agreement
<0	Less than chance agreement
0.01–0.20	Slight agreement
0.21– 0.40	Fair agreement
0.41–0.60	Moderate agreement
0.61–0.80	Substantial agreement
0.81–0.99	Almost perfect agreement

Table 3.1 – Interpretation of Fleiss' kappa

The formula to calculate Fleiss' kappa is as follows:

$$\frac{P_0 - P_e}{1 - P_e}$$

Here, P_0 is the relative observed agreement among raters and P_e is the hypothetical probability of chance agreement.

- **Krippendorff's alpha:** The problem with Fleiss' kappa is that it requires the total number of answers for each item (e.g., a tweet) to be equal. This is clearly not possible when annotating tweets with multiple emotions because the number of emotions chosen for each tweet can vary. In these situations, Krippendorff's alpha is used because it can cope with various sample sizes, categories, and numbers of annotators. It is also able to handle cases where data is missing – for example, when an annotator has left an answer blank. Krippendorff's alpha is also more reliable than other measures because, in contrast to other measures that are based on agreement, Krippendorff's alpha is a ratio that is based on the observed and the expected *disagreement*. This is one reason why it is believed to be more reliable. It has been reported that, in practice, the results from both Krippendorff's alpha and Fleiss' kappa are similar (Gwet). This is unsurprising since in cases where exactly one label is assigned, they compute the same thing, but only Krippendorff's alpha works when a data point can have zero, one, or more labels.

The interpretation of Krippendorff's alpha is also more straightforward than that of Fleiss' kappa. The alpha value is a number ranging from 0 to 1, where 0 is perfect disagreement and 1 is perfect agreement. Krippendorff suggests that, ideally, the value should be greater than or equal to 0.8, but tentative conclusions are still acceptable when the value is greater than or equal to 0.667 (Klaus). However, this would be the lowest acceptable value. It should be noted that while Krippendorff's alpha can measure the overall reliability of the annotation process, it does not inform on which annotators or which instances are problematic if the alpha is low. For that, further analysis may be conducted – for example, comparing the annotations of each pair of annotators, or looking at the instances where disagreement occurred.

The formula to calculate Krippendorff's alpha is as follows:

$$1 - \frac{D_0}{D_e}$$

Here, D_0 is the disagreement observed and D_e is the disagreement expected by chance.

That's enough theory. Let's work through an example using Krippendorff's alpha.

Calculating Krippendorff's alpha

Recall that Fleiss' kappa does not support multi-label input, hence Krippendorff's alpha is computed for multi-label classification. In this section, a fictitious example, heavily based on Krippendorff's paper, is set up to work through a simple Krippendorf's alpha calculation.

Consider the scenario where two annotators, A1 and A2, are asked to provide 10 (N) binary (yes/no) labels to the same set of two data points. The *reliability data matrix* then shows the combined responses from each annotator across both data points, where the rows are the annotators, and the columns are their labels:

	1	2	3	4	5	6	7	8	9	10
A1	0	1	0	0	0	0	0	0	1	0
A2	1	1	1	0	0	1	0	0	0	0

Using this matrix, a *coincidence matrix* is created that accounts for all values in the reliability data matrix.

> **Note**
>
> These matrices are slightly different from the typical coincidence matrices found in AI and ML in that they are used to record and analyze relationships between two or more categorical variables and show items that appear together. The typical coincidence matrix used in ML presents a table showing the different outcomes of the prediction and results of a classification problem.

The reliability data matrix is hence used to create a 2X2 coincidence matrix using the following template:

	0	1	
0	0_{00}	0_{01}	n_0
1	0_{10}	0_{11}	n_1
	n_0	n_1	2 x N

In the coincidence matrix, the values are entered twice – for example, once as $(0, 1)$ and once as $(1, 0)$. Hence, in the example, 1 is entered as a 0-1 pair of values and also as a 1-0 pair of values:

	0	1	
0	10	4	14
1	4	2	6
	14	5	20

These values are derived as follows:

- 0_{00} (**10**): The reliability data matrix shows that there are five 0-0 pairs. However, each pair is represented twice, hence 10.

- 0_{01} (**4**): There are four 0-1 pairs.

- 0_{10} (**4**): The four 1-0 pairs are the same as the four 0-1 pairs.

- 0_{11} (**2**): There is one 1-1 pair, hence 2.

Now, it is a simple matter of using the formula and substituting the values to calculate the alpha:

$$\alpha = 1 - \frac{D_0}{D_e}$$

$$\alpha = 1 - (2N - 1)\frac{0_{01}}{n_0 \times n_1}$$

$$\alpha = 1 - (20 - 1)\frac{4}{14 \times 6} = 0.095$$

Luckily, we do not need to code this ourselves since the NLTK metrics package has functions to calculate inter-annotator agreement values. The `nltk.metrics.agreement` module requires its input to be in the form of a list of triples, where each triple contains a label to identify the annotator (e.g., A1 and A2), an item to indicate the label (e.g., 1, 2, 3, etc.) and the annotator label (e.g., 0, 1).

The corresponding Python code for the preceding simple example is as follows:

```
import nltk
data = [
    ['A1', 1, 0],
    ['A1', 2, 1],
    ['A1', 3, 0],
    ['A1', 4, 0],
    ['A1', 5, 0],
    ['A1', 6, 0],
    ['A1', 7, 0],
    ['A1', 8, 0],
```

```
        ['A1', 9, 1],
        ['A1', 10, 0],
        ['A2', 1, 1],
        ['A2', 2, 1],
        ['A2', 3, 1],
        ['A2', 4, 0],
        ['A2', 5, 0],
        ['A2', 6, 1],
        ['A2', 7, 0],
        ['A2', 8, 0],
        ['A2', 9, 0],
        ['A2', 10, 0]
        ]
task = nltk.metrics.agreement.AnnotationTask(data=data)
print (task.alpha())
```

This generates the same result as in the worked example:

```
0.0952380952381
```

Debrief

It is a good idea to follow up with your annotators after the task to ascertain their views about the overall task and whether they experienced any particular difficulties with any emotions. For example, tweets may contain several different emotions and hence it may be difficult to pinpoint the prevalent ones. There may also have been occasions where emotive words were seen but the annotator did not feel that this led them to strongly lean toward any particular emotion. It is sensible to obtain an understanding of these types of situations as early as possible as changes to the procedures for collecting data are likely to change the nature of what is collected. Typically, annotators refer to tweets being short and informal as a primary reason for being unable to determine a definitive emotion for a tweet. It is, therefore, ironic that when tweets are overly lengthy, annotators mention that it is hard to restrict themselves to selecting a sensible set of emotions, as in this example:

Who is responsible for this tampering? !!! At the University of Nora !! Meeting with His Excellency the #MinisterofEducation

Summary

There is no doubt that data annotation is a challenge, but with the right tools and techniques, these problems can be minimized and the process streamlined, resulting in a well-labeled dataset that is fit for purpose.

In this chapter, we started by understanding why labeling must be high quality, and what the consequences are of even minor errors. The data labeling process usually begins by getting humans to use their domain expertise, intelligence, sense, and perception to make a decision about data that is unlabeled. We explored the process and key considerations and discussed the options when there is not enough data available. Data labeling is a tedious but necessary process and is prone to errors by the annotators. It is thus important to improve its effectiveness and accuracy by identifying and then following good practices. We then discussed the various ways to label data and their pros and cons. A common technique is to crowdsource, hence we introduced techniques such as gold tweets and competency tasks to improve outcomes when following this technique. We also presented a scenario for labeling, discussed the labels that might be used and the skills an annotator needs, and presented a simple architecture and UI for the data labeling task. Finally, we presented the criteria for building or buying a labeling tool, worked through the theory behind inter-annotator reliability, and presented the corresponding Python code.

In the next chapter, we will look at competition-based research and evaluation strategies, discover how it is not always necessary to create your own dataset, and explore how existing datasets can be transformed in ways to make them useful for the emotion analysis task.

References

To learn more about the topics that were covered in this chapter, take a look at the following resources:

- T.N. Ahmad and A. Ramsay. *Classification of Tweets using Multiple Thresholds with Self-Correction and Weighted Conditional Probabilities.* 2020.

- S. M. Mohammad and S. Kiritchenko. *Understanding Emotions: A Dataset of Tweets to Study Interactions between Affect Categories.* In Proceedings of the 11th Edition of the Language Resources and Evaluation Conference, Miyazaki, Japan, 2018.

- H. E. Tinsley and D. J. Weiss. *Interrater reliability and agreement. In Handbook of applied multivariate statistics and mathematical modeling,* pages 95–124. Elsevier, 2000.

- M. Joyce. *Picking the best intercoder reliability statistic for your digital activism content analysis.* In *Digital Activism Research Project: Investigating the Global Impact of Comment Forum Speech as a Mirror of Mainstream Discourse,* volume 243, 2013.

- Gwet, Kilem. (2015). *On Krippendorff's Alpha Coefficient.*

- K. Klaus. *Content analysis: An introduction to its methodology,* 1980.

- K. Krippendorff. *Computing Krippendorff's alpha-reliability.* 2011.

4

Preprocessing – Stemming, Tagging, and Parsing

Before we can start assigning emotions to texts, we have to carry out a range of preprocessing tasks to get to the elements that carry the information we want. In *Chapter 1*, *Foundations*, we briefly covered the various components of a generic NLP system, but without looking in detail at how any of these components might be implemented. In this chapter, we will provide sketches and partial implementations of the tools that are most likely to be useful for sentiment mining – where we give a partial implementation or a code fragment for something, the full implementation is available in the code repository.

We will look at the earlier stages of the language processing pipeline in detail. The texts that are most often used for sentiment mining tend to be very informal – tweets, product reviews, and so on. This material is often ungrammatical and contains made-up words, misspellings, and non-text items such as emoticons, images, and emojis. Standard parsing algorithms cannot deal with this kind of material, and even if they could, the analyses that they produce would be very hard to work with: what would the parse tree for *@MarthatheCat Look at that toof! #growl* look like? We will include material relating to tagging (which is generally only useful as a precursor to parsing) and parsing, but the focus will be largely on the lowest level steps – reading the text (not as straightforward as it seems), decomposing words into parts, and identifying compound words.

In this chapter, we will cover the following topics:

- Readers
- Word parts and compound words
- Tokenizing, morphology, and stemming
- Compound words
- Tagging and parsing

Readers

Before we can do anything, we need to be able to read the documents that contain the texts – in particular, the training data that will be used by the preprocessing algorithms and the sentiment mining algorithms themselves. These documents come in two classes:

- **Training data for the preprocessing algorithms**: A number of the algorithms that we use for finding words, decomposing them into smaller units, and combining them into larger groups require training data. This can be raw text or it can be annotated with suitable labels. In either case, we need a lot of it (for some tasks, you need hundreds of millions of words, maybe more), and it is often more convenient to use data from external sources than to try to compile it yourself. Unfortunately, externally supplied data does not always come in a single agreed format, so you need **readers** to abstract away from the details of the format and organization of this data. To take a simple example, data for training a program to assign part-of-speech tags to text needs to be given text that has been labeled with such tags. We will carry out some experiments here using two well-known corpora: the **British National Corpus (BNC)** and the **Universal Dependency Tre ebanks (UDT)**. The BNC provides text with complex XML-like annotations, such as the following:

```
<w c5=NN1  hw=factsheet  pos= SUBST >FACTSHEET </w>
<w c5=DTQ  hw=what  pos= PRON >WHAT </w>
```

This says that *factsheet* is an NN1 and *what* is a pronoun.

The UDT provides text as tab-separated files where each line represents information about a word:

```
1    what    what    PRON    PronType=Int,Rel   0        root    _
2    is      be      AUX     Mood=Ind           1        cop     _
```

This says that *what* is a pronoun and *is* is an auxiliary. To use these to train a tagger, we have to dig out the information that we want and convert it into a uniform format.

- **Training data for the sentiment analysis algorithms**: Almost all approaches to assigning emotions to texts employ machine learning algorithms, and hence again require training data. As noted in *Chapter 2, Building and Using a Dataset*, it is often convenient to use externally supplied data, and as with the data used for the preprocessing algorithms, this data can come in a variety of formats.

Training data may be supplied as text files, as directory trees with text files as leaves, or as SQL or other databases. To make matters more complex, there can be very large amounts of data (hundreds of millions of items, even billions of items), to the point where it is not convenient to have all the data in memory at once. Therefore, we start by providing a reader generator function that will traverse a directory tree until it reaches a leaf file whose name matches an optional pattern and then uses an appropriate reader to return items one at a time from this file:

```
def reader(path, dataFileReader, pattern=re.compile('.*')):
    if isinstance(pattern, str):
        pattern = re.compile(pattern)
```

```
if isinstance(path, list):
    # If what you're looking at is a list of file names,
    # look inside it and return the things you find there
    for f in path:
        for r in reader(f, dataFileReader, pattern=pattern):
            yield r
elif os.path.isdir(path):
    # If what you're looking at is a directory,
    # look inside it and return the things you find there
    for f in sorted(os.listdir(path)):
        for r in reader(os.path.join(path, f),
                        dataFileReader, pattern=pattern):
            yield r
else:
    # If it's a datafile, check that its name matches the pattern
    # and then use the dataFileReader to extract what you want
    if pattern.match(path):
        for r in dataFileReader(path):
            yield r
```

reader will return a generator that walks down through the directory tree specified by path until it finds leaf files whose names match pattern and then uses dataFileReader to iterate through the data in the given files. We use a generator rather than a simple function because corpora can be very large and reading all the data contained in a corpus into memory at once can become unmanageable. The disadvantage of using a generator is that you can only iterate through it once – if you want to solidify the results of using a reader, you can use list to store them as a list:

```
>>> r = reader(BNC, BNCWordReader, pattern=r'.*\.xml')
>>> l = list(r)
```

This will create a generator, r, for reading words from the **BNC**. The BNC is a widely used collection of documents, though its status as a resource for training, and especially testing, taggers is slightly unclear since the tags for the vast majority of the material were assigned programmatically by the CLAWS4 tagger (Leech et al., 1994). This means that any tagger trained on it will be learning the tags assigned by CLAWS4, so unless these are 100% accurate (which they are not), then it will not be learning the "real" tags. Nonetheless, it is an extremely useful resource, and can certainly be used as a resource for training usable taggers. It can be downloaded from https://ota.bodleian. ox.ac.uk/repository/xmlui/handle/20.500.12024/2554.

Then, we solidify this generator to a list, l, for ease of use. The BNC contains about 110 million words, which is a manageable amount of data on a modern computer, so storing them as a single list makes sense. However, for larger corpora, this may not be feasible, so having the option of using a generator can be useful.

The BNC is supplied as a directory tree with subdirectories, A, B, …, K, which contain A0, A1, …, B0, B1, …, which, in turn, contain A00.xml, A01.xml, …:

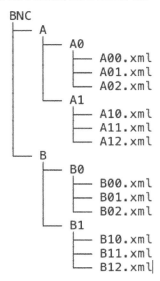

Figure 4.1 – Structure of the BNC directory tree

The leaf files contain header information followed by sentences demarcated by <s n=???>...</s>, with the words that make up a sentence marked by <w c5=??? hw=??? pos=???>???</w>. Here's an example:

```
<s n= 1 ><w c5= NN1  hw= factsheet  pos= SUBST >FACTSHEET </w><w c5=
DTQ  hw= what  pos= PRON >WHAT </w><w c5= VBZ  hw= be  pos= VERB >IS
</w><w c5= NN1  hw= aids  pos= SUBST >AIDS</w><c c5= PUN >?</c></s>
```

To read all the words in the BNC, we need something to dig out the items between <w ...> and </w>. The easiest way to do this is by using a regular expression:

```
BNCWORD = re.compile('<(?P<tagtype>w|c).*?>(?P<form>.*?)\s*</
(?P=tagtype)>')
Get raw text from BNC leaf files


def BNCWordReader(data):
    for i in BNCWORD.finditer(open(data).read()):
        yield i.group( form )
```

The pattern looks for instances of either <w ...> or <c ...> and then looks for the appropriate closing bracket since the BNC marks words with <w ...> and punctuation marks with <c ...>. We have to find both and make sure that we get the right closing bracket.

Given this definition of BNCWordReader, we can, as we did previously, create a reader to extract all the raw text from the BNC. Other corpora require different patterns for extracting the text – for example, the **Penn Arabic Tree Bank (PATB)** (this is a useful resource for training and testing Arabic NLP tools. Unfortunately, it is not free – see the Linguistic Data Consortium (https://www.ldc.upenn.edu/) for information about how to obtain it – however, we will use it for illustration when appropriate) contains leaf files that look like this:

```
INPUT STRING: فـي
LOOK-UP WORD: fy
     Comment:
        INDEX: P1W1
* SOLUTION 1: (fiy)  [fiy_1]  fiy/PREP
     (GLOSS): in
  SOLUTION 2: (fiy~a) [fiy_1] fiy/PREP+ya/PRON_1S
     (GLOSS): in + me
  SOLUTION 3: (fiy)  [fiy_2]  Viy/ABBREV
     (GLOSS): V.

INPUT STRING: سوسة
LOOK-UP WORD: swsp
     Comment:
        INDEX: P1W2
* SOLUTION 1: (suwsap) [suws_1] suws/NOUN+ap/NSUFF_FEM_SG
     (GLOSS): woodworm:licorice + [fem.sg.]
  SOLUTION 2: (suwsapu) [suws_1] suws/NOUN+ap/NSUFF_FEM_SG+u/CASE_DEF_
NOM
     (GLOSS): woodworm:licorice + [fem.sg.] + [def.nom.]

...
```

To extract words from this, we would need a pattern like this:

```
PATBWordPattern = re.compile("INPUT STRING: (?P<form>\S*)")
def PATBWordReader(path):
    for i in PATBWordPattern.finditer(open(path).read()):
        yield i.group( form )
```

This will return the following when applied to the PATB:

لونغ بيتش (الولايات المتحدة) 7-15 (اف ب ... ...

Given the similarity between `BNCWordReader` and `PATBWordReader`, we could have simply defined a single function called `WordReader` that takes a path and a pattern and bound the pattern as required:

```
def WordReader(pattern, path):
    for i in pattern.finditer(open(path).read()):
        yield i.group( form )

from functools import partial
PATBWordReader = partial(WordReader, PATBWordPattern)
BNCWordReader = partial(WordReader, BNCWordPattern)
```

The same technique can be applied to extract the raw text from a wide range of corpora, such as the UDT (`https://universaldependencies.org/#download`), which provides free access to moderate amounts of tagged and parsed data for a large number of languages (currently 130 languages, with about 200K words per language for the commoner languages but rather less for others).

Similarly, the training data for sentiment assignment algorithms comes in a variety of formats. As noted in *Chapter 1*, *Foundations*, Python already provides a module, `pandas`, for managing training sets for generic sets of training data. `pandas` is useful if your training data consists of sets of data points, where a data point is a set of `feature:value` pairs that describe the properties of the data point, along with a label that says what class it belongs to. The basic object in `pandas` is a DataFrame, which is a collection of objects where each object is described by a set of `feature:value` pairs. As such, a DataFrame is very much like a SQL table, where the names of the columns are the feature names and an object corresponds to a row in the table; it is also extremely like a nested Python dictionary, where the keys at the top level are the feature names and the values associated with those names are index-value pairs. And it's also very like a spreadsheet, where the top row is the feature names and the remaining rows are the data points. DataFrames can be read directly from all these formats and more (including from a table in a SQL database), and can be written directly to any of them. Consider the following extract from a set of annotated tweets stored as a MySQL database:

```
mysql> describe sentiments;
+-----------+--------------+------+-----+---------+-------+
| Field     | Type         | Null | Key | Default | Extra |
+-----------+--------------+------+-----+---------+-------+
| annotator | int(11)      | YES  |     | NULL    |       |
| tweet     | int(11)      | YES  |     | NULL    |       |
| sentiment | varchar(255) | YES  |     | NULL    |       |
+-----------+--------------+------+-----+---------+-------+
3 rows in set (0.01 sec)

mysql> select * from sentiments where tweet < 3;
```

```
+-----------+-------+-----------------------+
| annotator | tweet | sentiment             |
+-----------+-------+-----------------------+
|        19 |     1 | love                  |
|         1 |     1 | anger+dissatisfaction |
|         8 |     1 | anger+dissatisfaction |
|         2 |     2 | love+joy              |
|        19 |     2 | love                  |
|         6 |     2 | love+joy+optimism     |
+-----------+-------+-----------------------
```

The sentiments table contains rows representing the ID of the annotator who annotated a given tweet, the ID of the tweet itself, and the set of emotions that the given annotator assigned to it (for example, annotator 8 assigned anger and dissatisfaction to tweet 1). This table can be read directly as a DataFrame and can be transformed into a dictionary, a JSON object (very similar to a dictionary), a string in CSV format, and more:

```
>>> DB = MySQLdb.connect(db= centement , autocommit=True, charset=
UTF8 )
>>> cursor = DB.cursor()
>>> data = pandas.read_sql( select * from sentiments where tweet < 3 ,
DB)
```

```
>>> data
    annotator  tweet               sentiment
0          19      1                    love
1           1      1   anger+dissatisfaction
2           8      1   anger+dissatisfaction
3           2      2                love+joy
4          19      2                    love
5           6      2       love+joy+optimism
```

```
>>> data.to_json()
'{ annotator :{ 0 :19, 1 :1, 2 :8, 3 :2, 4 :19, 5 :6}, tweet :{
0 :1, 1 :1, 2 :1, 3 :2, 4 :2, 5 :2}, sentiment :{ 0 : love , 1 :
anger+dissatisfaction , 2 : anger+dissatisfaction , 3 : love+joy , 4 :
love , 5 : love+joy+optimism }}'
```

```
>>> print(data.to_csv())
,annotator,tweet,sentiment
0,19,1,love
1,1,1,anger+dissatisfaction
2,8,1,anger+dissatisfaction
3,2,2,love+joy
```

```
4,19,2,love
5,6,2,love+joy+optimism
```

We therefore do not have to worry too much about actually reading and writing the data to be used to train the emotion classification algorithms – DataFrames can be read from, and written to, in almost any reasonable format. Nonetheless, we still have to be careful about what features we are using and what values they can have. The preceding MySQL database, for instance, refers to the IDs of the tweets and the annotators, with the text of each tweet being kept in a separate table, and it stores each annotator's assignment of emotions as a single compound value (for example, love+joy+optimism). It would have been perfectly possible to store the text of the tweet in the table and to have each emotion as a column that could be set to 1 if the annotator had assigned this emotion to the tweet and 0 otherwise:

```
ID    Tweet                         anger   sadness   surprise
0     2017-En-21441 Worry is a dow    0       1          0
1     2017-En-31535  Whatever you d   0       0          0
2     2017-En-22190  No but that's    0       0          1
3     2017-En-20221  Do you think h   0       0          0
4     2017-En-22180  Rooneys effing   1       0          0
6830  2017-En-21383  @nicky57672 Hi   0       0          0
6831  2017-En-41441  @andreamitchel   0       0          1
6832  2017-En-10886  @isthataspider   0       1          0
6833  2017-En-40662  i wonder how a   0       0          1
6834  2017-En-31003  I'm highly ani   0       0          0
```

Here, each tweet has an explicit ID, as well as a position in the DataFrame; the tweet itself is included, and each emotion is a separate column. The data here was supplied as a CSV file, so it was read directly as a DataFrame without any trouble, but the way it is presented is completely different from the previous set. Therefore, we will need preprocessing algorithms to make sure that the data we are using is organized the way the machine learning algorithms want it.

Fortunately, DataFrames have database-like options for selecting data and merging tables, so converting from one way of presenting the data into another is reasonably straightforward, but it does have to be carried out. There are, for instance, advantages to having a single column per emotion and advantages to having a single column for all emotions but allowing compound emotions – having a single column per emotion makes it easy to allow for cases where a single object may have more than one emotion associated with it; having just one column for all emotions makes it easy to search for tweets that have the same emotions. Some resources will provide one and some the other, but almost any learning algorithm will require one or the other, so it is necessary to be able to convert between them.

Word parts and compound words

The key to identifying emotions in texts lies with the words that make up those texts. It may turn out to be useful to classify words, find similarities between words, and find out how the words in a given text are related, but the most important things are the words themselves. If a text contains the words *love* and *happy*, then it's very likely to be positive, whereas if it contains the words *hate* and *horrible*, it's very likely to be negative.

As noted in *Chapter 1, Foundations*, however, it can be difficult to specify exactly what counts as a word, and hence difficult to find the words that make up a text. While the writing systems of many languages use white space to split up text, there are languages where this does not happen (for example, written Chinese). But even where the written form of a language does use white space, finding the units that we are interested in is not always straightforward. There are two basic problems:

- Words are typically made up of a core lexeme and several affixes that add to or alter the meaning of the core. *love, loves, loved, loving, lover,* and *lovable* are all clearly related to a single concept, though they all look slightly different. So, do we want to treat them as different words or as variations on a single word? Do we want to treat *steal, stole,* and *stolen* as different words or as variations of the same word? The answer is that sometimes we want to do one and sometimes the other, but when we do want to treat them as variations of the same word, we need machinery to do so.

- Some items that are separated by white space look as though they are made out of several components: *anything, anyone,* and *anybody* look very much as though they are made out of *any* plus *thing, one,* or *body* – it is hard to imagine that the underlying structures of *anyone could do that* and *any fool could do that* are different. It is worth noting that in English, the stress patterns of the spoken language match up with the presence or absence of white space in text – *anyone* is pronounced with a single stress on the first syllable, /en/, while *any fool* has stress on /en/ and /fool/, so there is a difference, but they also have the same structure.

It is tempting to try to deal with this by looking at each White space-separated item to see whether it is made out of two (or more) other known units. *Stock market* and *stockmarket* seem to be the same word, as do *battle ground* and *battleground*, and looking at the contexts in which they occur bears this out:

```
            as well as in a stock market
     in share prices in the stock market
    to the harsher side of stock market life
          apart from the stock market crash of two

       There was a huge stockmarket crash in October
of being replaced in a sudden stockmarket coup
 in the days that followed the stockmarket crash of October
                  The stockmarket crash of 1987 is
```

```
                    was to be a major battle ground between
         of politics as an ideological battle ground and by her
         likely to form the election battle ground
         likely to form the election battle ground


                     surveying the battleground with quiet
         Industry had become an ideological battleground
         of London as a potential savage battleground is confirmed by
         previous evening it had been a battleground for people who
```

However, there are also clear examples where the compound word is not the same as the two words put next to one another. A *heavy weight* is something (anything) that weighs a lot, whereas a *heavyweight* is nearly always a boxer; if something is *under study*, then someone is studying it, whereas an *understudy* is someone who will step in to fill a role when the person who normally performs it is unavailable:

```
         an example about lifting a heavy weight and doing a
                I was n't lifting a heavy weight
              's roster there was a heavy weight of expectation for the
    half-conscious levels he was a heavy weight upon me of a perhaps


                        the heavyweight boxing champion of the
         up a stirring finale to the heavyweight contest
    of the main contenders for the heavyweight Bath title
a former British and Commonwealth heavyweight boxing champion


    a new sound broadcasting system under study
            many of the plants now under study phase come to fruition '
     to the Brazilian auto workers under study at that particular time
       in Guanxi province has been under study since the 1950s


                     and Jack 's understudy can take over as the maid
    to be considered as an England understudy for the Polish expedition
            His Equity-required understudy received $800 per —
                    will now understudy all positions along the
```

This is particularly important for languages such as Chinese, which are written without white space, where almost any character can be a standalone word but sequences of two or more characters can also be words, often with very little connection to the words that correspond to the individual characters.

These phenomena occur in all languages. Some languages have very complex rules for breaking words into smaller parts, some make a great deal of use of compounds, and some do both. These examples gave a rough idea of the issues as they arise in English, but in the following discussion of using algorithms to deal with these issues, we will look at examples from other languages. In the next section, *Tokenizing, morphology, and stemming*, we will look at algorithms for splitting words into parts – that is, at ways of recognizing that the word *recognizing* is made up of two parts, *recognize* and *-ing*. In the section, *Compound words*, we will look at ways of spotting compounds in languages where they are extremely common.

Tokenizing, morphology, and stemming

The very first thing we have to do is split the input text into **tokens** – units that make an identifiable contribution to the message carried by the whole text. Tokens include words, as roughly characterized previously, but also punctuation marks, numbers, currency symbols, emojis, and so on. Consider the text *Mr. Jones bought it for £5.3K!* The first token is *Mr.*, which is a word pronounced /m i s t uh/, while the next few are *Jones*, *bought*, *it*, and *for*, then the currency symbol, *£*, followed by the number *5.3K* and the punctuation mark, *!*. Exactly what gets treated as a token depends on what you are going to do next (is *5.3K* a single number or is it two tokens, *5.3* and *K*?), but there is very little you can do with a piece of text without splitting it into units along these lines.

The easiest way to do this is by defining a regular expression where the pattern specifies the way the text is to be split. Consider the preceding sentence: we need something for picking out numbers, something for abbreviations, something for currency symbols, and something for punctuation marks. This suggests the following pattern:

```
ENGLISHPATTERN = re.compile(r"""(?P<word>(\d+,?)+((\.|:)\
d+)?K?|(Mr|Mrs|Dr|Prof|St|Rd)\.?|([A-Za-z_](?!n't))*[A-Za-
z]|n't|\.|\?|,|\$|£|&|:|!|"|-|-|[^a-zA-Z\s]+)""")
```

The first part of this pattern says that a number can consist of some digits, possibly followed by a comma (to capture cases such as 120,459 for one hundred and twenty thousand four hundred and fifty-nine), followed by a point and some more digits, and then finally possibly followed by the letter K; the second part lists several abbreviations that will normally be followed by a full stop; the next two, n't and ([A-Za-z](?!n't))*[A-Za-z], are fairly complex; n't recognizes *n't* as a token, while ([A-Za-z](?!n't))*[A-Za-z] picks out sequences of alphabetic characters not ending with *n't* so that *hasn't* and *didn't* are each recognized as two tokens, *has + n't* and *did + n't*. The next few just recognize punctuation marks, currency symbols, and similar; the last one recognizes sequences of non-alphabetic symbols, which is useful for treating sequences of emojis as tokens.

Looking for instances of this pattern in English texts produces results like this:

```
>>> tokenise("Mr. Jones bought it for £5.3K!")
['Mr.', 'Jones', 'bought', 'it', 'for', '£', '5.3K', '!']
```

```
>>> tokenise("My cat is lucky the RSPCA weren't open at 3am last
night!!!
#fuming 😠 🐱")
['My', 'cat', 'is', 'lucky', 'the', 'RSPCA', 'were', "n't", 'open',
'at', '3', 'am', 'last', 'night', '!', '!', '!', '#', 'fuming', '😠
🐱']
```

Using regular expressions for tokenization has two advantages: regular expressions can be applied extremely fast, so large amounts of text can be tokenized very quickly (about three times as fast as the NLTK's built-in `word_tokenize`: the only major difference between the output of the two is that `tokenise` treats words such as *built-in* as being made of three components, *built*, -, and *in*, whereas the NLTK treats them as single compounds, *built-in*); and the patterns are completely self-contained, so they can be changed easily (if, for instance, you would rather treat each emoji as a separate token, just remove + from `[^a-zA-Z\s]+`, and if you would rather treat *built-in* as a single compound unit, just remove – from the list of options) and can also be easily adapted to other languages, such as by replacing the character range, `[a-z]`, with the Unicode range of characters used by the required language:

```
ARABICPATTERN = re.compile(r"(?P<word>(\d+,?)+(\.\d+)?|[
ﺀﻱ]+|\.|\?|,|\$|£|&|!|'|\"|\S+)")
CHINESEPATTERN =
re.compile(r"(?P<word>(\d+,?)+(\.\d+)?|[一-
顧]|.|\?|,|\$|£|&|!|'|\"|)")
```

Once we have tokenized our text, we are likely to have tokens that are minor variants of the same lexeme – *hating* and *hated* are both versions of the same lexeme, *hate*, and will tend to carry the same emotional charge. The importance (and difficulty) of this step will vary from language to language, but virtually all languages make words out of a core lexeme and a set of affixes, and finding the core lexeme will generally contribute to tasks such as emotion detection.

The obvious starting point is to produce a list of affixes and try to chop them off the start and end of a token until a known core lexeme is found. This requires us to have a set of core lexemes, which can be quite difficult to get. For English, we can simply use the list of words from WordNet. This gives us 150K words, which will cover most cases:

```
from utilities import *
from nltk.corpus import wordnet

PREFIXES = {"", "un", "dis", "re"}
SUFFIXES = {"", "ing", "s", "ed", "en", "er", "est", "ly", "ion"}
PATTERN = re.compile("(?P<form>[a-z]{3,}) (?P<pos>n|v|r|a) ")

def readAllWords():
    return set(wordnet.all_lemma_names())

ALLWORDS = readAllWords()
```

```
def stem(form, prefixes=PREFIXES, words=ALLWORDS, suffixes=SUFFIXES):
    for i in range(len(form)):
        if form[:i] in prefixes:
            for j in range(i+1, len(form)+1):
                if form[i:j] in words:
                    if form[j:] in suffixes:
                        yield ("%s-%s+%s"%(form[:i],
                            form[i:j], form[j:])).strip("+-")

ROOTPATTERN = re.compile("^(.*-)?(?P<root>.*?)(\+.*)?$")
def sortstem(w):
    return ROOTPATTERN.match(w).group("root")


def allstems(form, prefixes=PREFIXES, words=ALLWORDS,
suffixes=SUFFIXES):
    return sorted(stem(form, prefixes=PREFIXES,
        words=ALLWORDS, suffixes=SUFFIXES), key=sortstem)
```

This will look at the first few characters of the token to see whether they are prefixes (allowing for empty prefixes), and then at the next few to see whether they are known words, and then at the remainder to see whether it's a suffix. Writing it as a generator makes it easy to produce multiple answers – for example, if WORDS contains both *construct* and *reconstruct*, then stem1 will return ['-reconstruct+ing', 're-construct+ing'] to form *reconstructing*. stem1 takes around 2*10^{-06} seconds for a short word such as *cut* and 7*10^{-06} seconds for a longer and more complex case such as *reconstructing* – fast enough for most purposes.

To use stem1, use the following code:

```
>>> from chapter4 import stem1
>>> stem1.stem("unexpected")
<generator object stem at 0x7f947a418890>
```

stem1.stem is a generator because there might be several ways to decompose a word. For *unexpected*, we get three analyses because *expect*, *expected*, and *unexpected* are all in the base lexicon:

```
>>> list(stem1.stem("unexpected"))
['unexpected', 'un-expect+ed', 'un-expected']
```

For *uneaten*, on the other hand, we only get *un-eat+en*, because the lexicon does not contain *eaten* and *uneaten* as entries:

```
>>> list(stem1.stem("uneaten"))
['un-eat+en']
```

That's a bit awkward because it is hard to predict which derived forms will be listed in the lexicon. What we want is the root and its affixes, and it is clear that *expected* and *unexpected* are not the root forms. The more affixes you remove, the closer you get to the root. So, we might decide to use the output with the shortest root as the best:

```
>>> stem1.allstems("unexpected")
['un-expect+ed', 'un-expected', 'unexpected']
```

The quality of the output depends very heavily on the quality of the lexicon: if it contains forms that are themselves derived from smaller items, we will get analyses like the three for *unexpected*, and if it doesn't contain some form, then it won't return it (the WordNet lexicon contains about 150K entries, so this won't happen all that often if we use it!).

`stem1.stem` is the basis for several well-known tools – for example, the `morphy` function from the NLTK for analyzing English forms and the **Standard Arabic Morphological Analyzer (SAMA)**, (Buckwalter, T., 2007). There are, as ever, some complications, notably that the spelling of a word can change when you add a prefix or a suffix (for instance, when you add the English negative prefix *in-* to a word that begins with a *p*, it becomes *im-*, so *in-* + *perfect* becomes *imperfect* and *in-* + *possible* becomes *impossible*), and that words can have multiple affixes (for instance, French nouns and adjectives can have two suffixes, one to mark gender and one to mark number). We will look at these in the next two sections.

Spelling changes

In many languages (for example, English), the relationship between spelling and pronunciation is quite subtle. In particular, it can encode facts about the stress of a word, and it can do so in ways that change when you add prefixes and suffixes. The "magic e," for instance, is used to mark words where the final vowel is long – for example, *site* versus *sit*. However, when a suffix that begins with a vowel is added to such a word, the *e* is dropped from the version with a long vowel, and the final consonant of the version with a short vowel is doubled: *siting* versus *sitting* (this only happens when the final vowel of the root is both short and stressed, with *enter* and *infer* becoming *entering* and *inferring*). Such rules tend to reflect the way that spelling encodes pronunciation (for example, the magic e marks the preceding vowel as being long, while the doubled consonant in *inferring* marks the previous vowel as being short and stressed) or to arise from actual changes in pronunciation (the *im-* in *impossible* is the *in-* prefix, but it's difficult to say *inpossible* (try it!), so English speakers have lazily changed it to *im-*. See (Chomsky & Halle, 1968) for a detailed discussion of the relationship between spelling and pronunciation in English).

`morphy` deals with this by including all possible versions of the affixes and stopping as soon as one that matches is found:

```
MORPHOLOGICAL_SUBSTITUTIONS = {
    NOUN: [
        ('s', ''),
```

```
                ('ses', 's'),
                ('ves', 'f'),
                ('xes', 'x'),
                ('zes', 'z'),
                ('ches', 'ch'),
                ('shes', 'sh'),
                ('men', 'man'),
                ('ies', 'y'),
            ],
        VERB: [
                ('s', ''),
                ('ies', 'y'),
                ('es', 'e'),
                ('es', ''),
                ('ed', 'e'),
                ('ed', ''),
                ('ing', 'e'),
                ('ing', ''),
            ],
        ADJ: [('er', ''), ('est', ''), ('er', 'e'), ('est', 'e')],
        ADV: [],
    }
```

This table says, for instance, that if you see a word that ends with *s*, it might be a noun if you delete the *s*, and that if you see a word that ends with *ches*, then it might be a form of a noun that ends *ch*. Making these substitutions will work fine a lot of the time, but it does not deal with cases such as *hitting* and *slipped*. Due to this, morphy includes a list of exceptions (quite a long list: 2K for nouns and 2.4K for verbs) that includes forms like these. This will work, of course, but it does take a lot of maintenance and it does mean that words that obey the rules but are not in the exception list will not be recognized (for example, the basic word list includes *kit* as a verb, but does not including *kitting* and *kitted* as exceptions and hence will not recognize that *kitted* in *he was kitted out with all the latest gear* is a form of *kit*).

Instead of providing multiple versions of the affixes and long lists of exceptions, we can provide a set of spelling changes that are to be applied as the word is split:

```
SPELLINGRULES = """
ee X:(d|n) ==> ee + e X
C y X:ing ==> C ie + X
C X:ly ==> C le + X
i X:e(d|r|st?)|ly ==> y + X
X:((d|g|t)o)|x|s(h|s)|ch es ==> X + s
```

```
X0 (?!(?P=X0)) C X1:ed|en|ing ==> X0 C e + X1
C0 V C1 C1 X:e(d|n|r)|ing ==> C0 V C1 + X
C0 V C1 X:(s|$) ==> C0 V C1 + X
"""
```

In these rules, the left-hand side is a pattern that is to be matched somewhere in the current form and the right-hand side is how it might be rewritten. `C`, `C0`, `C1`, … will match any consonant, `V`, `V0`, `V1`, … will match any vowel, `X`, `X0`, `X1`, … will match any character, and `X:(d|n)` will match d or n and fix the value of `X` to be whichever one was matched. Thus, the first rule will match *seen* and *freed* and suggest rewriting them as *see+en* or *free+ed*, and the second last one, which looks for a consonant, a vowel, a repeated consonant, and any of *ed*, *en*, *er*, or *ing* will match *slipping* and *kitted* and suggest rewriting them as *slip+ing* and *kit+ed*.

If we use rules like these, we can find roots of forms where the ending has been changed without explicitly listing them:

```
>>> from chapter4 import stem2
>>> list(stem2.stem("kitted"))
['kit+ed']
```

As before, if we use it with a word where the derived form is explicitly listed as an exception, then we will get multiple versions, but again, using the one with the shortest root will give us the most basic version of the root:

```
>>> stem2.allstems("hitting")
['hit+ing', 'hitting']
```

The implementation of `allstems` in `chapter4.stem2` in this book's code repository also allows multiple affixes, so we can analyze words such as *unreconstructed* and *derestrictions*:

```
>>> stem2.allstems("unreconstructed")
['un-re-construct+ed', 'un-reconstruct+ed', 'un-reconstructed',
'unreconstructed']
>>> stem2.allstems("restrictions")
['restrict+ion+s', 'restriction+s', 're-strict+ion+s']
```

These rules can be compiled into a single regular expression, and hence can be applied very fast and will cover the vast majority of spelling changes at the boundaries between the morphemes that make up an English word (the use of regular expressions for this task was pioneered by (Koskiennemi, 1985)). Rules only apply at the junctions between morphemes, so it is possible to immediately check whether the first part of the rewritten form is a prefix (if no root has been found) or a root (if no root has been found so far), so they will not lead to multiple unjustified splits. This kind of approach leads to tools that can be much more easily maintained since you do not have to add all the forms that cannot be obtained just by splitting off some versions of the affixes as exceptions, so it may be worth considering if you are working with a language where there are large numbers of spelling changes of this sort.

Multiple and contextual affixes

The preceding discussion suggests that there is a fixed set of affixes, each of which can be attached to a suitable root. Even in English, the situation is not that simple. Firstly, there are several alternative past endings, some of which attach to some verbs and some to others. Most verbs take *–ed* for their past participles, but some, such as *take*, require *–en*: `morphy` accepts *taked* as well as *taken* as forms of *take*, and likewise for other *–en* verbs and completely irregular cases such as *thinked* and *bringed*. Secondly, there are cases where a word may take a sequence of affixes – for example, *unexpectedly* looks as though it is made out of a prefix, *un-*, the root, *expect*, and two suffixes, *-ed* and *-ly*. Both these issues become more significant in other languages. It probably doesn't matter that `morphy` returns *steal* as the root of *stealed* since it is very unlikely that anyone would ever write *stealed* (likewise, it doesn't matter that it accepts *sliping* as the present participle of *slip* since no one would ever write *sliping*). In other languages, failing to spot that some affix is the wrong kind of thing to attach to a given root can lead to incorrect readings. Likewise, there are not all that many cases in English of multiple affixes, certainly not of multiple inflectional affixes (in the preceding example, *un-*, *-ed*, and *-ly* are all derivational affixes – *-un* obtains a new adjective from an old one, *-ed* in this case obtains an adjective from a verb root, and *-ly* obtains an adverb from an adjective).

Again, this can matter more in languages such as French (and other Romance languages), where a noun is expected to take a gender marker and a number marker (*noir*, *noire*, *noirs*, and *noires*), and a verb is expected to take a tense marker and an appropriate person marker (*achetais* as the first person singular imperfect, *acheterais* as the first person singular conditional); and in languages such as Arabic, where a word may have varying numbers of inflectional affixes (for example, a present tense verb will have a tense prefix and a present tense person marker, while a past tense one will just have the past tense number marker) and also a number of clitic affixes (closed class words that are directly attached to the main word) – for example, the form ويكتبون (wyktbwn) consists of a conjunction, وَ/PART (wa), a present tense prefix, يَ/IV3MP, a present tense form of the verb, (كتُب/VERB_IMP), a present tense suffix, ونَ/IVSUFF_SUBJ:MP_MOOD:I, and a third person plural pronoun, هُم/IVSUFF_DO:3MP, with the whole thing meaning *and they are writing them*. The permitted constituents, the order they are allowed to appear in, and the form of the root, which can vary with different affixes and between different classes of nouns and verbs, are complex and crucial.

To capture these phenomena, we need to make a further change to the algorithm given previously. We need to say what each affix can combine with, and we need to assign words to lexical classes. To capture the first part of this, we must assume that a root is typically incomplete without certain affixes – that an English verb is incomplete without a tense marker, a French adjective is incomplete without a gender marker and a number marker, and so on. We will write A->B to denote an A character that is missing a following B – for example, an English verb root is of the type V->TNS, and A <-B denotes an A that is missing a preceding B. For example, *-ly* is an adverb missing a preceding adjective, so it is of the type ADV<-ADJ. Given this notion, we can require that items have to combine as they are found – for example, *sadly*, which is made of the adjective *sad* and the derivational affix *-ly* can be combined, but *dogly* is not a word because the noun *dog* is not what *-ly* requires. Thus, the standard set of English affixes becomes as follows:

```
PREFIXES = fixaffixes(
    {"un": "(v->tns)->(v->tns), (a->cmp)->(a->cmp)",
     "re": "(v->tns)->(v->tns)",
     "dis": "(v->tns)->(v->tns)"})
SUFFIXES = fixaffixes(
    {"": "tns, num, cmp",
     "ing": "tns",
     "ed": "tns",
     "s": "tns, num",
     "en": "tns",
     "est": "cmp",
     "ly": "r<-(a->cmp), r<-v",
     "er": "(n->num)<-(v->tns), cmp",,
     "ment": "(n->num)<-(v->tns)"
     "ness": "(n->num)<-(v->tns)"})
```

Here, the root forms of nouns, verbs, and adjectives are assigned the types n->num, v->tns, and a->cmp. Now, analyzing a word such as *smaller* involves combining *small* (adj->cmp) and the suffix, *–er* (cmp), while the analysis of *redevelopments* involves combining *re-* ((v->tns)->(v->tns)) and *develop* (v->tns) to produce a new untensed verb, *redevelop*, also of the (v->tns) type. Now, we can combine this with *–ment* ((n->num)<-(v->tns)) to produce a new noun root, *redevelopment* ((n->num)), and finally combine that with *-s* ((num)) to produce the plural noun *redevelopments*. If we pick the best analysis in each case, we will get the following:

```
>>> from chapter4 import stem3
>>> stem3.allstems("smaller")[0]
('small+er', ['a'])
>>> stem3.allstems("redevelopments")[0]
('re-develop+ment+s', ['n'])
>>> stem3.allstems("unsurprisingly")[0]
('un-surprise+ing++ly', ['r'])
>>> stem3.allstems("unreconstructedly")[0]
('un-re-construct+ed++ly', ['r'])
>>> stem3.allstems("reconstructions")[0]
('re-construct+ion+s', ['n'])
>>> stem3.allstems("unreconstructions")[0]
Traceback (most recent call last):
  File "<stdin>", line 1, in <module>
IndexError: list index out of range
```

Note that *unreconstructions* leads to an error because the *un-*, *re-*, and *-ion* affixes don't go together – *un-* produces an adjective from a verb, so *un-re-construct* is an adjective and *-ion* has to be attached to a verb root.

The more elements you can remove from a complex word, the more likely you are to arrive at a root that is known to carry an emotional charge. If you can work out that *disastrously* is *disaster+ous+ly*, then you will be able to make use of the fact that *disaster* is a highly negative word to detect the negative overtones of *disastrously*; if you can spot that *enthusiastic* and *enthusiastically* are *enthusiast+ic* and *enthusiast+ic+al+ly*, then these three words can be treated as though they were the same when learning and subsequently applying rules for detecting emotions. It is worth noting that some affixes reverse the meaning of the words to which they apply – for example, an unexpected event is one that was not expected. This has to be taken into account when understanding that *undesirable*, for instance, is *un+desire+able*, where *desire* is a generally positive term but the prefix reverses its meaning and hence suggests that a text that contains it will be negative.

Similar phenomena occur in many other languages, with affixes either adding information to the base word or changing its meaning and/or class. In many cases, such as in Romance languages, the root will require multiple affixes to complete itself. In the English cases mentioned previously, we saw several examples where a word was made out of multiple components, but all such cases involved at most one inflectional affix plus one or more derivational ones.

Consider, for instance, the adjective *noir*: this, like most French adjectives, has four forms – *noir*, *noire*, *noirs*, and *noires*. We can easily capture this pattern by saying that a French adjectival root is of the type (a->num)->gen (note the bracketing – the first thing that has to be found is the gender marker, and only once that has been found do we have a->num – that is, an adjective looking for a number marker). Now, let's say we have a set of affixes, like so:

```
FSUFFIXES = fixaffixes({
    "": "gen, num",
    "s": "num",
    "e": "gen",})
```

With this, we can easily decompose the various forms of *noir*. We will also need a set of spelling change rules since some adjectives change their form when we add the various suffixes – for example, adjectives that end with *-if* (*sportif*, *objectif*) change their feminine endings to *-ive* (singular) and *-ives* (plural), so we need spelling rules such as the following, which says that the *-ive* sequence could arise from adding *-e* to the end of a word that ends with *if*:

```
FSPELLING = """
ive ==> if+e
"""
```

This rule will account for the four forms (*sportif*, *sportive*, *sportifs*, and *sportives*), with the *e* marking the fact that *sportif* and *sportifs* are pronounced with an unvoiced following consonant and *sportive* and *sportives* are pronounced with the voiced version of the consonant.

The situation becomes considerably more complicated when we come to deal with verbs. Consider the following conjugation table for the regular verb *regarder*:

	Present	**Imperfect**	**Future**	**Conditional**	**Subjunctive**	**Imperfect subj.**
je	regarde	regardais	regarderai	regarderais	regarde	regardasse
tu	regardes	regardais	regarderas	regarderais	regardes	regardasses
il	regarde	regardait	regardera	regarderait	regarde	regardât
nous	regardons	regardions	regarderons	regarderions	regardions	regardassions
vous	regardez	regardiez	regarderez	regarderiez	regardiez	regardassiez
ils	regardent	regardaient	regarderont	regarderaient	regardent	regardassent

Figure 4.2 – Conjugation table for "regarder"

There are some easy-to-spot regularities in this table – for example, that the future and conditional forms all contain the *-er* suffix, and that the imperfect and conditional forms have the same set of person affixes. There are quite a lot of semi-regularities that don't carry over completely – for example, the subjunctive and imperfect subjunctive have very similar (but not identical) sets of person endings. It is very difficult to do anything useful with the semi-regularities, so the best that we can easily do is specify that a French verb requires a mood marker and a person marker – that is, that *regard* is of the (v->person)->mood type (as with the type for adjectives, this says that you have to supply the mood marker first to get something of the (v->person) type and then look for the person marker). Now, we can supply the collection of affixes, which can then be used to analyze input text:

```
FSUFFIXES = {
    "": "gen, num", "s": "num", "e": "gen, person",
    "er": "mood", "": "mood",
    "ez": "person", "ais": "person", "a": "person", "ai": "person",
    "aient": "person", "ait": "person", "as": "person","ât": "person",
    "asse": "person", "asses": "person", "ent": "person", "es":
"person",
    "iez": "person", "ions": "person", "ons": "person", "ont":
"person",
    }
```

These affixes can then be used to reduce verbs to their base forms – *regardions* and *regarderions*, for instance, become *regard+ions* and *regard+er+ions*, respectively – so that different variants of the same word can be recognized.

Simply using this table will overgenerate, incorrectly recognizing, for instance, *regardere* as *regard+er+e*. This may not matter too much since people don't generally write incorrect forms (and maybe if they do, it is helpful to recognize them anyway, as with the English examples of *stealed* and *sliping* mentioned previously). More significantly, different verbs have substantially different conjugation tables that require different sets of affixes:

	Present	**Imperfect**	**Future**	**Conditional**	**Subjunctive**	**Imperfect subj.**
je	faiblis	faiblissais	faiblirai	faiblirais	faiblisse	faiblisse
tu	faiblis	faiblissais	faibliras	faiblirais	faiblisses	faiblisses
il	faiblit	faiblissait	faiblira	faiblirait	faiblisse	faiblît
nous	faiblissons	faiblissions	faiblirons	faiblirions	faiblissions	faiblissions
vous	faiblissez	faiblissiez	faiblirez	faibliriez	faiblissiez	faiblissiez
ils	faiblissent	faiblissaient	faibliront	faibliraient	faiblissent	faiblissent

Figure 4.3 – Conjugation table for "faiblir"

Here, several (but not all) of the tense markers that were empty for *regard* are now *-iss*, the marker for the future and conditional tenses is *ir*, and some of the person markers for the present tense are different. We can add (and indeed will have to) these to our table, but we would also like to make sure that the right affixes get applied to the right verb.

To do this, we have to be able to say more about words and affixes than simply assigning them a single atomic label. In English, we want to be able to say that *–ly* attaches to participles but not to tensed forms (for example, that *unexpectedly* and *unsurprisingly* are *un+expect+ed+ly* and *un+surprise+ing+ly*, but that *unexpectly* and *unsurprisely* are not words). We want to be able to say that *regard* is an *er* verb and *faibl* is an *ir* verb, with an empty imperfect marker for *er* verbs and *iss* as the imperfect marker for *ir* verbs. In general, we want to be able to say quite detailed things about words and their affixes and to be able to copy information from one to the other (for example, that the verb root will get its tense and form from the tense affix).

We can do this by extending our notation to allow for features – that is, properties that distinguish one instance of a word from another. For example, we can say that *sleeps* is [hd=v, tense=present, finite=tensed, number=singular, person=third] and *sleeping* is [hd=v, tense=present, finite=participle]. We can, for instance, change the description of the base form of a verb from v->tns to v[tense=T, finite=F, number=N, person=P] ->tense[tense=T, finite=F, number=N, person=P], – i.e., a base verb isn't just something that needs a tense marker; it will also inherit the values of the features for tense, finiteness, number, and person from that affix. The verbal suffixes then become as follows:

```
SUFFIXES = fixaffixes(
    {"": "tense[finite=infinitive]; tense[finite=tensed, tense=present]"
     "ing": "tense[finite=participle, tense=present]",
     "ed": "tense[finite=participle, tense=present, voice=passive];
            tense[tense=past, voice=active]",
```

```
    "s": "tense[finite=tensed, tense=present, number=singular,
                person=third];
    "en": "tense[finite=participle]",
     ...
    "ly": "r<-v[finite=participle, tense=present]",
     ...
})
```

This code block says that adding an empty suffix to a verbal root will give you the infinitive form or the present tense, adding *-ing* will give you the present participle, and so on.

This general approach can be used to assign French verbs to the various classes of *-er*, *-ir*, *-re*, and irregular cases, to ensure that tense and agreement markers on Arabic verbs match each other, as well as to ensure that complex sequences of derivational and inflectional affixes are handled properly. If you want to get at the root of a surface form and see exactly what properties it has, you will have to do something like this. It does, however, come at a price:

- You have to say more about the words in your lexicon and a lot more about the affixes themselves. To realize that *kissed* can be the past tense or the past participle or the passive participle of *kiss* but that *walked* can only be the past tense or past participle of *walk*, you have to know what the *-ed* suffix does and you also have to know that *walk* is an intransitive verb and hence does not have a passive form. The more you want to know about the properties of a surface form, the more you have to say about its root and about the affixes that are attached to it. This is hard work and can make it very hard to maintain the lexicon. This can be seen in an extreme form in the lexicon for the most widely used morphological analyzer for Arabic, namely the SAMA lexicon (Buckwalter, T., 2007). A typical entry in the SAMA lexicon looks like this:

```
;--- Ab(1)
;; >ab~-ui_1
>b (أب) >ab~ (أَبّ) PV_V desire;aspire
>bb (أبب) >abab (أَبَب) PV_C desire;aspire
&b (ؤب) &ub~ (ؤُبّ) IV_Vd desire;aspire
>bb (أبب) >obub (أُبُب) IV_C desire;aspire
}b (ئب) }ib~ (ئِبّ) IV_Vd desire;aspire
>bb (أبب) >obib (أُبِب) IV_C desire;aspire
```

This entry contains six distinct variants for a verb meaning something such as desire. The first part of a variant is what the stem looks like with diacritics omitted (diacritics are things such as short vowels and other marks that affect the pronunciation of the word, and are generally omitted in written Arabic), the second part is what the stem would look like if the diacritics were written, the third is a label that specifies what affixes the stem will combine with, and the last is the English gloss. To add a single entry to the lexicon, you have to know what all the surface forms look like and which class they belong to – for example, the stem &b (ؤب) is the IV_Vd form of this word. To do that, you have to know what it means to say that something is the IV_Vd form of the word. And then, there are over 14K prefixes and nearly 15k suffixes, each with a complex label saying what stems it attaches to.

This is an extreme case: we need five inflectional affixes for English verbs and maybe another 10 derivational ones, and around 250 inflectional affixes for French verbs. Nonetheless, the point is clear: if you want to get complete and correct decompositions of complex words, you need to provide a lot of information about words and suffixes. (See Hoeksema, 1985, for more on describing words in terms that specify what they need to complete themselves.)

- Exploiting this information requires more work than just splitting the surface form into pieces, and can markedly slow things down. morphy runs at about 150K words/second, but it does very little with compound words such as *unexpectedly* – if a word like this is in the set of exceptions, then it is returned without being decomposed; if it is not (for example, *unwarrantedly*), then it will simply return nothing at all. The analyzer provided in the code repository runs at 27K words/ second if we use simple labels and no spelling rules, 17.2K words/second with simple labels and spelling rules, 21.4K words/second with complex labels and no spelling rules, and 14.7K words/second with complex labels and spelling rules, and the SAMA lexicon runs at about 9K words/second. The analyzer from the code repository and the SAMA lexicon also provide all the alternative analyses of a given form, whereas morphy just returns the first match it finds.

The lesson is clear: if you want words that have been stripped right down to their roots, you will have to provide a substantial amount of clear information about word classes and about the effects that the various affixes have. If you take a simple-minded approach and are not too worried about getting right to the heart of each form, and about finding out its exact properties, then you can do the task substantially faster, but even at 14.7K words/second, morphological analysis not going to be a major bottleneck.

Compound words

In the previous section, we looked at how to find the root element of a complex word. This is important for our overall task since a large part of the emotional content of a text is determined simply by the choice of words. A tweet such as *My joy at finding that you loved me as much as I love you has filled my heart with contentment* is overwhelmingly likely to be tagged as expressing **joy** and **love**, and the form *loved* will contribute as much to this as the form *love*. It can also happen, however, that a group of words expresses something quite different from what they express individually – that a tweet containing the phrases *greenhouse gases* and *climate change* is much more likely to be negative than one that just contains *greenhouse* and *change*, and that one that contains the phrase *crime prevention* is much more likely to be positive than one that just contains *crime* or *prevention*.

This is a fairly marginal effect in languages that use white space to separate tokens because compound words of this kind tend to be written either with no separator or with a dash: a *blackbird* is not just a bird that is black, and a *greenhouse* is neither a house nor green. In some languages, however, each token is potentially a word and each sequence of tokens is also potentially a word, with no white space to mark the boundaries around sequences. In Chinese, for instance, the words 酒 and 店 mean *wine* and *shop*, but the sequence 酒店 means *hotel*. Similarly, the word 奄 means *suddenly* but the sequence 奄奄 means *dying*. While it is easy enough to see the connection between *wine shop* and *hotel*, there is more to a hotel than just somewhere that sells wine; and it is all but impossible to see why *suddenly-*

suddenly would mean *dying*. Similarly, the four characters 新, 冠, 疫, and 情, which individually mean *new crown epidemic feeling*, meaning COVID-19, when taken as a group, are hard to predict. Also, a tweet about COVID-19 is much more likely to be negative than one about *new crown epidemic feeling*. Therefore, it is important to be able to detect such compounds even when there is no typographical evidence for them, particularly since they are fluid, with new ones being created all the time (新冠疫情 would not have meant COVID-19 in 2018!).

The key to finding such compounds is observing that the elements of a compound will occur next to each much more frequently than you would expect just by chance. The standard way to detect this is by using **pointwise mutual information** (PMI) (Fano, r. M., 1961). The idea here is that if two events, E1 and E2, are unconnected, then the likelihood of E2 occurring immediately after E1 should be the same as the likelihood of E2 occurring immediately after some other event. If E1 and E2 have nothing to do with each other, then the likelihood of E2 occurring immediately after E1 is *prob(E1)*prob(E2)*. If we find that they are occurring together more often than that, we can conclude that they have some connection. If E1 and E2 are words, we can hypothesize that if they co-occur much more often than expected, then they may be a compound. Therefore, we can calculate the PMI of two words as *log(prob(W1+W2)/(prob(W1)*prob(W2))* (taking logs smooths out values that are returned but this is not crucial to the approach).

The machinery for doing this is implemented in `chapter4.compounds`. If we apply it to a collection of 10 million words from the BNC, we will see that the top 20 pairs that occur at least 300 times are largely fixed phrases, often Latin (*inter-alia*, *vice-versa*, *ad-hoc*, *status-quo*, and *de-facto*) or technical/medical terms (*ulcerative-colitis*, and *amino-acids*). The following scores are of the (`<PMI-score>`, `<pair>`, `<freq>`) form:

```
>>> from basics.readers import *
>>> from chapter4 import compounds
>>> l = list(reader(BNC, BNCWordReader, pattern=".*/[A-Z\d]*\.xml"))
>>> pmi, pmiTable, words, pairs = compounds.doItAllPMI(l)
111651731 words
760415 distinct words found (111651731 tokens)
Getting pairs
67372 pairs found
Calculating PMI

>>> thresholded = compounds.thresholdpmi(pmi, 300)
>>> printall(thresholded[:20])
(14.880079898248782, 'inter-alia', 306)
(14.10789557602586, 'ulcerative-colitis', 708)
(13.730483221346029, 'vice-versa', 667)
(13.600053898897935, 'gall-bladder', 603)
(13.564948792663655, 'amino-acids', 331)
(13.490100806659854, 'ad-hoc', 485)
(12.956064741908307, 'carbon-dioxide', 976)
```

```
(12.935141767901545, 'sq-km', 499)
(12.872023194200782, 'biopsy-specimens', 306)
(12.766406621309034, 'da-da', 499)
(12.55829842681955, 'mentally-handicapped', 564)
(12.46079297927814, 'ethnic-minorities', 336)
(12.328294856503494, 'et-al', 2963)
(12.273447636994682, 'global-warming', 409)
(12.183953515076327, 'bodily-harm', 361)
(12.097267289044826, 'ozone-layer', 320)
(12.083121068394941, 'ha-ha', 665)
(12.01519057467734, 'activating-factor', 311)
(12.005309794347232, 'desktop-publishing', 327)
(11.972306035897368, 'tens-thousands', 341)
```

Even in English, pairs such as `crime-prevention` and `greenhouse-gases`, which have high PMI scores (the median pair in our set is (`5.48, needs-help, 121`), and `crime-prevention` and `greenhouse-gases` are both in the top 2% of the entire set), can carry an emotional weight that is different from the emotions associated with the components:

```
>>> pmiTable['crime-prevention']
(10.540598239864938, 202)
>>> pmiTable['greenhouse-gases']
(12.322885857554724, 120)
```

So, it may be worth looking at the emotional weights associated with particularly frequent compound terms even in English. For other languages, this may be even more important.

Tagging and parsing

We have spent quite a long time looking at individual words – finding tokens in text, decomposing those into smaller elements, looking at the way that spelling changes happen at the boundaries between word parts, and considering the problems that arise, particularly in languages that do not use white space to separate tokens when words come together to form compounds. A huge part of the task of emotion detection relies on identifying words that carry emotions, so it makes sense to be careful when looking at words.

As noted in *Chapter 1, Foundations*, for most NLP tasks, finding the relationships between words is just as important as finding the words themselves. For our current task, which involves finding the general emotional overtones of a short informal text, this may not be the case. There are two major questions to be answered here:

- Does assigning a set of relations between words help with emotion detection?

- Is it possible to assign relations to elements of informal text?

Normal texts are divided into sentences – that is, groups of words separated by punctuation marks that describe the words (or query a description of the words). A properly formed sentence has a main verb that denotes an event or a state and a set of satellite phrases that either describe the participants in this event or state or say something about where, when, how, or why it took place. Consider the second question: if we use a rule-based parser we get something similar to the following tree (the exact form of the tree will depend on the nature of the rules being used; we are using a parser that was designed to deal cleanly with out-of-position items (Ramsay, A. M., 1999), but any rule-based parser will produce something like this):

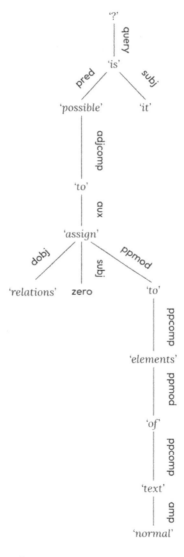

Figure 4.4 – Rule-based parse of "Is it possible to assign relations to elements of normal text"

This tree says that the given sentence is a query about the existence of a particular kind of possibility, namely the possibility of assigning relations to elements of normal text. To understand this sentence properly, we have to find these relations.

The preceding tree was generated by a rule-based parser (Ramsay, A. M., 1999). As noted in *Chapter 1, Foundations*, rule-based parsers can be fragile when confronted with texts that do not obey the rules, and they can be slow. Given that informal texts are, more or less by definition, likely not to obey the rules of normal language, we will consider using a data-driven parser to analyze them.

We will start by looking at two tweets that were chosen fairly randomly from the SEMEVAL training data:

```
@PM @KF Very misleading heading.
```

```
#anxious don't know why #worry (: slowly going #mad hahahahahahahaha
```

These tweets do not obey the rules of normal well-formed text. They contain elements that simply do not appear in normal language (usernames, hashtags, emojis, emoticons), they contain non-standard uses of punctuation, they very often have no main verb, they contain deliberate misspellings and words made out of repeated elements (*hahahahahahahaha*), and so on. Our rule-based parser will just fail if we try to use it to analyze them. What happens if we were to use a data-driven one (we use the NLTK pre-trained version of the MALT parser (Nivre, 2006) with the NLTK recommended tagger, but very little changes if we choose another data-driven parser or a different tagger)?

Just using MALT with the standard tagger, we get the following trees for *@PM @KF Very misleading heading.* and *#anxious don't know why .... #worry (: slowly going #mad hahahahahahahaha*:

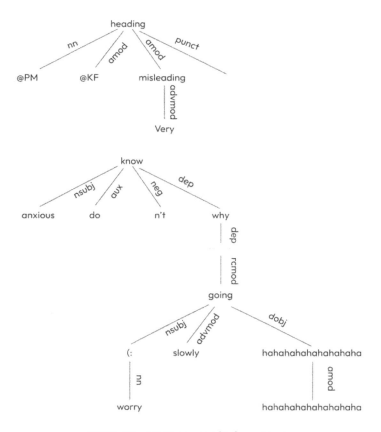

Figure 4.5 – MALT parses of informal texts

There are two problems here. The first is that the tagger and parser are data-driven – that is, the decisions they make are learned from a labeled corpus, and the corpus they have been trained on does not contain the kind of informal text that is found in tweets. Secondly, and more significantly, informal texts often contain fragments jumbled up together, so it is not possible to assign relationships to such a text in a way that makes a single coherent tree.

The first of these problems could be overcome by marking up a corpus of tweets. This would, of course, be tedious, but no more tedious than doing so for a corpus of standard texts. The second problem raises its head again here because to mark up a piece of text, you have to have an underlying theory of what POS tags to use and what kinds of relationships exist between the elements of the text. If you assume that the only POS tags that you can use are the standard NN, VV, JJ, DET, IN, CC, and PR, then you cannot assign the correct tags to tweet elements, since these are new and are not of the standard types. And if you assume that only the standard relations between words can be used, then you cannot assign the correct roles to tweet items since they do not tend to occupy these roles – the emoticon *(:* and the word *hahahahahahahaha* are not the kinds of things that can play these roles.

So, if we are going to mark up a collection of tweets to train a tagger and parser, we are going to have to come up with a theory of the structure of such texts. Constructing a treebank is not a theory-free activity. The guidelines given to the annotators are, by definition, an informal specification of a grammar, so unless you have a clear idea of what roles things such as hashtags and emojis can play, and a clear understanding of when, for instance, an emoji should be seen as a comment on the tweet as a whole and when it should be seen as a comment on a particular element, it is just not possible to construct a treebank.

Tweets often contain well-formed fragments, so maybe we can get some benefit from finding these:

Never regret anything that once made you smile :)   #positive

Literally hanging on by a thread need some taylor ray tonight loving a bad dog sucks #taylorrayholbrook #hurting @TRT

was one moron driving his oversize tonka truck with the big flag in the bed back and forth blaring country music. 😕 *#disappointment*

#ThingsIveLearned The wise #shepherd never trusts his flock to a #smiling wolf. #TeamFollowBack #fact #wisewords

There are a couple of things that are worth doing to start with. No existing parser, rule-based or data-driven, is going to do anything sensible with tags, usernames, emojis, or emoticons at the beginning or end of a sentence, so we may as well strip those off before attempting to find parseable fragments. Hashtags in the middle of a tweet are often attached to meaningful words, so we may as well remove those too. This will give us the following:

Never regret anything that once made you smile

was one moron driving his oversize tonka truck with the big flag in the bed back and forth blaring country music.

Literally hanging on by a thread need some taylor ray tonight loving a bad dog sucks

The wise shepherd never trusts his flock to a smiling wolf.

These all contain well-formed fragments: the first and fourth are, indeed, well-formed sentences, and the other two contain well-formed fragments. What happens if we try to parse them using our rule-based tagger and then use MALT?

The two parsers give essentially the same answers for the first and fourth of these (rule-based analysis on the left, MALT analysis on the right), save that the rule-based parser gives the wrong attachment to *to a smiling wolf*. No parser can be expected to get the attachment of such phrases right every time, and apart from that, the two behave perfectly sensibly given the rules that either explicitly or implicitly underly them:

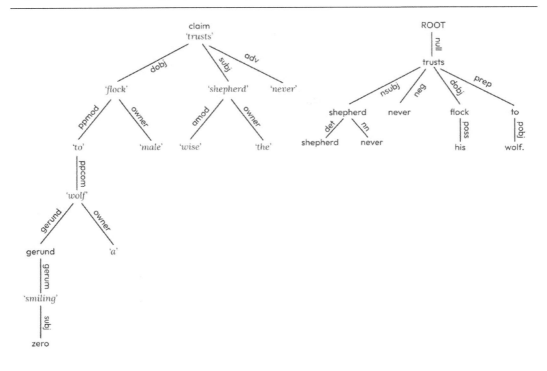

Figure 4.6 – Rule-based and MALT parses for "The wise shepherd never trusts his flock to a smiling wolf"

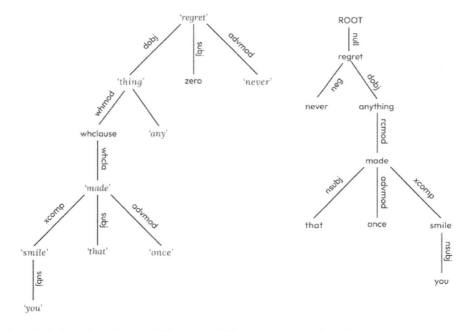

Figure 4.7 – Rule-based and MALT parses for "Never regret anything that once made you smile"

So, either approach will suffice for these examples. When we consider the other cases, the situation becomes more difficult. The rule-based parser fails to produce any overall analysis for *was one moron driving his oversize tonka truck with the big flag in the bed back and forth blaring country music* or *Literally hanging on by a thread need some taylor ray tonight loving a bad dog sucks*. Both these sentences are simply too long for it to handle because there are too many options to be explored. MALT produces analyses for both cases:

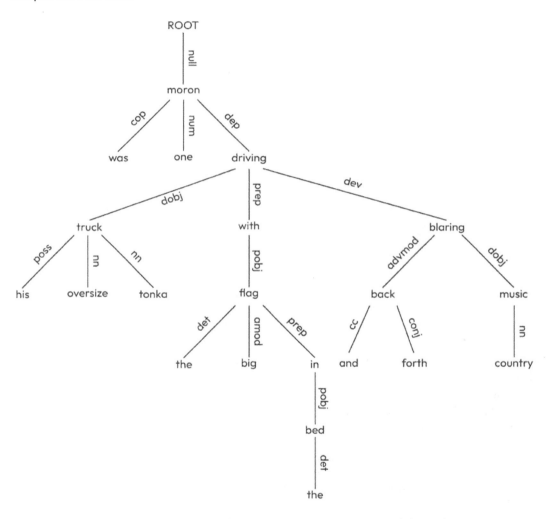

Figure 4.8 – MALT parse for "was one moron driving his oversize tonka truck with the big flag in the bed back and forth blaring country music"

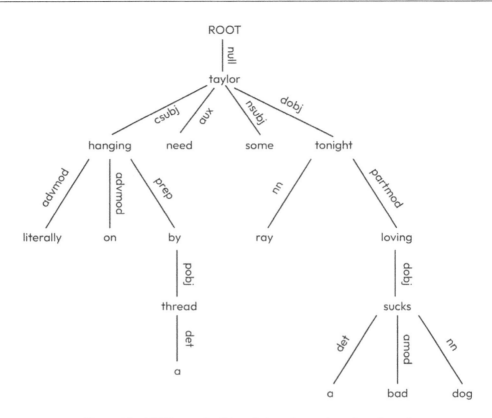

Figure 4.9 – MALT parse for "Literally hanging on by a thread need
some taylor ray tonight loving a bad dog sucks"

The first of these is reasonable – the analysis of *was* as a copula is questionable, and the attachment of *back and forth* is wrong, but by and large, it captures most of the relevant relationships. The second is just a mess. The problem with the second is that the text contains several disjoint elements – *Literally hanging on by a thread, need some taylor ray tonight* and *loving a bad dog sucks* – but the parser has been told to analyze the whole thing and hence it has analyzed the whole thing.

There is nothing to be done about this. Data-driven parsers are generally designed to be robust, so even if the text they are given is entirely ungrammatical or contains grammatical fragments but is not a single coherent whole, they will return a single tree **and there is no way of telling that what they return is problematic**. This holds pretty much by definition. If a text doesn't have a sensible structure – that is, it can't be assigned a sensible parse tree – then a robust parser will assign it a tree that is not sensible. A rule-based parser, on the other hand, will just fail if the text does not obey the rules it expects it to obey or is just too long and complex to handle.

So, there seems little point in including a parser in the preprocessing steps for sentiment mining. Rule-based parsers will frequently just fail when confronted with informal texts, even if they are preprocessed to strip non-textual items off the front and back and to do various other simple steps. Data-driven parsers will always produce an answer, but for text that does not obey the rules of normal language, this answer will often be nonsensical and **there is no easy way of telling which analyses are reasonable and which are not**. And if there is no point in including a parser, then there is also no point in including a tagger, since the sole function of a tagger is to preprocess the text for a parser. It might be possible to use a rule-based parser to check the output of a data-driven parser – if the output of the data-driven one is reasonable, then using it to guide the rule-based one will enable the rule-based one to verify that it is indeed acceptable without exploring vast numbers of dead-ends.

However, it is very unclear how a typical machine learning algorithm would be able to make use of such trees, even if they could be reliably found. The code repository for this book includes code for tagging tweets and running a data-driven parser on the results, and some examples can be explored further there, but since these are not generally useful steps for our overall goal, we will not discuss them further here.

Summary

In this chapter, we have looked at the issues that arise when you try to split a piece of text into words by looking at how to split text into tokens, how to find the basic components of words, and how to identify compound words. These are all useful steps for assigning emotions to informal texts. We also looked at what happens when we try to take the next step and assign grammatical relations to the words that make up an informal text, concluding that this is an extremely difficult task that provides comparatively little benefit for our overall task. We had to look quite carefully at this step, even though we believe it is not all that useful, since we need to understand why it is so hard and why the results of even the best parsers cannot be relied on.

References

To learn more about the topics that were covered in this chapter, take a look at the following resources:

- Buckwalter, T. (2007). *Issues in Arabic Morphological Analysis*. Arabic Computational Morphology, 23-42.

- Chomsky, N., & Halle, M. (1968). *The Sound Pattern of English*. MIT Press.

- Fano, R. M. (1961). *Transmission of Information: A Statistical Theory of Communications*. MIT Press.

- Hoeksema, J. (1985). *Categorial Morphology*. Garland Publishing.

- Koskiennemi, K. (1985). *A General Two-level Computational Model for Word-form Recognition and Production*. COLING-84, 178-181.

- Leech, G., Garside, R., & Bryant, M. (1994, August). *CLAWS4: The Tagging of the British National Corpus*. COLING 1994 Volume 1: The 15th International Conference on Computational Linguistics. `https://aclanthology.org/C94-1103`

- Nivre, J., Hall, J., & Nilsson, J. (2006). *MaltParser: A language-independent system for data-driven dependency parsing*. Proceedings of the International Conference on Language Resources (LREC), 6, 2216-2219.

- Ramsay, A. M. (1999). *Direct parsing with discontinuous phrases*. Natural Language Engineering, 5(3), 271-300.

Part 3: Approaches

In this part, you'll learn how we go about the task of EA. We will discuss various models, explain how they work, and evaluate the results.

This part has the following chapters:

- *Chapter 5, Sentiment Lexicons and Vector Space Models*
- *Chapter 6, Naïve Bayes*
- *Chapter 7, Support Vector Machines*
- *Chapter 8, Neural Networks and Deep Neural Networks*
- *Chapter 9, Exploring Transformers*
- *Chapter 10, Multiclassifiers*

5

Sentiment Lexicons and Vector-Space Models

We now have the machinery that we need to make systems that find emotions in texts – **natural language processing (NLP)** algorithms for converting raw texts into feature sets and machine learning algorithms for extracting patterns from feature sets. Over the next few chapters, we will develop a series of emotion mining algorithms, very simple ones to start with, leading up to sophisticated algorithms that use a variety of advanced techniques.

While doing so, we will use a collection of datasets and a variety of measures to test each algorithm and compare the effectiveness of the various preprocessing steps. So, this chapter will start by considering the datasets and metrics that we will be using as we develop the various algorithms. Once we have the datasets and metrics in place, we will consider very simple classifiers based purely on sentiment lexicons, and we will look at ways of calculating how strongly an individual word expresses a sentiment. This will provide us with a baseline for looking at the performance of more sophisticated algorithms in later chapters.

In this chapter, we will cover the following topics:

- Datasets and metrics
- Sentiment lexicons
- Extracting a sentiment lexicon from a corpus
- Vector-space models

Datasets and metrics

Over the next few chapters, we will look at several emotion-mining algorithms. Before we do so, we need to consider exactly what these algorithms are designed to do. There are several slightly different tasks for emotion mining algorithms, and we need to be clear about which of these tasks a given algorithm is aimed at:

- You might just want to know whether the texts you are looking at are positive or negative, or you might want a finer-grained classification.

- You might assume that each text expresses exactly one emotion, or at most one emotion, or that a text can express several (or no) emotions.

- You might want to know how strongly a text expresses an emotion. For example, *I'm a bit irritated by that* and *That makes me absolutely furious* both express anger, but the second clearly expresses it much more strongly.

We will concentrate on algorithms that aim to assign multiple (or no) labels to each tweet, with the labels drawn from some collection of candidate emotions, ranging from just positive and negative to larger sets drawn from Plutchik's wheel. We will refer to datasets where a single tweet can have zero or more labels as **multi-label** datasets. This is to be distinguished from **multi-class** datasets, where there are several labels available but exactly one is assigned to each tweet. Multi-label datasets are significantly more difficult than simple multi-class ones, and the task also gets harder as the set of labels gets larger (it may, for instance, be difficult to distinguish between anger and disgust, but they are both negative); and it also gets harder if we don't have a preconception about how many emotions are expressed. Since most of the learning algorithms depend on comparing some score obtained from the text with a threshold, we can usually use this score to assess how strongly a text expresses an emotion rather than just whether it expresses it or not. We will mainly concentrate on deciding whether a text expresses an emotion rather than how strongly.

We will use a selection of the datasets listed in *Chapter 2, Building and Using a Dataset*, to train and test the various models that we will develop:

- The **Workshop on Computational Approaches to Subjectivity, Sentiment & Social Media Analysis (WASSA)** dataset, which contains 3.9K English tweets, each labeled with one of anger, fear, joy, and sadness.

- The Semeval 2018 Task E_c dataset, which contains a moderate number of tweets in English, Arabic, and Spanish, where a fairly high percentage of tweets contain emojis, with each tweet labeled with 0 or more emotions from a standard set of 11 emotions. This dataset contains 7.7K English tweets, 2.9K Arabic tweets, and 4.2K Spanish tweets. We will refer to this as the SEM-11 set.

- The Semeval 2016 Task El-reg and El-oc dataset, where the El-reg dataset has tweets labeled with a score from 0 to 1 for each of a set of four emotions, and the El-oc dataset has tweets ranked in terms of which emotion they express. The combinations of these datasets, which we will refer to as the SEM4 set, contain 7.6K English tweets, 2.8K Arabic, and 2.6K Spanish.

- The CARER dataset is large (slightly over 400K tweets) and has labels for six emotions (anger, fear, joy, love, sadness, and surprise). Each tweet is assigned exactly one emotion.

- The IMDb dataset contains 50K negative and positive film reviews and provides an interesting test of the robustness of the various algorithms since it is split into just two categories (positive and negative), which makes the task of learning to classify documents easier. The reviews contain anything from 100 to 1,000 words, which is much longer than a tweet and poses a different set of problems.

- A collection of Kuwaiti tweets, annotated either by assigning a label if all three annotators unanimously assigned that label (KWT.U) or if at least two of them did (KWT.M). This set is particularly interesting because, in a large number of cases, the annotators agreed that a tweet expressed no emotions and in some, it expressed several, which poses a substantial challenge for classifiers that assign a single label to every observation.

These datasets provide enough variation to help us verify that a given approach to the task of finding emotions is robust across different conditions:

- The WASSA, SEM4, and SEM11 datasets contain emojis, which makes the task of emotion mining slightly easier because the main (sole?) point of using emojis is to express emotions, though they are sometimes used in slightly surprising ways.

- The SEM4 and SEM11 datasets are multilingual, with data supplied in English, Arabic, and Spanish. This helps when trying out approaches that are intended to be language-independent since the methodology for collecting the three languages is the same.

- The SEM11 set contains tweets with differing numbers of emotions, including none, which can make the task of assigning emotions considerably harder.

- The CARER dataset is very large, though it does not contain any emojis or hashtags: this makes it possible to carry out investigations into how performance varies with the size of the training data.

- The IMDb set has just two labels, but very long texts.

- The KWT sets have tweets with zero, one, or more emotions, but this time, a very large proportion have zero.

Given that these datasets are supplied in different formats, we need, as usual, a common format for representing them. We will use two basic classes:

- A tweet is an object with a sequence of tokens, a term frequency table, and possibly a Gold Standard set of labels, along with several bookkeeping properties:

```
class TWEET:

    def __init__(self, id=False, src=False,
                 text=False, tf=False,
                 scores=False, tokens=False,
```

```
                    args=False):
        self.id = id
        self.src = src
        self.text = text
        self.GS = scores
        self.tokens = tokens
        self.tf = ormalize(tf)
        self.ARGS = args


    def __repr__(self):
        return self.text
```

- A dataset is a set containing a set of tweets, a list of emotion names, the Gold Standard labels for the tweets, and, again, some bookkeeping properties. The most useful of these is an index that assigns each word in the dataset a unique index. We will frequently use this in later sections, so it is worth looking at how we do it here. The basic idea is that we read the dataset word by word. If the word we have just read is already in the index, there is nothing to be done. If it is not, then we assign it the current length of the index: this ensures that every word gets assigned a unique identifier; once we have added the current word, the length of the index will be incremented by one, so the next new word will get a new index:

```
def makeIndex(self):
    index = {}
    for tweet in self.tweets:
        for token in tweet.tokens:
            if not token in index
                index[token] = len(index)
    return index
```

This will generate an index, as shown here, where each word has a unique identifier:

```
{..., 'days': 6, 'sober': 7, 'do': 8, "n't": 9, 'wanna': 10,  ...}
```

Given makeIndex, we can construct a DATASET class as follows:

```
class DATASET:

    def __init__(self, emotions, tweets, idf, ARGS, N=sys.
maxsize):
        self.emotions = sorted(emotions)
        self.tweets = tweets
        self.GS = [tweet.GS for tweet in self.tweets][:N]
        self.idf = idf
        self.words = [w[0] for w in reversed(sortTable(idf))]
        self.makeIndex()
        self.ARGS = ARGS
```

We will need to convert the format of a given dataset into these representations, but once that has been done, we will use them throughout this and the following chapters. We will do this in stages.

First, we will convert the dataset so that it looks like the SEM11 dataset – that is, a tab-separated file with a header that specifies that the first and second fields as the ID and the tweet itself, with the remaining columns as the various emotions, followed by a line per tweet with 0s and 1s in the appropriate columns (the following example has the tweet and the columns for emotions truncated, so it will fit on the page).

This format is a variant of the standard **one-hot** representation used in neural networks, where a choice from several discrete labels is represented by a vector where each position in the vector represents a possible option. Suppose, for instance, that the possible labels were {**angry, sad, happy, love**}. In this case, we could represent **angry** with the vector <1, 0, 0, 0>, **sad** with <0, 1, 0, 0>, **happy** with <0, 0, 1, 0>, and **love** with <0, 0, 0, 1>.

The advantage of the SEM11 version of this format is that it makes it easy to allow tweets to have an arbitrary number of labels, thus allowing us to treat multi-label datasets and single-label datasets uniformly:

```
ID       Tweet                    anger   disgust   fear
21441    Worry is a down payment    0        1        0
1535     it makes you #happy.       0        0        0
```

Exactly how we convert a given dataset into this format depends on how the dataset is supplied. The following code shows how we do it for the CARER dataset – the others are similar, but because their original format is slightly different, the code for converting it into the SEM11 format will be slightly different

The CARER dataset comes as two files: a file called `dataset_infos.json` containing information about the dataset and another called `data.jsonl` containing the actual data. We convert this into SEM11 format by finding the names of the labels in `dataset_infos.json` and then converting the entries in `data.jsonl` so that they have a 1 in the appropriate column and a 0 in the others.

`data.jsonl` looks as follows:

```
{"text":"i feel awful about it","label":0}
{"text":"i really do feel proud of myself","label":1}
...
```

We want to convert this into the following:

ID	text	sadness	joy	love	anger	fear	surprise
0	i feel awful about it	1	0	0	0	0	0
1	i really do feel proud of myself	0	1	0	0	0	0

We do this by using the set of labels provided in `dataset_infos.json` as the header line, and then writing each entry in `data.jsonl` with a 1 in the column specified by its label (for example, in the first (sadness) column for tweet 1 and the second (joy) column for tweet 2):

```
def convert(self):
    # extract the labels from dataset_infos.json
    with open(os.path.join(self.DOWNLOAD,
                           "dataset_infos.json")) as jsfile:
        infos = json.load(jsfile)
        self.labels = infos["default"]["features"]\
                                    ["label"]["names"]
    # read the data line by line from data.jsonl
    with open(os.path.join(self.PATH, "data.jsonl"))\
            as input:
        d = [json.loads(line) for line in input]
    # initialise the output with a header line
    csv = "ID\ttext\t%s\n"%("\t".join(self.labels))
    # Go through the data writing each line as the ID,
    # the text itself and an appropriate set of 0s and 1s
    for i, x in enumerate(d):
        cols = ["1" if x['label'] == i else "0"\
                        for i in range(len(self.labels))]
        csv += "%s\t%s\t%s\n"%(i, x['text'],"\t".join(cols))
    # Save this as wholething.csv inside CARER/EN
    with open(os.path.join(self.PATH, "wholething.csv"), "w") as out:
        out.write(csv)
```

Once we have the data in SEM11 format, we can read it as a dataset. We read the data line by line, using the first line as a header where the first two items are `ID` and `tweet` and the remainder are the emotions, and then use `makeTweet` to convert subsequent lines into `tweets`. We then remove duplicates and shuffle the data, construct document frequency and inverse document frequency tables, and wrap the whole thing up as a `dataset`:

```
def makeDATASET(src, N=sys.maxsize, args=None):
    dataset = [line.strip() for line in open(src)][:N]
    emotions = None
    tweets = []
    for tweet in dataset:
        if emotions is None:
            emotions = tweet.split()[2:]
        else:
            tweets.append(makeTweet(tweet, args=args))
    pruned = prune(tweets)
    random.seed(0); random.shuffle(pruned)
```

```
df = counter()
index = {}
for i, tweet in enumerate(tweets):
    for w in tweet.tokens:
        df.add(w)
"""
remove singletons from the idf count
"""
idf = {}
for w in list(df.keys()):
    idf[w] = 1.0/float(df[w]+1)
return DATASET(emotions, tweets, df, idf, args=args)
```

makeTweet does quite a lot of work. It splits the line that was read from the file (which is, at this point, still just a tab-separated string) into its component parts and converts the 0s and 1s into a NumPy array; does tokenization and stemming as required (for example, for Arabic, the default is to convert the text into a form using Latin characters, tokenize it by just splitting it at white space, and then use the stemmer described in *Chapter 4, Preprocessing – Stemming, Tagging, and Parsing* to find roots and affixes, with similar steps for other languages); and then finally make a term frequency table for the tweet and wrap everything up in tweet. All of these functions have an argument called args that contains a set of parameters that are supplied at the top level and that control what happens – for example, what language we are using, which tokenizer and stemmer we want to use, and so on:

```
def makeTweet(tweet, args):
    tweet = tweet.strip().split("\t")
    scores = numpy.array([int(score) for score in tweet[2:]])
    tweet, text tweet[0], tweet[1]
    if args["language"] == "AR":
        tokens = a2bw.convert(text, a2bw.a2bwtable).split()
        if args["stemmer"] == "standard":
            tokens = stemmer.stemAll(tokens, stemmer.TWEETGROUPS)
    elif args["language"] == "ES":

    elif args["language"] == "EN":

    tf = counter()
    for w in tokens:
        tf.add(word)
    return TWEET(id=tweet,tf=tf,scores=scores,tokens=tokens,args=args)
```

We must also define an abstract class for classifiers:

```
class BASECLASSIFIER():
    def applyToTweets(self, dataset):
        return [self.applyToTweet(tweet) for tweet in dataset.tweets]
```

As we continue, we will define several concrete types of classifiers. These all need a method so that they can be applied to sets of tweets, though how they are applied to individual tweets will vary. Therefore, we will provide this abstract class, which says that to apply any classifier to a set of tweets, you just apply its `applyToTweet` method to each tweet in the dataset. BASECLASSIFIER lets us capture this in an abstract class: we will never actually make a BASECLASSIFIER, and indeed it does not have a constructor, but all our concrete classifiers will be subclasses of BASECLASSIFIER and hence will have this method.

The abstract class has no constructor and just one method, which simply says that to apply a classifier to a dataset, you must use its `applyToTweet` method on each tweet in the dataset, but it will prove useful as we continue. Different concrete subclasses of this class will each define a version of `applyToTweet`, but it is useful to have a generic method for applying a classifier to an entire dataset.

We will use the Jaccard score, macro-F1, and micro-F1 as performance measures. As noted in *Chapter 2, Building and Using a Dataset*, micro-F1 tends to be very forgiving in situations where there is one class that predominates and the learning algorithm performs well on this class but less so on the smaller classes. This is a useful measure if you want to know how well the algorithm performs overall, but if you wish to make sure that it performs well on all the classes, then macro-F1 is more reliable (and is typically lower). Again, from *Chapter 2, Building and Using a Dataset* Jaccard and micro-F1 are monotonically linked – if the micro-F1 for one experiment is higher than the micro-F1 for another, then the Jaccard measure will also be higher. So, these two measures will always provide the same ranking for sets of classifiers, but since some papers report one and some the other, it makes sense to include both when comparing a new classifier with others in the literature.

Sentiment lexicons

Now that we have all the machinery for reading and managing datasets, it is time to start trying to develop classifiers. The first one we will look at is based on the simple observation that individual words carry emotional weight. It may be, as we will see later, that exactly how they contribute to the overall content of the message depends on their relationships with other words in the text, but simply looking at the presence of emotionally laden words (and emojis and suchlike) will give you a pretty good idea:

I feel like she is a really sweet person as well (from the CARER dataset)

I feel like she is a really horrible person as well (one word changed)

I feel gracious as he hands me across a rough patch (from the CARER dataset)

I feel irritated as he hands me across a rough patch (one word changed)

So, the simplest imaginable emotion-mining algorithm would simply involve labeling words with sentiments and seeing which sentiment scored the most highly for each text. Nothing could be simpler to implement, so long as you have a lexicon that has been labeled with emotions.

How could you get such a lexicon? You could make one by hand (or find one that someone else has made by hand), or you could try to extract one from a labeled corpus.

Both these approaches involve a large amount of work. You either have to go through a long list of words and assign a set of emotion labels to each, possibly with a score (for example, *sweet* and *love* both express joy, but *love* probably expresses it more strongly than *sweet*, and quantifying just how much more strongly it does so would be very difficult); or you have to go through a long list of tweets and assign a set of emotion labels to them, again possibly with a score. Both of these require a considerable amount of work, which you can either do yourself or get someone else to do (for example, by crowdsourcing it via a platform such as Amazon's Mechanical Turk). If someone else has already done it and made the results available, then so much the better. We will start by considering a well-known resource, namely the NRC Word-Emotion Association Lexicon (also known as **EMOLEX**) (Mohammad & Turney, 2013). This consists of a list of English forms, each labeled with zero or more labels from a set of eight emotions (**anger, anticipation, disgust, fear, joy, sadness, surprise,** and **trust**) plus two polarities (**negative** and **positive**):

	anger	anticipation	disgust	fear	joy	negative	positive	sadness	surprise	trust
aback	0	0	0	0	0	0	0	0	0	0
abacus	0	0	0	0	0	0	0	0	0	1
abandon	0	0	0	1	0	1	0	1	0	0
abandoned	1	0	0	1	0	1	0	1	0	0
abandonment	1	0	0	1	0	1	0	1	1	0
abate	0	0	0	0	0	0	0	0	0	0
abatement	0	0	0	0	0	0	0	0	0	0
abba	0	0	0	0	0	0	1	0	0	0
abbot	0	0	0	0	0	0	0	0	0	1
...	...	...	...	...	...	...	...	...	...	...

Figure 5.1 – EMOLEX labels

To use this with a given dataset, we have to match the emotions in the lexicon with the labels in the dataset – we cannot use the lexicon for any emotions that it does not contain, and emotions that are in the lexicon but not in some dataset cannot be used for extracting emotions from that dataset.

We will start by reading the lexicon and converting it into a Python dictionary. This is very straightforward – read the lexicon line by line, where the first item on a line is a word and the remainder are the scores for the 11 emotions. The only complications are that the dataset we want to use it with may have a different set of emotions from the eleven in the lexicon; and that we might want to use a stemmer to get the root form of a word – for example, to treat *abandon* and *abandoned* as a single item. This may make little difference for English, but it can be important when using the non-English equivalents that are provided for several languages.

EMOLEX comes in various forms. We are using the one where the first column is an English word, the next 11 are the values for each emotion, and the last is a translation of the given English word into some other language. The default is the one where the other language is Arabic, but we have done some experiments with a Spanish corpus, for which we need a Spanish stemmer. The way to extend this to other languages should be obvious.

ARGS is a set of parameters for applying the algorithm in different settings – for example, for specifying which language we are using. The two major issues here are as follows:

- EMOLEX contains inflected forms of words, but our classifiers typically require the root forms
- The emotions in EMOLEX are not necessarily the same as the ones used in the datasets

To deal with the first of these, we have to use a stemmer – that is, one of the ones from *Chapter 4, Preprocessing – Stemming, Tagging, and Parsing*. For the second, we have to find the emotions that are shared between EMOLEX and the dataset and restrict our attention to those:

```
EMOLEX="CORPORA/NRC-Emotion-Lexicon/Arabic-NRC-EMOLEX.txt"
def readNRC(ifile=EMOLEX, targets=None, ARGS=False):
    lines = list(open(ifile))

    # emotions is the list of emotions in the EMOLEX file
    # targets is the list of emotions in the dataset that
    # the classifieris going to be applied to.

    emotions = lines[0].strip().split("\t")[1:-1]
    emotionIndex = [True if e in targets else False for e in emotions]
    targetIndex = [True if e in emotions else False for e in targets]
    lex = {}
    # add entries line by line
    for line in lines[1:]:
        line = line.split("\t")
        # if we're doing it for English
        if ARGS.Language == "EN":
            form = line[0]
            if ARGS.Stemmer.startswith("justRoot"):
                form = justroot(form)
```

```
        elif ARGS.Stemmer.startswith("morphyroot"):
            form = morphyroot(form)
    ...
    else:
        raise Exception("Unknown language: %s"%(ARGS.Language))

    # The line we just read is a string, so the values
    # for the emotions are "0" and "1". We want them as
    # ints, and we also only want the ones that appear
    # in emotionIndex, i.e. ones that are present in
    # the lexicon and in the target dataset

    lex[form] \
            = [int(x) for (x, y) in zip(line[1:-1], emotionIndex) if
y]
    return lex, emotionIndex, targetIndex
```

The following table shows what happens when we use this lexicon with our English datasets (SEM4, SEM11, WASSA, CARER), simply tokenizing the text by splitting it at white space:

	Precision	Recall	Micro-F1	Macro-F1	Jaccard
SEM4-EN	0.418	0.683	0.519	0.489	0.350
SEM11-EN	0.368	0.401	0.383	0.333	0.237
WASSA-EN	0.435	0.738	0.547	0.524	0.376
CARER-EN	0.229	0.524	0.318	0.287	0.189

Figure 5.2 – EMOLEX-based classifiers, no stemming

These scores provide a baseline for comparing the more sophisticated models to be developed later. It is worth observing that the scores for SEM4 are better than those for SEM11 – this is unsurprising given that SEM4 only has four fairly basic emotions (**anger**, **fear**, **joy**, and **sadness**), whereas SEM11 adds several more challenging ones (**surprise**, **trust**, and **anticipation**).

Some of the classifiers that we will look at later can take a long time to train, and it may be that losing a bit of accuracy is worth it if training the more accurate classifiers takes an infeasible amount of time. What matters is whether the classifier is any good at the task we want it to carry out. A classifier that takes a second to train but gets almost everything wrong is no use. Nonetheless, if two algorithms have very similar results but one is much faster to train than the other, it may make sense to choose the faster one. It is hard to imagine anything much faster than the EMOLEX-based one – less than a thousandth of a second to process a single tweet, so that's a tenth of a second to train on our largest (411K) training set.

The basic EMOLEX-based classifier, then, is very fast but produces fairly poor results. Are there things we can do to improve its scores?

The first extension involves using the tokenizer and stemmer described in *Chapter 4, Preprocessing – Stemming, Tagging, and Parsing*. This has a fairly substantial effect in that it improves the scores, as shown here (we will mark the highest score that we have seen to date in bold; since all the scores in the table that use stemming are better than the ones without, they are all marked in bold here):

	Precision	Recall	Micro-F1	Macro-F1	Jaccard
SEM4-EN	**0.461**	**0.622**	**0.530**	**0.538**	**0.360**
SEM11-EN	**0.411**	**0.430**	**0.420**	**0.363**	**0.266**
WASSA-EN	**0.465**	**0.666**	**0.547**	**0.545**	**0.377**
CARER-EN	0.378	0.510	0.434	0.378	0.278

Figure 5.3 – EMOLEX-based classifiers with stemming

EMOLEX also provides a route into other languages by including a target language equivalent for each English word:

	anger	...	negative	positive	sadness	surprise	trust	Spanish
Aback	0	...	0	0	0	0	0	detrás
Abacus	0	...	0	0	0	0	1	ábaco
Abandon	0	...	0	0	1	0	0	abandonar
Abandoned	1	...	1	0	1	0	0	abandonado
...	...	...	...	...	...	...	...	...

Figure 5.4 – EMOLEX entries with Spanish translations

In some cases, this can be leveraged to provide a classifier for the target language: the missing section from the previous definition of readNRC is given here – the key changes are that we use the last item in the line as the form and that we use the appropriate stemmer for the given language:

```
elif ARGS.Language == "AR":
    form = line[-1].strip()
    form = a2bw.convert(form, a2bw.a2bwtable)
    if ARGS.Stemmer == "SEM":
        form = stemArabic(form)
elif ARGS.Language == "ES":
    form = line[-1].strip()
    if ARGS.Stemmer.startswith("stemSpanish"):
        form = stemSpanish(form)
```

By trying this on the SEM4 and SEM11 Spanish and Arabic datasets, we obtain the following results:

	Precision	Recall	Micro-F1	Macro-F1	Jaccard
SEM4-ES	0.356	0.100	0.156	0.144	0.085
SEM11-ES	0.272	0.070	0.111	0.096	0.059
SEM4-AR	0.409	0.362	0.384	0.372	0.238
SEM11-AR	0.267	0.259	0.263	0.232	0.151

Figure 5.5 – EMOLEX-based classifiers for Spanish and Arabic, no stemming

The recall for the Spanish sets is very poor, but apart from that, the scores are surprisingly good considering that we just have the English dataset with one translation of each English word, where the translation is in the canonical form (that is, Spanish verbs are in the infinitive, Arabic nouns are singular, and where a noun has both masculine and feminine forms, then the masculine is used). If we simply use the Spanish and Arabic stemmers from *Chapter 4 , Preprocessing – Stemming, Tagging, and Parsing* (which do not, remember, make use of any lexicon), we get the following:

	Precision	Recall	Micro-F1	Macro-F1	Jaccard
SEM4-ES	0.406	0.164	0.234	0.224	0.132
SEM11-ES	0.255	0.105	0.149	0.121	0.080
SEM4-AR	0.452	0.536	0.490	0.469	0.325
SEM11-AR	0.284	0.348	0.313	0.276	0.185

Figure 5.6 – EMOLEX-based classifiers for Spanish and Arabic, stemmed

Using the stemmed forms improves the recall in every case, and generally improves the precision. The key here is that by using stemmed forms, things that look different but have the same underlying form get matched – for example, if the lexicon contains قدرة (*qdrp*, using the Buckwalter transliteration scheme (Buckwalter, T, 2007)) and some tweet contains القدرات (*AlqdrAt*, the plural form of the same word with a definite article added) – then whatever emotions قدرة is associated with will be found for القدرات. This will improve the recall since more words in the lexicon will be retrieved. It is more surprising that it generally improves the precision: to see why this happens, consider a case where the unstemmed form retrieves one word that is linked with **anger** and **surprise** but the stemmed form retrieves that word plus one that is just linked with **anger**. In the first case, the tweet will be labeled overall as **anger+surprise**, while in the second, it will be linked with just **anger**.

Using a better stemmer will improve the performance of the non-English versions of this approach, but the performance of the English version provides an upper limit – after all, there will be cases where the English word expresses some emotion that the translation doesn't, and in those cases, any inferences based on the translation will be wrong. Suppose, for instance, that the English word *sick* was marked as being positive (which it often is in informal texts, though EMOLEX doesn't recognize this); it is very unlikely that the French word *malade*, which is given as a translation, has the same informal interpretation. However, using EMOLEX, as described previously, would lead to the same emotions being ascribed to a French text that contains *malade* as those ascribed to an English one containing *sick*.

The EMOLEX lexicon for English is fairly large (14K words) and has been constructed following fairly strict guidelines, so it gives a reasonable indication of what can be achieved using a manually constructed lexicon. Can we do any better by extracting a lexicon from a training corpus?

Extracting a sentiment lexicon from a corpus

Extracting a lexicon from a corpus marked up for emotions is easy (once you have a corpus that has been marked up for emotions, which can be an extremely time-consuming and laborious thing to get). Just look at each tweet in the corpus: if it is annotated as contributing to some emotion, increment the number of times it has voted for that emotion, and at the end find out which emotion it has voted for most often. The corpus is used to make an instance of a class called SIMPLELEXCLASSIFIER, which is a realization of the BASECLASSIFIER class introduced previously. The key methods of this class are calculateScores, which iterates the training data (embodied as DATASET) to create the lexicon, and applyToTweet:

```
def calculateScores(self):
    for word, cols in self.dataset.index.items():

        # set up a list of zeros to correspond to the
        # emotions in the dataset

        self.scoredict[word] = [0]*len(self.emotions)

        # count the non-zero emotions for this word

        s = sum(len(col) for col in cols.values())
        if s > 0:
            for col in cols:

                # use s to rebalance the scores for
```

```
# emotions for this word so they add up
# to 1

self.scoredict[word][self.colindex[col]]
                            = len(cols[col])/s
```

This gives a range of scores for each word for each emotion – *sorry*, for instance, scores **anger**:0.62, **fear**:0.10, **joy**:0.00, **sadness**:0.29 – that is, it expresses mainly anger (most tweets containing it have been labeled as **anger**) but also sadness and, to a slight extent, fear.

Given this range of scores for individual words, we can expect complete tweets to contain a mixture of scores. So, we need to choose a threshold at which we say a tweet expresses an emotion. Thus, the definition of `applyToTweet` is as follows:

```
def applyToTweet(self, tweet):
    scores = [0]*len(self.emotions)
    for token in tweet.tokens:
        if token and token in self.scoredict:
            for i, x in enumerate(
            self.scoredict[token]):
                scores[i] += x
    m = max(scores)
    return [1 if x >= m*self.threshold else 0 for x in scores]
```

The choice of threshold is crucial. As we increase the threshold, the precision will go up (by definition, as the threshold goes up, fewer tweets will meet it; however, the ones that do meet or exceed it are more likely to be correct, so the proportion that is correctly assigned an emotion will increase) and the recall will go down (because fewer tweets will meet it and some of the ones that do not will be ones that should have been included). The following tables show what happens with different thresholds for our datasets (we have added the aclIMDB and KWT.M-AR sets at this point – neither of these worked at all with the EMOLEX-based classifier). The following table shows the scores we get for the various datasets using a threshold of 1 and no stemming. Note the extremely high score we obtain for aclIMDB: this is due largely to the fact that this dataset only contains two emotions, so if we simply made random guesses, we would expect to obtain a score of 0.5, whereas since the SEM11 datasets have 11 emotions, random guessing would have an expected score of 0.09:

	Precision	Recall	Micro-F1	Macro-F1	Jaccard
SEM4-EN	0.664	0.664	0.664	0.664	0.497
SEM11-EN	0.614	0.258	0.363	0.365	0.222
WASSA-EN	0.601	0.601	0.601	0.601	0.430
CARER-EN	0.503	0.503	0.503	0.503	0.336
aclImdb-EN	0.839	0.839	0.839	0.839	0.722
SEM4-AR	0.672	0.672	0.672	0.672	0.506
SEM11-AR	0.647	0.283	0.394	0.413	0.245
KWT.M-AR	0.768	0.757	0.762	0.768	0.616
SEM4-ES	0.541	0.664	0.596	0.542	0.425
SEM11-ES	0.486	0.293	0.365	0.367	0.224

Figure 5.7 – Simple lexicon-based classifier, threshold=1, no stemming

This contrasts with the results we get when we lower the threshold to 0.5, as shown in *Figure 5.8*.

	Precision	Recall	Micro-F1	Macro-F1	Jaccard
SEM4-EN	0.281	0.997	0.438	0.465	0.281
SEM11-EN	**0.365**	**0.767**	**0.494**	**0.487**	**0.328**
WASSA-EN	0.287	0.989	0.444	0.471	0.286
CARER-EN	0.365	0.803	0.502	0.508	0.335
aclImdb-EN	0.500	1.000	0.667	0.667	0.500
SEM4-AR	0.454	0.858	0.594	0.654	0.422
SEM11-AR	**0.430**	**0.728**	**0.541**	**0.546**	**0.371**
KWT.M-AR	**0.795**	**0.785**	**0.790**	**0.795**	**0.652**
SEM4-ES	0.311	0.879	0.460	0.516	0.299
SEM11-ES	**0.315**	**0.625**	**0.419**	**0.421**	**0.265**

Figure 5.8 – Simple lexicon-based classifier, threshold=0.5, no stemming

As expected, the precision decreases and the recall increases as we lower the threshold. The size of this effect varies from dataset to dataset, with different thresholds producing different Jaccard and macro-F1 scores – the Jaccard score for SEM4-EN at threshold 1 is better than the score for this dataset at threshold 0.5, whereas, for SEM-11-EN, the Jaccard score is better at 0.5 than at 1. Note that the scores for the SEM-11 and KWT.M cases are all better at the lower threshold: this happens because these cases all allow multiple emotions to be assigned to a single tweet. Lowering the threshold lets the classifier find more emotions, which is helpful if large numbers of tweets have multiple emotions. We will return to this issue in *Chapter 10, Multiclassifiers*.

We can attempt to find the best threshold automatically: find the lowest and highest scores that any tweet has and then try a range of thresholds between these two values. We apply this algorithm to a small section of the training data – we cannot apply it to the test data, but experimentation shows that we do not need the full training set to arrive at good values for the threshold:

```
def bestThreshold(self, test=None, show=False):
    if test is None:
        test = self.test.tweets

    # Apply this classifier to the tweets we are
    # interested in: setting probs=True forces it to
    # return the values actually calculated by the
    # classifier rather than the 0/1 version obtained
    # by using the threshold

    train = self.train.tweets[:len(test)]
    l = self.applyToTweets(train, threshold=0,
                           probs=True)

    # The optimal threshold must lie somewhere between
    # the smallest and largest scores for any tweet

    start = threshold = min(min(tweet.predicted) for tweet in
train)
    end = max(max(tweet.predicted) for tweet in train)
    best = []

    # Go from start to end in small steps using
    # increasing values for threshold

    while threshold <= end:
        l = self.applyToTweets(train,
                               threshold=threshold)
        # getmetrics returns macro F1, true positives,
        # false positives, false negatives
        (macroF, tp, fp, fn)
                = metrics.getmetrics([tweet.GS for tweet in test],
1)
        # Jaccard
        j = tp/(tp+fp+fn)
        best = max(best, [j, threshold])
        threshold += (end-start)/20
    return round(best[1], 5)
```

Using this to find the optimal threshold, we find that in every case, automatically extracting the lexicon produces a better score than the original scores with EMOLEX:

	Precision	Recall	Micro-F1	Macro-F1	Jaccard
SEM4-EN	**0.617**	**0.732**	**0.670**	**0.683**	**0.503**
SEM11-EN	**0.475**	**0.564**	**0.515**	**0.515**	**0.347**
WASSA-EN	**0.571**	**0.669**	**0.616**	**0.623**	**0.445**
CARER-EN	**0.487**	**0.554**	**0.518**	**0.522**	**0.350**
aclImdb-EN	**0.839**	**0.839**	**0.839**	**0.839**	**0.722**
SEM4-AR	**0.672**	**0.672**	**0.672**	**0.672**	**0.506**
SEM11-AR	**0.485**	**0.632**	**0.549**	**0.549**	**0.378**
KWT.M-AR	**0.816**	**0.812**	**0.814**	**0.817**	**0.687**
SEM4-ES	**0.541**	**0.664**	**0.596**	**0.542**	**0.425**
SEM11-ES	**0.372**	**0.493**	**0.424**	**0.429**	**0.269**

Figure 5.9 – Standard datasets, optimal thresholds, no stemming

Unsurprisingly, the scores here are as good as or better than the scores obtained with 1.0 or 0.5 as thresholds since we have tried a range of thresholds and chosen the best – if the best is indeed 1.0 or 0.5, then the score will be as in those tables, but if not, it must be better (or we would not have chosen it!).

Using the optimal thresholds with stemming produces worse results in several cases. In the English cases, the performance is, at best, fractionally better than when we do not do stemming, though it does help with some of the non-English cases:

	Precision	Recall	Micro-F1	Macro-F1	Jaccard
SEM4-EN	0.610	0.729	0.664	0.677	0.497
SEM11-EN	**0.478**	**0.562**	**0.516**	**0.518**	**0.348**
WASSA-EN	0.566	0.658	0.609	0.615	0.437
CARER-EN	**0.477**	**0.569**	**0.519**	**0.522**	**0.350**
aclImdb-EN	0.684	0.964	0.800	0.827	0.667
SEM4-AR	**0.651**	**0.701**	**0.675**	**0.683**	**0.509**
SEM11-AR	**0.497**	**0.635**	**0.557**	**0.554**	**0.386**
KWT.M-AR	0.802	0.793	0.797	0.801	0.663
SEM4-ES	0.516	0.692	0.591	0.531	0.420
SEM11-ES	**0.376**	**0.493**	**0.427**	**0.431**	**0.271**

Figure 5.10 – Standard datasets, optimal thresholds, stemmed

It is less surprising that we get the greatest improvement from the EMOLEX-based classifiers with the large dataset: EMOLEX contains 24.9K words, the lexicons extracted from the SEM4-EN, SEM11-EN, and WASSA datasets contain 10.8K, 17.5K, and 10.9K words, respectively, and the lexicon extracted from CARER contains 53.4K words. In other words, the increase in the size of the extracted lexicon is much greater for the large dataset, which is why the improvement over the hand-coded one is also greater.

The various lexicons all link emotionally loaded words with the emotions they express. Using the CARER dataset, we can see that we get sensible associations for some common words that would be used to express emotions:

	anger	fear	joy	love	sadness	surprise
adores	0.11	0.00	0.44	0.33	0.11	0.00
happy	0.08	0.05	0.62	0.05	0.17	0.03
hate	0.22	0.13	0.16	0.06	0.42	0.02
joy	0.07	0.05	0.53	0.12	0.21	0.04
love	0.09	0.07	0.42	0.19	0.21	0.03
sad	0.14	0.08	0.11	0.03	0.61	0.03
scared	0.04	0.71	0.07	0.01	0.14	0.02
sorrow	0.15	0.04	0.24	0.13	0.41	0.04
terrified	0.01	0.90	0.03	0.01	0.04	0.01

Figure 5.11 – Emotions associated with significant words, the CARER dataset

If we look at other words that would not be expected to have any emotional significance, however, we will find something surprising:

	anger	fear	joy	love	sadness	surprise
a	0.13	0.12	0.35	0.10	0.27	0.04
and	0.13	0.11	0.35	0.09	0.28	0.04
the	0.13	0.11	0.37	0.10	0.26	0.04

Figure 5.12 – Emotions associated with common words, the CARER dataset

The word *a* occurs in almost every text in this dataset – every text that expresses anger, every text that expresses fear, and so on. So, it contains scores that reflect the distribution of emotions in the dataset: *a*, *and*, and *the* all get scores of around 0.13 for anger, which simply reflects the fact that about 13% of the tweets express this emotion; they each get scores of about 0.11 for fear because about 11% of the tweets express fear, and so on.

There are three obvious things we can do to try to solve this problem:

- We can manually produce a list of stop words. This tends to be a poor way to proceed since it relies very heavily on intuitions, which are often unreliable when people are thinking about words in isolation.

- We can try to weed out words that do not contribute to the distinctive meaning of the text we are looking at.

- We can adjust the degree to which a word votes more strongly for one emotion than for others.

Let's discuss the last two in detail.

Weeding out words that do not contribute much to the distinctive meaning of a text: If a word occurs extremely frequently across a corpus, then it cannot be used as a good indicator of whether one text in the corpus is similar to another. This notion is widely used when computing similarity between texts, so it is worth looking at whether it can help us with the problem of common words voting for emotions.

The most commonly used measure for assessing the contribution that a word makes to the distinctiveness of a text is **term frequency/inverse document frequency** (**TF-IDF**) (Sparck Jones, 1972). Term frequency is the number of times the word in question occurs in a given document, whereas document frequency is the number of documents that it occurs in. So, if a word occurs frequently in a document, then it may be important for that document, but if it occurs in every single document, then it probably is not. It is customary to take the log of the document frequency to smooth out the effect of very common words, and it is essential to add 1 to the document frequency to make sure that we are not trying to take the log of 0:

$$TF - IDF(word, document, corpus) = \frac{|occurrences\ of\ word\ in\ document|}{log(|documents\ containing\ words\ |)}$$

Using this measure to weight the contributions of individual words produces the following:

	Precision	Recall	Micro-F1	Macro-F1	Jaccard
SEM4-EN	0.546	0.546	0.546	0.546	0.375
SEM11-EN	0.554	0.232	0.327	0.328	0.195
WASSA-EN	0.492	0.492	0.492	0.492	0.326
CARER-EN	0.518	0.518	0.518	0.518	0.350
aclImdb-EN	0.815	0.815	0.815	0.815	0.687
SEM4-AR	0.638	0.638	0.638	0.638	0.468
SEM11-AR	0.592	0.261	0.362	0.378	0.221
KWT.M-AR	0.804	0.789	0.797	0.802	0.662
SEM4-ES	0.503	0.661	0.571	0.510	0.400
SEM11-ES	0.439	0.279	0.341	0.348	0.206

Figure 5.13 – Using TF-IDF to adjust the weights

These scores are not an improvement on the originals: using TF-IDF does not help with our task, at least not in isolation. We will find that it can be useful when used in combination with other measures, but by itself, it is not useful.

Adjusting the degree to which a word votes more strongly for one emotion than for others: Revisiting the tables of weights for individual words, we can see that the weights for *a* are very evenly distributed, whereas the scores for *terrified* scores highly for **fear** and very low for anything else:

	anger	fear	joy	love	sadness	surprise
a	0.13	0.12	0.35	0.10	0.27	0.04
terrified	0.01	0.90	0.03	0.01	0.04	0.01

Figure 5.14 – Emotions associated with "a" and "terrified," the CARER dataset

If we subtract the average for a score from the individual scores, we end up with a much more sensible set of scores: a conditional probability classifier, CPCLASSIFIER, is a subclass of SIMPLELEXCLASSIFIER, which simply has the definition of calculateScores changed to the following:

```
def calculateScores(self):
    for word, cols in self.dataset.index.items():
        best = False
        bestscore = -1
        self.scoredict[word] = [0]*len(self.emotions)
        for col in cols:
            self.scoredict[word][self.colindex[col]]
                                    = len(cols[col])
        s = sum(self.scoredict[word])
        for i, x in enumerate(self.scoredict[word]):
            if s > 0:
                x = x/s-1/len(self.emotions))
                self.scoredict[word][i] = max(0, x)
```

In other words, the only change is that we subtract the average score for emotions for a given word from the original, so long as the result of doing that is greater than 0. This changes the values for a common word and an emotionally laden word, as shown here:

	anger	fear	joy	love	sadness	surprise
a	0.00	0.00	0.18	0.00	0.10	0.00
terrified	0.00	0.73	0.00	0.00	0.00	0.00

Figure 5.15 – Emotions associated with "a" and "terrified," the CARER dataset, bias emphasized

Here, the scores for *a* have been greatly flattened out, while *terrified* only votes for **fear**:

	Precision	Recall	Micro-F1	Macro-F1	Jaccard
SEM4-EN	**0.714**	**0.779**	**0.745**	**0.752**	**0.593**
SEM11-EN	**0.471**	**0.582**	**0.521**	**0.518**	**0.352**
WASSA-EN	**0.604**	**0.769**	**0.677**	**0.692**	**0.512**
CARER-EN	0.539	0.640	0.585	0.589	0.414
aclImdb-EN	0.798	0.883	0.838	0.847	0.721
SEM4-AR	0.592	0.747	0.661	0.684	0.493
SEM11-AR	0.476	0.624	0.540	0.540	0.370
KWT.M-AR	0.814	0.811	0.813	0.816	0.684
SEM4-ES	0.194	0.948	0.321	0.310	0.191
SEM11-ES	0.400	0.471	0.433	0.435	0.276

Figure 5.16 – Increased bias lexicon-based classifier, optimal thresholds, no stemming

Changing the weights in this way without stemming improves or has very little effect on the scores for nearly all the English cases:

	Precision	Recall	Micro-F1	Macro-F1	Jaccard
SEM4-EN	**0.718**	**0.772**	**0.744**	**0.750**	**0.593**
SEM11-EN	**0.479**	**0.573**	**0.522**	**0.520**	**0.353**
WASSA-EN	0.641	0.703	0.671	0.675	0.505
CARER-EN	0.512	0.633	0.566	0.570	0.395
aclImdb-EN	**0.799**	**0.882**	**0.839**	**0.848**	**0.722**
SEM4-AR	**0.651**	**0.709**	**0.679**	**0.686**	**0.513**
SEM11-AR	0.501	0.616	0.553	0.552	0.382
KWT.M-AR	0.801	0.797	0.799	0.803	0.666
SEM4-ES	0.189	0.733	0.301	0.284	0.177
SEM11-ES	**0.397**	**0.481**	**0.435**	**0.439**	**0.278**

Figure 5.17 – Increased bias lexicon-based classifier, optimal thresholds, stemmed

As ever, stemming sometimes helps with non-English examples and sometimes it doesn't.

So far in this chapter, we have looked at several ways of extracting a lexicon from a corpus that has been marked up with emotion labels and used this to assign emotions to unseen texts. The main lessons to be learned from these experiments are as follows:

- Lexicon-based classifiers can provide reasonable performance for very little computational cost, though the effort involved in making lexicons, either directly or by extracting them from annotated texts, is considerable.

- Refinements such as stemming and varying the weights associated with individual words can sometimes be useful, but what works for one corpus may not work for another. For this reason, it is sensible to divide your training data into training and development sets so that you can try out different combinations to see what works with your data, on the assumption that the data you are using for training is indeed similar to the data that you will be applying it on for real. For this reason, competition data is often split into training and development sets when it is distributed.

- Having a large amount of data can be useful but after a certain point, the improvements in performance tail off. It makes sense to plot data size against accuracy for subsets of your full dataset since this allows you to fit a curve of the relationship between the two. Given such a curve, it is possible to estimate what the accuracy would be if you were able to obtain more data, and hence to decide whether it is worth trying to do so. Such an estimate will only be an approximation, but if, for instance, it is clear that the curve has already flattened out, then it is unlikely that getting more data will make a difference.

One of the problems with this kind of approach is that the training data may not contain every emotion-bearing word. In the next section, we will try to extend lexicons of the kind we extracted previously by looking for "similar" words to fill in the gap.

Similarity measures and vector-space models

One of the problems that any lexicon-based classifier faces is that the lexicon may not contain all the words in the test set. For the English datasets we have been looking at, EMOLEX and the lexicon extracted from the training data contain the following percentages of the words in the development sets:

	% of words in the extracted dictionary	% of words in EMOLEX
SEM4-EN	0.46	0.20
SEM11-EN	0.47	0.19
WASSA-EN	0.55	0.21
CARER	0.95	0.44

Figure 5.18 – Words in the test sets that are in one of the lexicons

Many of the words that are missing from EMOLEX will be function words (*a*, *the*, *in*, *and*, and so on) and words that carry no emotion, but it seems likely that adding more words to the lexicon will be helpful. If we knew that *adore* was very similar to *love*, but *adore* was not in the lexicon, then it would be very helpful if we could use the emotional weight of *love* when a text contained *adore*. The number of words that are missing from the extracted lexicons is more worrying. As the training data increases, the number of missing words goes down – 54% of the words in the test sets for SEM4-EN are missing in the training data, whereas only 5% are missing from CARER, but virtually none of the missing words in these cases are function words, so many are likely to be emotion-bearing.

There are numerous ways of estimating whether two words are similar. Nearly all are based on the notion that two words are similar if they occur in similar contexts, usually using sentences or local windows as contexts, and they nearly all make use of vector-space models. In this section, we will explore these two ideas before looking at how they may be used to supplement the lexicons being used for emotion detection.

Vector spaces

It is often useful to represent things as vectors in some high-dimensional space. An obvious example is the representation of a sentence as a point in a space where each word of the language is a dimension. Recall that `makeIndex` lets us make an index linking each word to a unique identifier; for example:

```
{..., 'days': 6, 'sober': 7, 'do': 8, "n't": 9, 'wanna': 10,  ...}
```

We can then use `sentence2vector` to convert a string of words into a vector. We make a vector full of zeros that is large enough to accommodate every word in the index. Then, we can scan the sentence and add 1 to the appropriate position in the vector for each word that we see:

```python
def sentence2vector(sentence, index):
    vector = numpy.zeros(len(index))
    for word in sentence:
        vector[index[word]] += 1
    return vector
```

Given the preceding index, this would produce the following for the sentence *I don't want to be sober*:

```
>>> list(sentence2vector("I do n't want to be sober".split(), index))
[0., 0., 1., 0., 0., 0., 0., 1., 1., 1., ...]
```

Such vectors tend to be very sparse. The index we used for constructing this vector contained 18,263 words and the sentence contained 7 distinct words, so 18,256 entries in the vector are 0. This means that a lot of space is wasted, but also that calculations involving such vectors can be very slow. Python provides tools for handling such vectors: **sparse arrays**. The key to the way Python does this is that instead of keeping an array that contains a place for every value, you keep three arrays: the first contains the non-zero values, and the second and third contain the row and column where a value is to be found. For our example, we would have the following (we only need the column values because our array is just a vector):

```
>>> # v is the vector we just made; convert it to a sparse matrix
>>> s = sparse.csr_matrix(v)
>>> # it contains seven 1s
>>> list(s.data)
[1.0, 1.0, 1.0, 1.0, 1.0, 1.0, 1.0]
>>> # These are at positions 2, 7, 8, ...
>>> list(s.indices)
[2, 7, 8, 9, 119, 227, 321]
```

In other words, we have the value 1 at positions 2 (which was the index entry for *I*), 7 (*sober*), 8 (*do*), and so on.

Calculating similarity

The commonest use of vector representations is for calculating the similarity between two objects. We will illustrate this, and explore it a bit further, by considering it as a way of comparing sentences, but given the number of things that can be represented as vectors, the technique has a very wide range of applications.

Consider two vectors in a simple 2D space. There are two ways of assessing how similar they are: you can see how far apart their endpoints are, or you can calculate the angle between them. In the following diagram, it is clear that the angle between the two vectors <(0,0), (2.5, 2.5)> and <(0, 0), (4.6, 4.9)> is very small, but the distance between their endpoints is quite large. It is common practice when using vector-space representations to carry out normalization, by dividing the value in each dimension by the length of the vector:

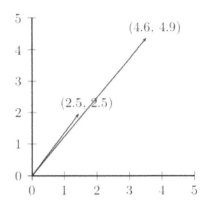

Figure 5.19 – Vectors to (2.5, 2.5) and (4.6, 4.9)

If we normalize these two vectors, we get *Figure 5.20*, where the angle between the vectors and the distance between their endpoints are both very small:

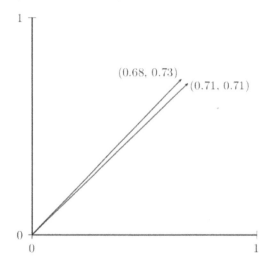

Figure 5.20 – Normalized versions of (2.5, 2.5) and (4.6, 4.9)

Most applications use the (*N*-dimensional) cosine of the angle between the vectors, but it is worth noting that for **normalized** vectors, the angle between V0 and V1 will be greater than that between V0 and V2 if and only if the Euclidean distance between the endpoints of V0 and V1 is greater than the distance between the endpoints of V0 and V2; so, the two measures will rank the similarity between sets of vectors identically. Calculating the cosine of the angle between two vectors in a high dimensional space is slightly confusing, but fortunately, the Python `sklearn.metrics.pairwise` library provides `cosine_similarity` for this task.

If we apply `sentence2vector` to the sentences *John ate some pasta, John ate the pasta, John ate some potatoes,* and *Mary drank some beer,* we get the following:

```
S0: John ate the pasta
[63, 2306, 3304, 7616]
S1: John ate some pasta
[229, 2306, 3304, 7616]
S2: John ate the potatoes
[63, 3304, 4162, 7616]
S3: Mary drank some beer
[229, 5040, 5176, 10372]
```

This means *John ate some pasta* is represented by a vector that has 1 as the value in the 63rd, 2,306th, 3,304th, and 7,616th dimensions and zero everywhere else, and similarly for the other sentences. If we compute the cosine similarity of each pair, we get the following:

	S0	S1	S2	S3
S0	1.00	0.75	0.75	0.25
S1	0.75	1.00	0.50	0.00
S2	0.75	0.50	1.00	0.25
S3	0.25	0.00	0.25	1.00

In other words, every sentence is identical to itself, S0, S1, and S2 are quite similar to one another, and S3 is fairly different from the others. This all seems fairly sensible, save that S0, S1, and S2 all have **identical** similarity scores. That doesn't seem quite as reasonable – surely *John ate some pasta* and *John ate the pasta* are more similar than *John ate some pasta* and *John ate some potatoes*.

The key here is that some words seem to be more important than others *when you are trying to calculate how similar two sentences are*. This is not to say that words such as *some* and *the* are not important when you are trying to work out what a sentence means, but if, for instance, you want to see whether two sentences are about the same general topic, then maybe these closed class items are less significant.

You could try to deal with this by providing a list of **stop words**, which should be ignored when you are turning a sentence into a vector. However, there are two problems with this approach:

- It is very hard to work out which words should be ignored and which ones shouldn't
- It's a very blunt instrument – some words seem to make very little difference when you are comparing sentences, some make a bit of difference but not much, and some are highly significant

What we want is a number that we can use to weight different words for their significance.

We will use TF-IDF to assign weights to words. There are several minor variations on how to calculate TF-IDF, with some working better with long documents and some with shorter ones (for example, when a document is just a single sentence), but the following is a reasonably standard version. We start by calculating an **inverse document frequency** table. We walk through the set of documents, getting the set of words in each document, and then increment a counter for each word in the set. This gives us a count of the number of documents each word appears in. We then make the inverse table by getting the reciprocal of the log of each entry – we need the reciprocal because we are going to want to divide by these values. We may as well do that now so that we can replace division with multiplication later on. It is standard practice to use the log at this point, though there is no very strong theoretical reason for doing so and there are cases (particularly with very short documents) where the raw value works better:

```
def getDF(documents, uselog=numpy.log):
    # adding something to df either sets or increments a counter
    df = counter()
    for document in enumerate(documents):
        # for each unique word in the document increment df
        for w in set(document.split()):
            df.add(w)
    idf = {}
    for w in df:
        idf[w] = 1.0/float(uselog(df[w])+1)
    return df, idf
```

This produces a pair of tables, df and idf, as follows when applied to the tweets in SEM4-EN, where *a* and *the* appear in large numbers of documents and *man*, *cat*, and *loves* appear in a fairly small set, so df for *a* and *the* is high and their idf (which is the measure of how important they are in this document) is low:

	DF	IDF
a	1521	0.001
the	1842	0.001
cat	5	0.167
loves	11	0.083
man	85	0.012

We can use this to change sentence2vector so that it increments the scores by the IDF value for each word, rather than always incrementing by 1 (this is the same as multiplying the sum of a series of increments by the IDF value):

```
def sentence2vector(sentence, index, idf={}):
    vector = numpy.zeros(len(index))
    for word in sentence:
        inc = idf[word] if word in idf else 1
```

```
        vector[index[word]] += inc
    return vector
```

John ate the pasta is now represented by a vector with values that represent how common the words in question are, and hence how much importance they should be given when comparing vectors:

```
>>> list(S1.data)
[0.008, 0.3333333333333333, 0.1, 0.5]
>>> list(S1.indices)
[229, 2306, 3304, 7616]
```

Using this weighted version of the various vectors, our similarity table for the four sentences becomes as follows:

	S0	S1	S2	S3
S0	1.0000	0.9999	0.5976	0.0000
S1	0.9999	1.0000	0.5976	0.0003
S2	0.5976	0.5976	1.0000	0.0000
S3	0.0000	0.0003	0.0000	1.0000

Figure 5.21 – Similarity table

S0 and S1 are now very similar (so similar that we have had to print them to four decimal places for any difference to show up) because the weights for *some* and *the* are very low; S1 and S2 are fairly similar to one another, and S3 is different. By treating *the* and *some* as being less significant than *pasta* and *potatoes* for comparing similarity, we get a better measure of similarity.

We can use cosine similarity and TF-IDF weights to compare any items that can be represented as sequences of words. We will use this to calculate how similar two words are. We can represent a word using a **cooccurrence table** – that is, the set of words that occur in the same context, where a context could be an article, a sentence, a tweet, or a window around the word's position in a text – it could also be defined by requiring the two words to be syntactically related (for example, *eat* and *cake* could be seen as occurring in the same context in *he ate some very rich cake* because *cake* is the object of *ate*, even though they are some way apart in the text). We can either simply count the cooccurrences or we can weigh them using an IDF table if we have one.

Let's assume that `getPairs` returns a cooccurrence table of words that have occurred in the same context:

```
king  {'king': 144, 'new': 88, 'queen': 84, 'royal': 69, 'made':
68,...}
queen  {'mother': 123, 'speech': 86, 'king': 84, 'royal': 62, ...}
```

There are various ways of obtaining such a table. For the next few examples, we will use the fact that the BNC is already tagged to collect open class words (nouns, verbs, adjectives, and adverbs) that occur inside a window of three words on either side of the target word – for example, from the sentence, *It*-PN *is*-VB *often*-AV *said*-VV *that*-CJ *you*-PN *can*-VM *discover*-VV *a*-AT *great*-AJ *deal*-NN, we would get `{'often': {'said': 1}, 'said': {'often': 1}, 'discover': {'great': 1, 'deal': 1}, 'great': {'discover': 1, 'deal': 1}, 'deal': {'discover': 1, 'great': 1}}` because *often* and *said* are within a window of three positions of each other and so are *discover*, *great*, and *deal*. We save this table in `pairs0`.

We then make a document frequency table and reduce this so that it only contains the top *N* words (we do this by sorting it, getting the *N* highest-scoring cases, and then reconstructing it as a table), and we use the reduced table to get a cooccurrence table (`pairs1`) that only contains the top *N* words. If we only consider the top 10,000 words, we will get comparisons between most words that we are likely to be interested in and we will reduce the amount of computation to be carried out when constructing the similarity table. We weight the scores in this table by the document frequency for the words that it contains (we use a version of TF-IDF in which we do not take logs since this seems to work better in this case), storing this in `pairs2`. Finally, we convert `pairs2` into a sparse matrix and use `cosine_similarity` to calculate the similarity scores for every word in the matrix:

```
class TF-IDFMODE():

    def __init__(self, uselog=log, corpus=corpora.BNC, N=10000):
        self.pairs0 = getPairs(corpus)
        self.df = sortTable(getDF(self.pairs0))[:N]
        self.df = {x[0]:x[1] for x in self.df}
        self.pairs1 = {}
        for word in self.pairs0:
            if word in self.df:
                self.pairs1[word] = {}
                for other in self.pairs0[word]:
                    if other in self.df:
                        self.pairs1[word][other]\
                            = self.pairs0[word][other]
        self.pairs2 = applyIDF(self.pairs1, df=self.df, uselog=uselog)
        self.dimensions, self.invdimensions, self.matrices\
            = pairs2matrix(self.pairs2)
        self.similarities = cosine_similarity(
            self.matrices)
```

Applying this to the entire BNC (approximately 100 million words), we get an initial DF table and set of cooccurring pairs with just over 393K entries each, which means that if we do not reduce them to the commonest 10K words, the cooccurrence table would potentially have 393,000**2 entries – that is, about 15G entries. Reducing this so that only the top 10K words are included reduces the potential size of the cooccurrence table to 100M entries, but this table is fairly sparse, with the sparse representation containing just under 500K entries.

Typical entries in the cooccurrence table look as follows (just showing the highest scoring co-occurring entries for each word). These all look reasonable enough – they are all words that you can imagine cooccurring with the given targets:

```
cat:   mouse:0.03, litter:0.02, ginger:0.02, stray:0.02, pet:0.02
dog:   stray:0.05, bark:0.03, pet:0.03, shepherd:0.03, vet:0.02
eat:   sandwiches:0.03, foods:0.03, bite:0.03, meat:0.02, cake:0.02
drink: sipped:0.08, alcoholic:0.03, pints:0.03, merry:0.02,
relaxing:0.02
```

Calculating the pairwise similarities between rows in this table is remarkably quick, taking about 1.3 seconds on a standard MacBook with a 2.8 GHz processor. To make use of the similarity table, we have to map words to their indices to get into the matrix and then map indices back to words to interpret the results, but apart from that, finding the "most similar" words to a given target is very simple:

```
def nearest(self, word, N=6):
    similarwords = self.similarities[self.dimensions[word]]
    matches = list(reversed(sorted([x, i]\
                   for i, x in enumerate(similarwords))))[1:N]
    return [(self.invdimensions[i], s) for [s, i] in matches]
```

Looking at a set of common words, we can see that the most similar ones have quite a lot in common with the targets, so it seems plausible that calculating word similarity based on whether two words occur in the same contexts may be useful for a range of tasks:

```
Best matches for cat:
dog:0.39,cats:0.25,keyboard:0.23,bin:0.23,embryo:0.22
Best matches for dog:
dogs:0.42,cat:0.39,cats:0.35,hairs:0.26,bullet:0.24
Best matches for eat:
ate:0.35,eaten:0.35,cakes:0.28,eating:0.28,buffet:0.27
Best matches for drink:
brandy:0.41,beer:0.41,coffee:0.38,lager:0.38,drinks:0.36
```

Some of these are just the inflected forms of the originals, which shouldn't be too surprising – *eat*, *ate*, *eaten*, and *eating* are all very similar words! The ones that are not just inflected forms of the targets contain some plausible-looking pairs (*cat* and *dog* are returned as being very similar and the matches for *drink* are all things you can drink), along with some oddities. We will return to the question of whether this is useful for our task shortly.

Latent semantic analysis

Using TF-IDF weights makes it possible to discount items that occur in large numbers of contexts, and which therefore are unlikely to be useful when distinguishing between contexts. An alternative strategy is to try to find combinations of weights that produce **fixed points** – that is, those that can be used to recreate the original data. If you remove the least significant parts of such combinations, you can approximate the essence of the original data and use that to calculate similarities.

We will learn how to use neural networks for this purpose later. For now, we will consider an approach known as **latent semantic analysis** (**LSA**) (Deerwester et al., 1990), which uses matrix algebra to produce lower-dimensional approximations of the original data. The key here is that given any MxN matrix, A, you can find an MxM matrix, U, a vector, S, of length M where the elements of U are given in decreasing order, and an NxM matrix, V, such that A = (U * S) dot V. U, S, and V provide a fixed point of the original data. If S' is obtained from S by setting some of the lower values of S to 0, then (U * S') dot V becomes an approximation of A, where S' is of a lower dimension than S.

As an example, we will start with a 6x8 array of random integers:

```
61.0    26.0    54.0    90.0     9.0    19.0
34.0    53.0    73.0    21.0    17.0    67.0
59.0    75.0    33.0    96.0    59.0    24.0
72.0    90.0    79.0    88.0    48.0    45.0
77.0    24.0    88.0    65.0    33.0    94.0
44.0    0.00    55.0    61.0    71.0    92.0
```

U, S, and V are as follows:

```
-0.4     0.1     0.3     0.3     0.3    -0.8
-0.4    -0.5    -0.5     0.6     0.1     0.2
-0.3     0.3     0.5     0.2     0.4     0.6
-0.5     0.7    -0.5    -0.2    -0.1     0.0
-0.4    -0.5     0.1    -0.7     0.2     0.0
-0.4    -0.1     0.3     0.1    -0.8     0.0

356.95    103.09    90.57    61.44    53.85    14.53

-0.4    -0.4    -0.3    -0.4    -0.3    -0.3    -0.3    -0.4
-0.4    -0.1     0.7    -0.4    -0.0     0.2    -0.2     0.4
```

```
  0.2   -0.5    0.0   -0.1    0.0   -0.5    0.4    0.5
  0.1   -0.2   -0.0    0.3   -0.8    0.3   -0.1    0.3
  0.7   -0.4    0.1   -0.3    0.2    0.2   -0.5   -0.1
 -0.3   -0.5   -0.4    0.1    0.4    0.6    0.2    0.1
```

If we set the last element of S to 0 and calculate (U * S) dot V, we get the following:

```
 76.8   42.8   51.1   46.5   35.2   45.4   40.1   78.9
 72.8   76.4    2.0   78.6   10.9   65.3   16.4   19.8
 59.7   13.3   52.3   22.7   27.5   25.6   36.2   79.2
 26.2   98.3   93.2   36.9   60.7   84.6   19.9   69.9
 92.2   74.3   14.2   57.9   85.8   22.6   52.9   35.9
 44.1   64.1   29.1   69.0   31.9   17.9   76.0   78.0
```

This is a reasonable approximation to the original.

LSA works by applying this notion to cooccurrence matrices of the kind we have been looking at. Given the size of such matrices, it can be difficult to calculate S in full. So, we must restrict the number of entries that we want on S, rather than calculating the full set and then zeroing some out.

By restricting the length of S to 1,000, we get the following nearest neighbors for *cat*, *dog*, *drink*, and *eat*:

```
Best matches for cat:
cats:0.66,hairs:0.62,dog:0.61,dogs:0.60,hair:0.54
Best matches for dog:
dogs:0.72,cats:0.68,cat:0.61,pet:0.54,bull:0.46
Best matches for eat:
meat:0.77,sweets:0.75,ate:0.75,chicken:0.73,delicious:0.72
Best matches for drink:
pint:0.84,sherry:0.83,brandy:0.83,beer:0.81,drank:0.79
```

The changes from the original set are not dramatic – the inflected forms of *eat* have been demoted with various things that you can eat appearing high in the list, but apart from that, the changes are not all that significant.

However, calculating the SVD of a cooccurrence matrix, particularly if we allow less common words to appear as columns, becomes infeasible as the matrix gets larger, and hence alternative solutions are required if we want to handle gigabytes of training data, rather than the 100 million words of the BNC. The **GLoVe** (Pennington et al., 2014) model of word similarity essentially calculates the SVD of the matrix using an algorithm that is not as badly affected by the size of the cooccurrence matrix, while the **word2vec** algorithm (Mikolov et al., 2013) works by using a deep neural network to learn to predict a word from the context, and then uses the excitation levels in the penultimate layer in the network when a word is input as the vector-space model of that word (we will discuss neural networks in *Chapter 8, Neural Networks and Deep Neural Nets*; in the following examples, we will use the gensim (https://radimrehurek.com/gensim/intro.html) version of word2vec).

Returning to our task, the problem we were considering was that the training data may not contain all the words that appear in the test data. If a word in the test data should contribute to the emotional tag assigned to a sentence but is missing from the training data, then we cannot calculate its contribution to the emotion of that sentence. We can try to use these notions of similarity to fill in the gaps in our lexicons: if we have a word in the target text that does not appear in the emotion lexicon, we could substitute it with the nearest word according to our similarity metric that does. If the similarity lexicon returns words that have similar emotional associations, then that should improve the recall, and possibly the precision, of our emotion mining algorithms.

We can extend the method for calculating the scores for a given tweet like so. The key is that if some word is not in the sentiment lexicon, we use chooseother to select the nearest word according to the similarity metric:

```
def chooseother(self, token):

    # If the classifier has a model, use that to find
    # the 5 most similar words to the target and go
    # through these looking for one that is in the
    # sentiment lexicon

    if self.model:
        try:
            for other in self.model.nearest(token, topn=5):
                other = other[0]
                if other in self.scoredict:
                    return other
        except:
            pass
    return False


def applyToTweet(self, tweet):
    scores = [0]*len(self.emotions)
    for token in tweet.tokens:
        if not token in self.scoredict:
            token = self.chooseother(token)
        if token in self.scoredict:
            for i, x in enumerate(self.scoredict[token]):
                scores[i] += x
    m = max(scores)
    return [1 if x >= m*self.threshold else 0 for x in scores]
```

The following results show what happens when we combine a `word2vec` model derived from the entire BNC with the classification algorithm that we get by extracting a lexicon from the training data without stemming. The first table is just the one we had earlier for the English datasets (the `word2vec` model trained on the BNC will only work with the English datasets) with optimal thresholds, repeated here for ease of comparison:

	Precision	Recall	Micro-F1	Macro-F1	Jaccard
SEM4-EN	**0.718**	**0.772**	**0.744**	**0.750**	**0.593**
SEM11-EN	**0.474**	**0.579**	**0.521**	**0.520**	**0.353**
WASSA-EN	**0.641**	**0.703**	**0.671**	**0.675**	**0.505**
CARER-EN	**0.512**	**0.633**	**0.566**	**0.570**	**0.395**

Figure 5.22 – Lexicon-based classifier, basic English datasets, optimal thresholds, no stemming, no model

When we try to use a `word2vec` model trained on the entire BNC, we get the following:

	Precision	Recall	Micro-F1	Macro-F1	Jaccard
SEM4-EN	0.699	0.753	0.725	0.731	0.569
SEM11-EN	0.471	0.574	0.518	0.515	0.349
WASSA-EN	0.618	0.682	0.648	0.654	0.480
CARER-EN	0.510	0.631	0.564	0.568	0.393

Figure 5.23 – Lexicon-based classifier, basic English datasets, optimal thresholds, no stemming, word2vec as the model

In every case, using the `word2vec` model makes things worse. Why? We can look at the words that are substituted for missing words and the emotions that they carry:

```
...
cat chosen for kitten: anger:0.05, fear:0.10, joy:0.00, sadness:0.00
fall chosen for plummet: anger:0.00, fear:0.04, joy:0.04, sadness:0.02
restrain chosen for evict: anger:0.72, fear:0.00, joy:0.00,
sadness:0.00
arrogance chosen for cynicism: anger:0.72, fear:0.00, joy:0.00,
sadness:0.00
overweight chosen for obese: anger:0.00, fear:0.72, joy:0.00,
sadness:0.00, neutral:0.00
greedy chosen for downtrodden: anger:0.72, fear:0.00, joy:0.00,
sadness:0.00
sacred chosen for ancient: anger:0.00, fear:0.72, joy:0.00,
sadness:0.00

...
```

Most of the substitutions seem reasonable – *cat* is like *kitten*, *fall* is like *plummet*, and *overweight* is like *obese*. The trouble is that while the emotion associated with the substitution is often appropriate for the substitution, it cannot be relied on to be appropriate for the target. It is conceivable that cats are linked to **fear**, but kittens are surely more likely to be linked to **joy**, and while sacred objects might invoke **fear**, ancient ones surely don't.

The problem is that two words that are classified as being similar by one of these algorithms may not have similar emotional associations. The words that co-occur with a verb tend to be the kinds of things that can be involved when the action denoted by that verb is performed, the words that cooccur with a noun tend to be the kinds of actions it can be involved in, and the words that cooccur with an adjective tend to be the kinds of things that can have the property denoted by that adjective. If we look at the performance of our 100M-word `word2vec` model on a collection of emotionally laden words, the results are somewhat surprising:

```
love ['hate', 'kindness', 'joy', 'passion', 'dread']
hate ['adore', 'loathe', 'despise', 'hated', 'dislike']
adore ['loathe', 'hate', 'despise', 'detest', 'daresay']
happy ['pleased', 'nice', 'glad', 'lucky', 'unhappy']
sad ['funny', 'pathetic', 'miserable', 'depressing', 'strange']
furious ['stunned', 'angry', 'annoyed', 'shocked', 'horrified']
happiness ['sorrow', 'joy', 'fulfilment', 'enjoyment', 'dignity']
```

Figure 5.24 – Most similar words to common emotionally-laden words, 100M-word word2vec model

In five out of the seven cases, the most similar word carries exactly the opposite emotions from the target. The problem is that the kinds of things that you can love or hate are very similar, and the kinds of things that are sad or funny are very similar. Because the training corpus contains no information about emotions, its notion of similarity pays no attention to emotions.

This is not just an artifact of the way that `word2vec` calculates similarity or of the training set we used. We get very similar results with other algorithms and other training corpora. The following table shows the most similar words for a set of common words and for a set of emotionally-laden words with four algorithms – a simple TF-IDF model trained on the 110 million words in the BNC using a window of three words before and after the target as the "document" in which it appears; the same model after latent semantic analysis using 100 elements of the diagonal; `word2vec` trained on the same corpus; and a version of GloVe trained on a corpus of 6 billion words:

	man	woman	king	queen	eat	drink
GLOVEMODEL	woman	girl	prince	princess	consume	beer
W2VMODEL	woman	girl	duke	bride	cook	coffee
TF-IDFMODEL	woman	wise	emperor	grandmother	hungry	pour
LSAMODEL	priest	wise	bishop	bride	forget	bath

Figure 5.25 – Nearest neighbors for common words, various models

The words that are returned as the nearest neighbors of the targets by the various algorithms are all reasonable enough (you do have to weed out cases where the nearest neighbor is an inflected form of the target: GLoVe is particularly prone to this, with *eats* and *ate*, for instance, being the words that are found to be most similar to *eat*). For nouns, the words that are returned are things that can do, or have done to them, the same kinds of things; for verbs, they are largely actions that can be performed on the same kinds of things (GLoVe and word2vec both return things that you can drink for *drink*).

If similar words tend to involve, or are involved in, the same kinds of actions, what happens when we look at emotionally laden words?

	love	like	hate	detest	joy	sorrow
GLOVEMODEL	me	even	hatred	despise	sadness	sadness
W2VMODEL	envy	crush	despise	daresay	sorrow	sadness
TF-IDFMODEL	hate	think	love	--	pleasure	--
LSAMODEL	passion	want	imagine	--	pleasure	--

Figure 5.26 – Nearest neighbors for emotionally laden words

A number of the nearest neighbors simply carry no emotional weight – *me, even, think,* and *daresay.* In such cases, the strategy of looking for the nearest word that does carry such a weight would move on to the next case, but since this will produce different results with different lexicons, the effect is unpredictable until we choose a lexicon. In the remaining cases, we see the same phenomenon as before – some of the nearest neighbors carry the same emotions as the target (**hate**: *hatred* (GLoVe), *despise* (word2vec), **joy**: *pleasure* (TF-IDF, LSA), **sorrow**: *sadness* (GLoVe, word2vec)) and as many carry exactly the opposite weight (**love**: *envy* (word2vec), *hate* (TF-IDF), **hate**: *love* (TF-IDF), **joy**: *sadness* (GLoVe), *sorrow* (word2vec)). GLoVe trained on 6 billion words gives two words that carry the correct emotions, two that carry exactly the wrong ones, and two that carry none; word2vec trained on 100 million words gives two that carry the right emotions, two that carry the wrong ones and two that carry none; and TF-IDF and LSA do much the same. Using word similarity models that are trained on corpora that are not marked up for emotions can give very misleading information about emotions, and should only be used with extreme care.

Summary

What does all this add up to? You can make an emotion mining algorithm by making a lexicon with words marked up for emotions. Doing so by extracting the information from a corpus where texts, rather than words, have been marked will probably do better on target texts of the same kind than by using a lexicon where individual words have been marked. They are both time-consuming, labor-intensive activities, but you are going to have to do something like this because any machine learning algorithm is going to require training data. There are numerous minor variants that you can try – stemming, changing the bias, varying the threshold, or using a similarity metric for filling in gaps. They all produce improvements *under some circumstances*, depending on the nature of the corpus and the task, so it is worth trying combinations of techniques, but they do not produce large improvements. Lexicon-based algorithms form a good starting point, and they have the great advantage of being very easy to implement. To get substantially better performance, we will investigate more sophisticated machine learning algorithms in the following chapters.

References

To learn more about the topics that were covered in this chapter, take a look at the following resources:

- Buckwalter, T. (2007). *Issues in Arabic morphological analysis.* Arabic Computational Morphology, 23–42.

- Deerwester, S. C., Dumais, S. T., Landauer, T. K., Furnas, G. W., & Harshman, R. A. (1990). *Indexing by Latent Semantic Analysis.* Journal of the American Society of Information Science, 41(6), 391–407.

- Mikolov, T., Chen, K., Carrado, G., & Dean, J. (2013). *Efficient Estimation of Word Representations in Vector Space (1st ed.).* http://arxiv.org/pdf/1301.3781.pdf.

- Mohammad, S. M., & Turney, P. D. (2013). *Crowdsourcing a Word-Emotion Association Lexicon.* Computational Intelligence, 29 (3), 436–465.

- Pennington, J., Socher, R., & Manning, C. (2014). *GLoVe: Global Vectors for Word Representation.* Proceedings of the 2014 Conference on Empirical Methods in Natural Language Processing (EMNLP), 1,532–1,543. https://doi.org/10.3115/v1/D14-1162.

- Sparck Jones, K. (1972). *A statistical interpretation of term specificity and its application in retrieval.* Journal of Documentation, 28(1), 11–21.

6
Naïve Bayes

In *Chapter 5, Sentiment Lexicons and Vector-Space Models*, we investigated the use of simple lexicon-based classifiers, using both a hand-coded sentiment lexicon and extracting a lexicon from a corpus of marked-up texts. The results from this investigation were that such models can produce reasonable scores, with a variety of tweaks (using a stemmer or changing the way that weights are calculated, such as by using TF-IDF scores) that produce improvements in some cases but not in others. We will now turn to a range of machine learning algorithms to see whether they will lead to better results.

For most of the algorithms that we will be looking at, we will use the Python scikit-learn (`sklearn`) implementations. A wide range of implementations for all these algorithms are available. The `sklearn` versions have two substantial advantages: they are freely available with a fairly consistent interface to the training and testing data and they can be easily installed and run on a standard computer. They also have a significant disadvantage, in that some of them are slower than versions that have been designed to run on computers with fast GPUs or other highly parallel processors. Fortunately, most of them run reasonably quickly on a standard machine, and even the slowest with our largest dataset can train a model in about half an hour. So, for the tasks we are investigating here, where we are interested in comparing the performance of the various algorithms on identical datasets, the advantages outweigh the fact that on very large datasets, some of them will take an infeasibly long time.

In this chapter, we will look at the Naïve Bayes algorithm. We will look at the effects of the various preprocessing steps we used in *Chapter 5, Sentiment Lexicons and Vector Space Models* but we will not look at all the tweaks and parameter settings that are provided with this package. The various `sklearn` packages provide a range of options that can affect either the accuracy or the speed of the given algorithm, but we will not generally try out all the options – it is very easy to get distracted into playing with the parameters in the hope of gaining a few percentage points, but for our goal of looking at ways of carrying out sentiment mining, it is more useful to consider how changes to the data can affect performance. Once you have chosen your algorithm, then it may be worth investigating the effects of changing the parameters, but this book aims to see what the algorithms do with tweets that have been annotated with emotion labels, not to look at all the minutiae of the algorithms themselves.

We will start this chapter by looking at how to prepare our datasets to match the `sklearn` representation. We will then give a brief introduction to the Naïve Bayes approach to machine learning, and then apply the Naïve Bayes implementation from `sklearn.naive_bayes.MultinomialNB` to our datasets and consider why the algorithm behaves as it does and what we can do to improve its performance on our data. By the end of this chapter, you'll have a clear understanding of the theory behind Naive Bayes and the effectiveness of this as a way of assigning emotions to tweets.

In this chapter, we'll cover the following topics:

- Preparing the data for `sklearn`
- Naïve Bayes as a machine learning algorithm
- Naively applying Bayes' theorem as a classifier
- Multi-label and multi-class datasets

Preparing the data for sklearn

The `sklearn` packages expect training data consisting of a set of data points, where each data point is a real-valued vector, and a set of numerical labels representing the class to which each data point has been assigned. Our data consists of sets of tweets, where each tweet is represented by, among other things, a set of words and a set of values such as `[0, 0, 1, 1, 0, 0]`, where each element of the set corresponds to a single dimension. So, if the set of emotions in some training set were `['anger', 'fear', 'joy', 'love', 'sadness', 'surprise']`, then the `[0, 0, 1, 1, 0, 0]` set would indicate that the given tweet had been labeled as expressing joy and love. We will use the CARER dataset to illustrate how to convert our datasets into, as near as possible, the format required by the `sklearn` packages.

Initially, we will represent a dataset as a DATASET, as defined in *Chapter 5, Sentiment Lexicons and Vector Space Models*. To convert a dataset into a form that is suitable for `sklearn`, we have to convert the one-hot encoding of the assignment of labels to a tweet into a single numerical label and the tokens that represent a tweet into a sparse matrix. The first of these is straightforward: we just enumerate the list of values until we hit a non-zero case, at which point the index of that case is the required value. If there is more than one non-zero column, this encoding will just record the first that is found – this will distort the data, but it is inevitable if we use a one-hot encoding for data with multiple labels. The only complication arises when it is possible for a tweet to have no label assigned to it because in that case, we will get to the end of the list without returning a value. If `allowZeros` is set to `True`, then we will return a column beyond the actual range of possible cases – that is, we will encode the absence of a value as a new explicit value:

```
def onehot2value(l, allowZeros=False):
    for i, x in enumerate(l):
        if x == 1:
            return i
    if allowZeros:
        return len(l)
```

```
    else:
        raise Exception("No non-zero value found")
```

We can use this to help construct the sparse matrix representation of the training set, as discussed in the *Vector spaces* section in *Chapter 5, Sentiment Lexicons and Vector Space Models*. To make a sparse matrix, you must collect parallel lists of rows, columns, and data for all cases where the data is non-zero. So, what we have to do is go through the tweets one by one (tweet number = row number), and then go through the tokens in the tweet; we must look the token up in the index (token index = column number), work out what value we want to use for that token (either 1 or its idf), and add those to rows, columns, and data. Once we have these three lists, we can just invoke the constructor for sparse matrices. There are several forms of sparse matrices: csc_matrix makes a representation that is suitable when each row contains only a few entries. We must exclude words that occur no more than wthreshold times because including very rare words makes the matrix less sparse, and hence slows things down, without improving the performance of the algorithms:

```
from scipy import sparse
def tweets2sparse(train, wthreshold=1):
    rows = []
    data = []
    columns = []
    for i, tweet in enumerate(train.tweets):
        t = sum(train.idf[token] for token in tweet.tokens)
        for token in tweet.tokens:
            if train.df[token] > wthreshold:
                rows.append(i)
                columns.append(train.index[token])
                if useDF:
                    s = train.idf[token]/t
                else:
                    s = 1
                data.append(s)
    return sparse.csc_matrix((data, (rows, columns)),
                             (len(train.tweets[:N]),
                              len(train.index)))
```

Once we can convert the representation of the labels assigned to a tweet into a one-hot format and we can convert a set of tweets with Gold Standard labels into a sparse matrix, we have all we need for making a classifier. Exactly what we do with these structures will depend on the type of classifier and the one-hot values for the data points to single class identifiers. All our sklearn classifiers will be subclasses of a generic class called SKLEARNCLASSIFIER: the definition of SKLEARNCLASSIFIER does not include a constructor. We will only ever make instances of subclasses of this class, so it is in some ways like an abstract class – it provides some methods that will be shared by several subclasses, such as for making Naïve Bayes classifiers, support vector machine classifiers, or deep neural network classifiers, but we will never actually make a SKLEARNCLASSIFIER class. The first thing we will need in SKLEARNCLASSIFIER is something for reading the training data and converting it into a sparse matrix. readTrainingData does this by using makeDATASET from *Chapter 5*, *Sentiment Lexicons and Vector-Space Models*, and then converting the training data into a sparse matrix and the labels associated with the training data into one-hot format:

```
class SKLEARNCLASSIFIER(classifiers.BASECLASSIFIER):

    def readTrainingData(self, train, N=sys.maxsize,
                         useDF=False):
        if isinstance(train, str):
            train = tweets.makeDATASET(train)
        self.train = train
        self.matrix = tweets.tweets2sparse(self.train, N=N,
                                           useDF=useDF)
        # Convert the one-hot representation of the Gold
        # Standard for each tweet to a class identifier
        emotions = self.train.emotions
        self.values = [tweets.onehot2value(tweet.GS,
                                           emotions)
                       for tweet in train.tweets[:N]]
```

We will need a function to apply a classifier to a tweet. The default value for this, defined as a method of SKLEARNCLASSIFIER, wraps up the predict method for the underlying sklearn class and returns the result in one of several formats, depending on what is wanted:

```
    def applyToTweet(self, tweet, resultAsOneHot):
        p = self.clsf.predict(tweets.tweet2sparse(tweet,
                                                  self))[0]
        if resultAsOneHot:
            k = [0 for i in self.train.emotions]+[0]
            k[p] = 1
            return k
        else:
            return p
```

All our classifiers that make use of sklearn will be subclasses of this generic type. They will all make use of readTrainingData – that is, the machinery for converting sets of tweets into sparse matrices – and they will all require a version of applyToTweet. SKLEARNCLASSIFIER provides the default versions of these, though some of the classifiers may override them. The first classifier that we will develop using SKLEARNCLASSIFIER as a base class will involve using Bayes' theorem as a way of assigning probabilities to events. First, we will look at the theory behind Bayes' theorem and its use for classification before turning to the details of how this may be implemented.

Naïve Bayes as a machine learning algorithm

The key idea behind the Naïve Bayes algorithm is that you can estimate the likelihood of some outcome given a set of observations by using **conditional probabilities** and linking the individual observations to the outcome. Defining what conditional probability is turns out to be surprisingly slippery because the notion of probability itself is very slippery. Probabilities are often defined as something similar to proportions, but this view becomes difficult to maintain when you are looking at unique or unbounded sets, which is usually the case when you want to make use of them.

Suppose, for instance, that I am trying to work out how likely it is that France will win the FIFA 2022 World Cup (this is being written 2 days before the final, between France and Argentina, is to be played). In some sense, it is reasonable to ask about this probability – if the bookmakers are offering 3 to 1 against France and the probability that they will win is 0.75, then I should place a bet on that outcome. But this probability *cannot* be defined as *#(times that France win the 2022 World Cup)/#(times that France play in the 2022 World Cup final)*. Right now, both those numbers are 0, so the probability appears to be 0/0, which is undefined. By the time you are reading this, the first of them will be either 0 or 1 and the second will be 1, so the probability that France has won the World Cup will be either 0 or 1. Bookmakers and gamblers will make estimates of this likelihood, but they cannot do so by actually counting the proportion of times the outcome of this yet-to-be-played match comes out in France's favor.

So, we cannot define the likelihood of an outcome for a future one-off event in terms of the proportion of times that the event has the given outcome since we have not yet observed the outcome, and we cannot sensibly define the likelihood of an outcome for a past one-off event this way either, since it is bound to be either 0 or 1 once the event has occurred.

But we also cannot define the likelihood of an outcome, for instance, of a series of apparently similar events as a proportion. The fact that I have seen it become lighter in the morning every day of my life – that is, 25,488 out of 25,488 times – does not mean that the likelihood of it getting lighter tomorrow morning is 1. Tomorrow morning might be different. The sun may have turned into a black hole and have stopped emitting radiation. There may have been an enormous volcanic eruption and the sky might be completely blotted out. *Tomorrow may not be the same as today.*

And we also can't define the likelihood that a member of an unbounded set satisfies some property in terms of the proportion of times that members of a finite subset of that property satisfy it. Consider the likelihood that a randomly chosen integer is prime. If we plot the number of occurrences of a prime number in the first few integers, we get a plot similar to the following:

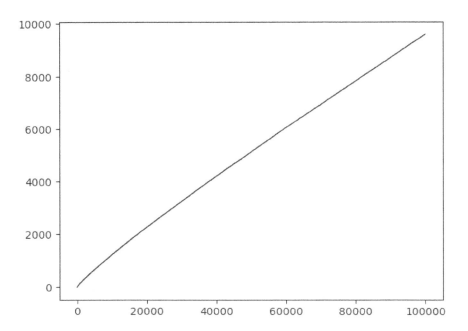

Figure 6.1 – The number of primes in the first N integers

It looks as though the number of primes in the first 10,000 integers goes up linearly, with about 10% of numbers being prime. If we look at the first 100,000,000, then about 6% are prime. What is the true probability? It cannot be defined as the ratio of the number of primes to the number of integers because these two are both infinite and ∞/∞ is undefined. It looks as though the proportion declines as we look at more cases, so it probably tends to 0, but it isn't 0. It turns out to be very hard to either define or estimate probabilities involving unbounded sets.

We can *estimate* the probability of the first two kinds of events. We can look at all football matches between teams that we believe to be similar to the current French and Argentinian teams and use the number of times that the team that is like the current French one beat the one that is like the current Argentinian one. I can look back at all the days of my life and say that if tomorrow is just like all the others *in all relevant respects*, then my estimate of the likelihood that it will get lighter in the morning is 1. But these are just estimates and they depend on the next event being the same as the previous ones in all relevant respects.

This has been a thorny issue in probability theory and statistics since the 19th century. Due to this, Thomas Bayes, among other people, defined probability as being, essentially, the odds that someone might reasonably assign for an outcome (Bayes, T, 1958). Counting previous experience might well be an important part of the information that such a person might use in coming up with their reasonable assignment, but since it is not possible to know that the next event will be similar to past ones in all relevant aspects, it cannot be used as the definition.

So, we cannot say what the probability of a given outcome is. What we can do, however, is define how such a probability should behave if we had it. If your reasonable estimate does not obey these constraints, then you should revise it!

What should a probability distribution be like? Assuming that we have a finite set, $\{O1, ... On\}$, of distinct possible outcomes, any probability distribution should satisfy the following constraints:

- $p(Oi) >= 0$ for all outcomes Oi

- $p(O1) + ... + p(On) = 1$

- $p(Oi \text{ or } Oj) = p(Oi) + p(Oj)$ for $i \neq j$

The first two constraints taken together mean that $p(Oi) <= 1$ for all Oi, and the second and third mean that $p(not(Oi)) = 1 - p(Oi)$ (since $not(Oi)$ is $O1$ or $O2$ or ... or $Oi-1$ or $Oi+1$ or .. or On).

These constraints say nothing about the likelihood of Oi and Oj both occurring. Given the initial conditions, this is not possible since $O1, ... On$ were specified as distinct possible outcomes. The most that we can say about multiple outcomes is that if we have two *completely distinct and unconnected* sets of events, each with a set of possible outcomes, $O1, ... On$ and $Q1, ..., Qm$, then the probability of Oi and Qj occurring must be $p(Oi) \times p(Qj)$. In the same way that we could not tell whether the event we are concerned with is like all the others in the set in all relevant ways, we cannot tell whether two sets of events are indeed unconnected, so, again, this is a constraint on how a probability measure should behave rather than a definition.

Given all this, we can define the conditional probability of some event, A, given that we know that some other event, B, has occurred (or indeed that we know that B will occur):

- $p(A \mid B) = p(A \& B)/p(B)$

How likely is A given that we know B? Well, it's how likely that they occur together divided by how likely B is by itself (so, if they occur together 5% of the time and B occurs 95% of the time, then seeing B will not make us much more likely to expect A, since A only occurs 1 in 19 times that B does; however, if they occur together 5% of the time but B itself only occurs 6%, then seeing B will be a strong clue that A will happen since A occurs 5 in 6 times that B does).

This definition leads very straightforwardly to **Bayes' theorem**:

- $p(A \mid B) = p(A \& B)/p(B)$ definition
- $p(B \mid A) = p(B \& A)/p(A)$ definition
- $p(A \& B) = p(B \& A)$ constraint on A and B
- $p(B \& A) = p(B \mid A) \times p(A)$ rearrange (2)
- $p(A \mid B) = p(B \mid A) \times p(A)/p(B)$ substitute (4) into (1)

If we have a set of events, *B1, ... Bn*, then we can use Bayes' theorem to say that *p(A | B1 & ... Bn)* = *p(B1 & ...Bn | A)×p(A)/p(B1 & ...& Bn)*. And *if the Bi are completely unconnected*, we can say that *p(A | B1 & ... Bn)* = *p(B1 | A) ×p(Bn | A)×p(A)/(p(B1) ×p(Bn))*.

This can be very convenient. Suppose that *A* is "this tweet is labeled as angry" and *B1, ..., Bn* are "this tweet contains the word *furious*," "this tweet contains the word *cross*," ..., "this tweet contains the word *irritated*." We may have never seen a tweet that contains these three words before, so we cannot estimate the likelihood of *A* by counting. However, we will have seen tweets that contain these words individually, and we can count how many tweets that have been labeled as **angry** contain *furious* (or *cross* or *irritated*), how many in total have been labeled as **angry**, ignoring what words they contain, and how many contain **furious** (or *cross* or *irritated*), ignoring how they are labeled. So, we can make sensible estimates of these, and we can then use Bayes' theorem to estimate *p(A | B1 & .. Bn)*.

This way of applying Bayes' theorem assumes that the events, *B1, ... Bn*, are completely unconnected. This is rarely true: a tweet that contains the word *cross* is much more likely to also contain *irritated* than one that doesn't. So, while we can indeed *naively* misuse Bayes' theorem in this way to get usable estimates of some outcome given a set of observations, we should never lose sight of the fact that these estimates are intrinsically unreliable. In the next section, we'll look at how to implement this kind of naïve application of Bayes' theorem as a classifier and investigate how well it works with our various datasets. The key to the success of this approach is that while the estimates of the likelihood of some outcome are not reliable, the ranking of different outcomes is often sensible – if the estimates of the probability that some tweet is **angry** or **sad** are 0.6 and 0.3, respectively, then it is indeed more likely to be **angry** than **sad**, even if the actual numbers cannot be relied on.

Naively applying Bayes' theorem as a classifier

sklearn.naive_bayes.MultinomialNB does these sums for us (they are not very difficult sums, but it is handy to have a package that does them very fast). Given this, the class of NBCLASSIFIER is very simple to define:

```
class NBCLASSIFIER(sklearnclassifier.SKLEARNCLASSIFIER):

    def __init__(self, train, N=sys.maxsize, args={}):
        # Convert the training data to sklearn format
        self.readTrainingData(train, N=N, args=args)
        # Make a naive bayes classifier
        self.clsf = naive_bayes.MultinomialNB()
        # Train it on the dataset
        self.clsf.fit(self.matrix, self.values)
```

That's all we need to make a Naïve Bayes classifier: make SKLEARNCLASSIFIER using sklearn.naive_bayes.MultinomialNB.

How well does this work? We will try this out on our datasets, using stemming for the non-English datasets but not for the English ones (we will do this from here on since those seemed to be generally the right choices in *Chapter 5 , Sentiment Lexicons and Vector Space Models*):

	Precision	Recall	Micro F1	Macro F1	Jaccard
SEM4-EN	0.873	0.873	0.873	0.873	0.775
SEM11-EN	0.625	0.262	0.369	0.373	0.227
WASSA-EN	0.830	0.830	0.830	0.830	0.709
CARER-EN	0.874	0.874	0.874	0.874	0.776
IMDB-EN	0.849	0.849	0.849	0.849	0.738
SEM4-AR	0.694	0.694	0.694	0.694	0.531
SEM11-AR	0.628	0.274	0.381	0.393	0.236
KWT.M-AR	0.667	0.655	0.661	0.664	0.494
SEM4-ES	0.525	0.535	0.530	0.462	0.360
SEM11-ES	0.508	0.296	0.374	0.380	0.230

Figure 6.2 – Naïve Bayes, one emotion per tweet

The first thing to note is that both making and applying a Naïve Bayes classifier is very quick – 10K tweets can be classified per second, and even training on a dataset containing 400K tweets takes just under 10 seconds. But, as before, what matters is whether the classifier is any good at the task we want it to carry out. The preceding table shows that for most of the English datasets, the scores are better than the scores in *Chapter 5, Sentiment Lexicons and Vector Space Models* with the improvement for the CARER dataset being particularly marked and the score for SEM11-EN being substantially worse than in *Chapter 5, Sentiment Lexicons and Vector Space Models*.

Recall the main differences between CARER and the others: CARER is much bigger than the others, and, in contrast to SEM11, every tweet has exactly one label associated with it. To see whether the issue is the size of the training set, we will plot the accuracy for this dataset against an increasing training size:

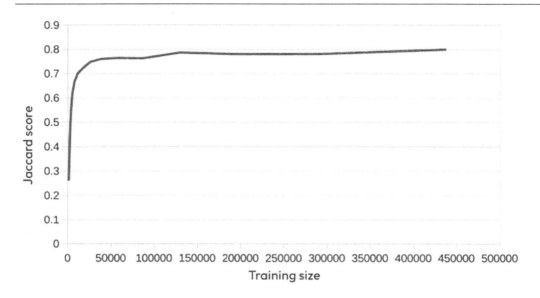

Figure 6.3 – Jaccard score against training size, Naïve Bayes, with the CARER dataset

The Jaccard score increases steadily from quite a low base, and while it is beginning to flatten out as we get to around 400K training tweets, it is clear that Naïve Bayes does require quite a lot of data. This is likely to be at least part of the reason why it is less effective for the other datasets: they simply do not contain enough data.

It is worth looking in some detail at the inner workings of this algorithm. Just like the lexicon-based classifiers, Naïve Bayes constructs a lexicon where each word has associated scores for the various emotions:

	anger	fear	joy	love	sadness	surprise
a	0.0187	0.0194	0.0203	0.0201	0.0190	0.0172
and	0.0291	0.0284	0.0311	0.0286	0.0308	0.0247
the	0.0241	0.0238	0.0284	0.0275	0.0245	0.0230
angry	0.0020	0.0003	0.0001	0.0001	0.0003	0.0001
happy	0.0005	0.0003	0.0014	0.0004	0.0005	0.0004
hate	0.0007	0.0005	0.0002	0.0003	0.0007	0.0002
irritated	0.0013	0.0000	0.0000	0.0000	0.0000	0.0000
joy	0.0001	0.0001	0.0002	0.0002	0.0001	0.0001

	anger	fear	joy	love	sadness	surprise
love	0.0009	0.0009	0.0019	0.0030	0.0011	0.0011
sad	0.0005	0.0003	0.0002	0.0002	0.0010	0.0003
scared	0.0001	0.0019	0.0001	0.0001	0.0002	0.0001
terrified	0.0000	0.0014	0.0000	0.0000	0.0000	0.0000

Figure 6.4 – Scores for individual words, Naïve Bayes, with the CARER dataset

As with the lexicon-based models, the scores for *a*, *and*, and *the* are quite high, reflecting the fact that these words occur in most tweets, and hence the conditional probability that they will occur in tweets that express the various emotions is also quite high. These words will get largely canceled out when we divide the contributions that they make by their overall frequencies. The others all have very small scores, but by and large, they do match the expected emotions – *angry* and *irritated* are most strongly linked to **anger**, *joy* is (just about) most strongly linked to **joy**, and so on. The differences in the levels of association to different emotions are much less marked than was the case for the simple lexicon-based algorithms, so the improved performance must be caused by the improvement in the way that Bayes' theorem combines scores. It is clear that these words are not independently distributed: the proportion of tweets in the CARER dataset that contain *angry* and *irritated* and both *angry* and *irritated* are 0.008, 0.003, and 0.0001, respectively. If we take these as estimates of the respective probabilities, we will find that p(*angry* + *irritated*)/p(*angry*) X p(*irritated*) = 3.6, where it should be 1 if these words were distributed independently. This is hardly surprising – you are much more likely to use two words that express the same emotion in a single tweet than you are to use ones that express different emotions or that have nothing to do with each other. Nonetheless, Bayes' theorem is robust enough to give us useful results even when the conditions for applying it soundly do not apply, so long as we have enough data.

Multi-label datasets

The key difference between SEM11 and the other datasets is that tweets in the SEM11 sets can be assigned any number of emotions – they are multi-label datasets, as defined in *Chapter 5, Sentiment Lexicons and Vector-Space Models*. The actual distributions are as follows:

	0	1	2	3	4	5	6	7	8	9	10
SEM11-EN	205	997	2827	2151	662	100	11	0	0	0	0
SEM11-AR	17	544	1005	769	210	33	3	0	0	0	0
SEM11-ES	179	1499	1605	479	52	1	1	0	0	0	0

Figure 6.5 – Number of tweets with 0, 1, 2, … emotion labels for each SEM11 dataset

In each case, most tweets have two or more labels. This makes it all but impossible for any algorithm that assigns exactly one label to each tweet to score highly – there has to be a false positive for every tweet that has zero labels, and there have to be K-1 false negatives for every tweet that has K labels (since, at most, one of these, K, has been picked, and hence K-1 was not). Suppose we have N tweets, where Z has no labels, O has exactly one label, and M has more than one label. So, even if we assume that our classifier gets one of the labels right whenever a tweet has at least one label, the best Jaccard score that can be obtained is $(O+M)/(O+2*M+Z)$ – there will be $O+M$ true positives (all the cases that ought to be assigned one label, plus all the cases that ought to have more than one, by the assumption), at least Z false positives (one for each tweet that should have no labels), and at least M false negatives.

Thus, the best Jaccard score that can be obtained by an algorithm that assigns exactly one label per tweet for the SEM11-EN dataset is 0.41 (if every label that was assigned to any of the tweets that have one or more labels in their Gold Standards set was correct, then we would have 6,748 true positives, 205 false positives, and 9,570 false negatives). If that is the maximum possible Jaccard score for an algorithm, then the scores of around 0.2 that we obtained previously are not too bad.

But they are not as good as the scores we got for these datasets in *Chapter 5, Sentiment Lexicons and Vector Space Models*. We need to somehow make Naïve Bayes return multiple labels.

This turns out to be fairly straightforward. We can use Bayes' theorem to provide an estimate of the probability of each possible outcome. `sklearn.naive_bayes.MultinomialNB` usually picks the outcome with the highest probability, but it has a method, `predict_log_proba`, that returns the log of the probabilities for each possible outcome (it is often convenient to use the log of the probabilities since working with logs allows us to replace multiplications with additions, which are significantly faster). We can use this to pick, for instance, every outcome whose probability exceeds some threshold, or to pick the best two rather than just the best one. We will look at these two options in turn. For the first, we will use the same constructor as for `NBCLASSIFIER`, and we will just change `applyToTweet` so that it uses `predict_log_proba` rather than `predict`:

```
class NBCLASSIFIER1(NBCLASSIFIER):
    def applyToTweet(self, tweet, resultAsOneHot=True):
        tweet = tweets.tweet2sparse(tweet, self)
        # use predict_log_proba
```

```
p = self.clsf.predict_log_proba(tweet)[0]
# compare to previously defined threshold
threshold = numpy.log(self.threshold)
return [1 if i > threshold else 0 for i in p]
```

The following table is just a copy of the earlier table for Naïve Bayes that deals with the multi-label cases for ease of comparison:

	Precision	Recall	Micro F1	Macro F1	Jaccard
SEM11-EN	0.625	0.262	0.369	0.373	0.227
SEM11-AR	0.628	0.274	0.381	0.393	0.236
KWT.M-AR	0.667	0.655	0.661	0.664	0.494
SEM11-ES	0.508	0.296	0.374	0.380	0.230

Figure 6.6 – Naïve Bayes, one emotion per tweet, multi-class cases

The following table shows what happens when we allow the classifier to assign more than one emotion to a tweet:

	Precision	Recall	Micro F1	Macro F1	Jaccard
SEM11-EN	0.515	0.356	0.421	0.424	0.267
SEM11-AR	0.494	0.381	0.430	0.444	0.274
KWT.M-AR	0.645	0.704	0.673	0.677	0.507
SEM11-ES	0.419	0.394	0.406	0.415	0.255

Figure 6.7 – Naïve Bayes, multiple outcomes with an optimal threshold, SEM11 datasets

In each case, we have improved the recall considerably (because we are now allowing more than one label per tweet to be picked), at the cost of worsening precision. The Jaccard scores have increased slightly, but not to the point where they are better than the scores obtained in *Chapter 5, Sentiment Lexicons and Vector Space Models*.

We can also simply demand to have two labels per tweet. Again, this will improve the recall since we have two labels for all the cases that should have two labels, two for all the cases that should have three, and two for all the cases that should have four – that is, we will potentially decrease the number of false negatives. We will also inevitably increase the number of false positives since we will have two where we should have either none or one. This is an extremely simplistic algorithm since it pays no attention to when we should allow two labels – we just assume that this is the right thing to do in every case:

```
class NBCLASSIFIER2(NBCLASSIFIER):
    def applyToTweet(self, tweet, resultAsOneHot=True):
        tweet = tweets.tweet2sparse(tweet, self)
        p = self.clsf.predict_log_proba(tweet)[0]
        # pick the second highest score in p
        threshold = list(reversed(sorted(list(p))))[2]
        return [1 if i > threshold else 0 for i in p]
```

This produces a further slight improvement for the SEM11 cases, but still not enough to improve over the *Chapter 5, Sentiment Lexicons and Vector Space Models* results, and is disastrous for KWT.M-AR, where there are a small number of cases with multiple assignments and a large number with no assignments at all – forcing the classifier to choose two assignments when there should be none will have a major effect on the precision!

	Precision	Recall	Micro F1	Macro F1	Jaccard
SEM11-EN	0.477	0.404	0.437	0.429	0.280
SEM11-AR	0.474	0.413	0.441	0.440	0.283
KWT.M-AR	0.461	0.906	0.611	0.612	0.440
SEM11-ES	0.370	0.431	0.398	0.395	0.249

Figure 6.8 – Naïve Bayes, best two outcomes, multi-label datasets

So, we have two very simple ways of turning Naïve Bayes into a classifier with multiple (or zero) outcomes. In both cases, the improvement over the standard version is minor but useful. And in both cases, it requires us to know something about the training set – the first requires us to choose a threshold to compare the individual scores with, and the second requires us to know the distribution of the number of outcomes per tweet. This means that, in both cases, we have to use the training data for two things – to find the conditional probabilities, as in the standard case, and then to pick the best possible threshold or to look at the distribution of the number of outcomes; for this, we have to split the training data into two parts, a training section to find the basic probabilities and then a **development** section to find the extra information. This is common in situations where you have to tune a basic model. No rule says that you *must* keep the training and development sections distinct like you must keep the training and test sets distinct, but pragmatically, it turns out that doing so usually produces better results than using the training set as the development set.

The scores for the multi-label datasets are still, however, worse than in *Chapter 5, Sentiment Lexicons and Vector Space Models*. We can try combinations of these two strategies, such as by demanding the best two outcomes so long as they both satisfy some threshold, but no amount of fiddling around is going to transform Naïve Bayes into a good classifier for multi-label problems. We will return to this issue in *Chapter 10, Multiclassifiers.*

We also need to try to work out why Naïve Bayes produces a considerable improvement over the lexicon-based approaches for the SEM4, CARER, and IMDB datasets but a worse performance for WASSA. We have already seen that the performance of Naïve Bayes improves substantially for CARER as we increase the training data. The dataset sizes for these three datasets are SEM4-EN 6812, WASSA-EN 3564, and CARER-EN 411809. What happens if we restrict the training data for all three cases to be the same as for WASSA? The following table is a copy of the relevant part of the original table, using the full dataset in each case:

	Precision	Recall	Micro F1	Macro F1	Jaccard
SEM4-EN	0.873	0.873	0.873	0.873	0.775
WASSA-EN	0.830	0.830	0.830	0.830	0.709
CARER-EN	0.874	0.874	0.874	0.874	0.776
IMDB-EN	0.849	0.849	0.849	0.849	0.738

Figure 6.9 – Naïve Bayes, English single-class datasets – full training sets

When we reduce the amount of data available to be the same as for WASSA, the results get worse, as expected:

	Precision	Recall	Micro F1	Macro F1	Jaccard
SEM4-EN	0.837	0.837	0.837	0.837	0.719
WASSA-EN	0.830	0.830	0.830	0.830	0.709
CARER-EN	0.732	0.732	0.732	0.732	0.577
IMDB-EN	0.825	0.825	0.825	0.825	0.703

Figure 6.10 – Naïve Bayes, English single-class datasets – restricted training sets

The improvements that we've made over the results from *Chapter 5, Sentiment Lexicons and Vector Space Models* for the SEM4-EN, CARER-EN, and IMDB-EN datasets are now less marked, particularly for CARER-EN: the loss of information when we restrict the size of the dataset is significant.

Is there anything else that might explain the differences? Having more classes will make the problem more difficult. If you have, for instance, 10 classes, then making a random choice will get it right 10%

of the time whereas with 5 classes, a random choice will get it right 20% of the time. However, both SEM4-EN and WASSA-EN have the same set of labels, namely **anger**, **fear**, **joy**, and **sadness**, with CARER-EN having these four plus **love** and **surprise**, so if this were the key factor, we would expect the versions of SEM4-EN and WASSA to produce similar results and CARER to be a bit worse, which is not what we find. It is also likely that having a set where the distribution between classes is very uneven may make a difference. However, the distributions of the various emotions between SEM4-EN and WASSA-EN are fairly similar:

SEM4-EN: anger: 834, fear: 466, joy: 821, sadness: 1443

WASSA-EN: anger: 857, fear: 1098, joy: 823, sadness: 786

SEM4-EN has more tweets that express sadness and WASSA-EN has more that express fear, but the differences are not of a kind that would lead you to expect a difference in the performance of a classifier. The two also have almost identical vocabulary sizes (75723 versus 75795) and almost identical average numbers of tokens per tweet (both 21.2). Sometimes, it just seems that one classifier is well suited to one task, and a different classifier is better suited to another.

Summary

In this chapter, we saw that Naïve Bayes can work extremely well as a classifier for finding emotions in tweets. It works particularly well with large training sets (and takes very little time to train since it simply counts occurrences of words and the emotions associated with the tweets they appear in). It can be adapted fairly straightforwardly to work with datasets where a single tweet may have any number of labels (including zero) but is outperformed on the test sets with this property by the lexicon-based approaches from *Chapter 5, Sentiment Lexicons and Vector Space Models*. *Figure 6.11* shows the best classifiers so far for the various datasets:

	LEX	CP	NB (single)	NB (multi)
SEM4-EN	0.503	0.593	0.775	*0.778*
SEM11-EN	0.347	*0.353*	0.227	0.267
WASSA-EN	0.445	0.505	*0.709*	0.707
CARER-EN	0.350	0.395	*0.776*	0.774
IMDB-EN	0.722	0.722	0.738	*0.740*
SEM4-AR	0.506	0.513	0.531	*0.532*
SEM11-AR	0.378	*0.382*	0.236	0.274
KWT.M-AR	*0.687*	0.666	0.494	0.507
SEM4-ES	*0.425*	0.177	0.360	0.331
SEM11-ES	0.269	*0.278*	0.230	0.255

Figure 6.11 – Best classifiers so far

In general, Naïve Bayes is the best classifier for datasets where each tweet has only one label, with marginal differences in these datasets between the version of Naïve Bayes that assumes there is only one label per tweet and the version that allows for multiple labels. For the multi-label datasets, the version that allows for multiple labels always outperforms the one that doesn't, but in all these cases, one of the lexicon-based classifiers from *Chapter 5, Sentiment Lexicons and Vector Space Models* is best. For now, the biggest lesson from this chapter is that when trying to solve a classification problem, you should try various approaches and take the one that works best. We will see what happens when we look at more sophisticated machine learning algorithms in the following chapters.

References

To learn more about the topics that were covered in this chapter, take a look at the following resources:

- Bayes, T. (1958). *An essay towards solving a problem in the doctrine of chances*. Biometrika, 45(3–4), 296–315. `https://doi.org/10.1093/biomet/45.3-4.296`.

7
Support Vector Machines

In *Chapter 6, Naive Bayes*, we looked at using Bayes' Theorem to find the emotions that are associated with individual tweets. The conclusion there was that the standard Naive Bayes algorithm worked well with some datasets and less well with others. In the following chapters, we will look at several other algorithms to see whether we can get any improvements, starting in this chapter with the well-known **support vector machine (SVM)** (Boser et al., 1992) approach.

We will start this chapter by giving a brief introduction to SVMs. This introduction will take a geometric approach that may be easier for you than the standard presentation. Bennett and Bredensteiner (see the *References* section) give detailed formal proof that the two approaches are equivalent – the discussion in this chapter is intended simply to provide an intuitive grasp of the issues. We will then show you how to use the `sklearn.svm.LinearSVC` implementation for our current task. As with the previous approaches, we will start with a simple application of the approach that will work well for some examples but less so for others; we will then introduce two ways of refining the approach to work with multi-label datasets, and finally, we will reflect on the results we have obtained.

In this chapter, we'll cover the following topics:

- The basic ideas behind SVMs
- Application of simple SVMs for standard datasets
- Ways of extending SVMs to cover multi-label datasets

A geometric introduction to SVMs

Suppose we have two groups of entities, called B and R, where each entity is described by a pair of numerical coordinates. B includes objects with coordinates (6.38, -10.62), (4.29, -8.99), (8.68, -4.54), and so on and R contains objects with coordinates (6.50, -3.82), (7.39, -3.13), (7.64, -10.02), and so on (the example used in this discussion has been taken from `https://scikit-learn.org/stable/modules/svm.html#classification`). Plotting these points on a graph gives us the following:

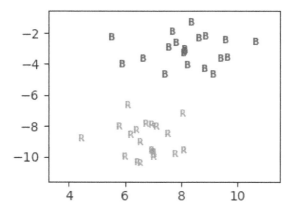

Figure 7.1 – Plot of the R and B points

It looks as though you should be able to draw a straight line to separate the two groups, and if you could, then you could use it to decide whether some new point was an instance of R or B.

There are numerous ways of finding such a line for a simple case like this. One approach would be to find the **convex hulls** (Graham, 1972) for the two groups – that is, the polygons that include them. The easiest way to visualize this involves taking the leftmost point in the set as a starting point. Then, you should pick the most clockwise point from there and set that as the next point on the list, and then do the same again with that one until you get back to the original.

To see how to pick the most clockwise point from a given starting point, consider the two diagrams shown here:

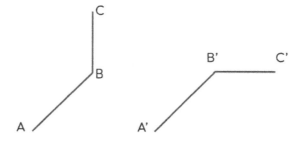

Figure 7.2 – Turning counter-clockwise and clockwise

In the left-hand diagram, the slope from A to B is less steep than the slope from B to C, which means that you have to turn counter-clockwise when you get to B if you want to go from A to B to C, which, in turn, means that C is further counter-clockwise from A than B is. In the right-hand diagram, the slope from A' to B' is steeper than the slope from B' to C', which means that C' is less counter-clockwise from A' than B' is. Thus, to see whether C is more or less counter-clockwise from A than B is, we need to calculate the slopes of the lines joining them and see which is steeper: the slope of the line from A to C is (C[1]-A[1])/(C[0]-A[0]), and likewise for the line joining A and B, so C is further counter-clockwise from A than B if (C[1]-A[1])/(C[0]-A[0]) > (B[1]-A[1])/(B[0]-A[0]). Rearranging this gives us ccw, as follows:

```
def ccw(a, b, c):
    return (b[1]-a[1])*(c[0]-b[0]) < (b[0]-a[0])*(c[1]-b[1])
```

We can then use this to find the convex hull. We sort the points by their Y and X coordinates, which lets us find the lowest point, p (picking the leftmost of these if there is a tie). This point must lie on the hull, so we add it to the hull. We then pick the next item, q, in the list of points (or go back to the beginning if p was the last point – (p+1)%n will be 0 if p is n and p+1 otherwise). We now go through the entire list of points starting at q using ccw to see whether going from p to i to q satisfies the constraint given previously: if it does, then i is further counter-clockwise from p than q is, so we replace q with it. At the end of this, we know that q is the furthest counter-clockwise point from p, so we add it to the hull and continue.

The complexity of this algorithm is $o(H*N)$, where H is the size of the hull and N is the total number of points – H because the main loop terminates after the hull has been constructed by adding one item for each iteration, N because on each pass through the main loop, we have to look at every point to find the most counter-clockwise one. There are more complicated algorithms that are more efficient than this under certain circumstances, but the one given here is efficient enough for our purposes:

```
def naiveCH(points):
    points.sort()
    p = 0
    hull = []
    while True:
        # Add current point to result
        hull.append(points[p])
        # Pick the next point (or go back to the beginning
        # if p was the last point)
        q = (p + 1) % n
        for i in range(len(points)):
# If i is more counterclockwise
# than current q, then update q
            if(ccw(points[p], points[i], points[q])):
                q = i;

# Now q is the most counterclockwise with respect to p
# Set p as q for next iteration, so that q is added to 'hull'

        p = q
# Terminate when you get back to that start and close the loop
```

```
        if(p == 0):
            hull.append(points[0])
            break
    return hull
```

The following figure illustrates how this algorithm progresses around the set of B points in our example:

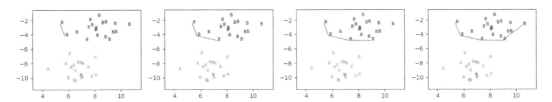

Figure 7.3 – Growing the convex hull for B

There are more efficient algorithms for growing the hull (see `scipy.spatial.ConvexHull`: `https://docs.scipy.org/doc/scipy/reference/generated/scipy.spatial.ConvexHull.html`), but this one is simple to understand. We use it to calculate the convex hulls of R and B:

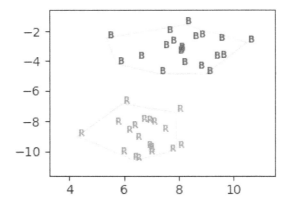

Figure 7.4 – Convex hulls of B and R

If any lines separate R and B (if they are **linearly separable**), then at least one of the segments of the convex hull must be one. If we pick the edge from the hull of B that is nearest to some edge from the hull of R, we can see that it is a separator – all the B items are above or on the dashed orange line and all the R ones are below it, and likewise, all the R items are on or below the dotted green line and all the B ones are above it:

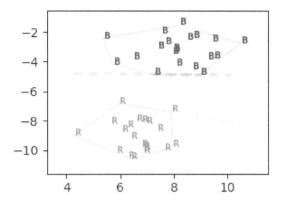

Figure 7.5 – Hull segments as candidate separators for R and B

But they are not very good separators. All items that fell just below the dashed orange line would be classified as R, even if they were only just below this line and hence were much nearer to the Bs than to the Rs; and all items that appeared just above the dotted green line would be classified as B, even if they were only just above it.

So, we want some way of finding a separator that will deal with cases that fall between these two extreme lines appropriately. We can do this by finding the line from the closest point on one of the segments to the other (the dotted gray line) and then drawing our separator through the middle of, and perpendicular to, this line (the solid black line):

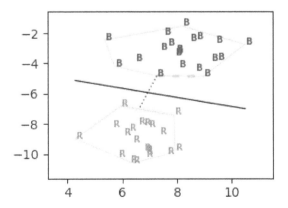

Figure 7.6 – Optimal separator for R and B

The solid black line is an optimal separator in that it makes the separation between the two groups as great as possible: the distance from the nearest point in each group to the line is as great as possible, so any unseen point that falls above it will be assigned to B, which is the best place for it to go, and any point that falls below it will be assigned to R.

This is what we want. Unfortunately, it will all go wrong if some points are outliers – that is, if some R points fall within the main body of B points or some B points fall within the main body of R points. In the following example, we have switched two so that there is a B near the top left of the Rs and an R near the bottom of the Bs:

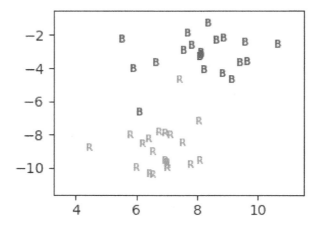

Figure 7.7 – One R point and one B point switched

The convex hulls of the two groups now overlap, and cannot sensibly be used for finding separators:

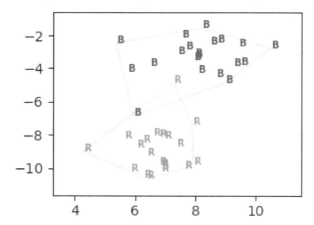

Figure 7.8 – Convex hulls with outliers

We can try to identify outliers and exclude them from their groups, for example, by finding the center of mass of the entire group, marked as black ovals, and removing a point from it if it is nearer to the center of mass of the other group:

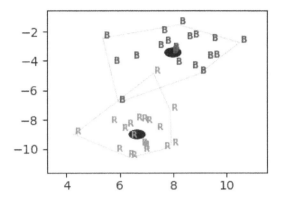

Figure 7.9 – Centers of mass of the two groups

It is clear that the outliers are nearer to the centers of mass of the "wrong" groups, and hence can be identified and removed from consideration when trying to find the separators. If we remove them both, we get non-overlapping hulls. The separator does not put the outliers on the "right" sides, but then no straight line could do that – any straight line that included the outlying R with the other Rs would have to include the outlying B and vice versa:

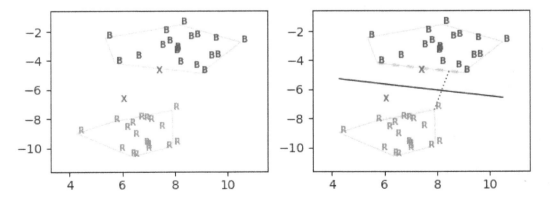

Figure 7.10 – Non-overlapping convex hulls and a separator
ignoring the two outliers (brown Xs are ignored)

However, we can also get non-overlapping hulls by ignoring just one of them:

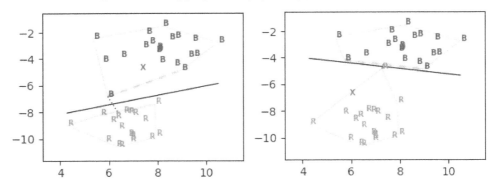

Figure 7.11 – Non-overlapping convex hulls and a separator ignoring outlying R (left) and B (right) points

This time, we are ignoring just one of the outlying points when calculating the hulls. In each case, we get two non-overlapping hulls and a separator, but this time, we have used more of the original data points, with just one of them lying on the wrong side of the line.

Which is better? To use more of the data points when trying to find the separator, to have more of the data points lying on the right-hand side of the line, or to minimize the total distance between the line and the points in the two sets? If we do decide to ignore a point, which one should we choose (is the separator at the top of *Figure 7.11* better than the one at the bottom)? Is the bottom left B point a normal member of B or is it an outlier? If we did not have the outlying R point then there would never have been any reason to doubt that this one was indeed a B.

We need to have a view of how important each of these issues is, and then we have to optimize our choice of points to get the best outcome. That turns this into an optimization algorithm, where we make successive changes to the sets of points to try to optimize the criteria given previously – how many points are included, how close the separator is to the nearest points, and in the most general case what the equation that defines the separator should be (there are tricks to allow for circular or curved separators or to allow the separator to be a bit bendy). If the separating line is straight – that is, the classes are linearly separable – then for the 2-dimensional cases, the line will have an equation such as $A*x + B*y + C = 0$. When we move to three dimensions, the separator becomes a plane with an equation such as $A*x + B*y + C*z + D = 0$. When we move to even higher dimensions, it becomes a **hyperplane**, with an equation such as $A1*x1 + A2*x2 + ...+An*xn + B = 0$.

The simple programs that we used for illustration purposes are not powerful enough to deal with all these issues. We are going to want to work with very high-dimensional spaces where, in most cases, most of the dimensions are zero. Fortunately, there are plenty of efficient implementations that we can use. We will use the Python `LinearSVC` implementation from `sklearn.svm` – there are plenty of other implementations in Python, but `sklearn` packages tend to be stable and well-integrated with other parts of `sklearn`, and `LinearSVC` is known to be particularly efficient for large sparse linear tasks.

Using SVMs for sentiment mining

We have now seen how SVMs provide classifiers by finding hyperplanes that separate the data into classes and have seen a graphical explanation of how such hyperplanes can be found, even when the data is not linearly separable. Now, we'll look at how SVMs can be applied to our datasets to find the boundaries between sentiments, with an analysis of their behavior on single-label and multi-label datasets and a preliminary investigation into how their performance on multi-label datasets might be improved.

Applying our SVMs

As with the previous classifiers, we can define the SVMCLASSIFIERs class as a subclass of SKLEARNCLASSIFIER by using the following initialization code (useDF is a flag to decide whether to use the TF-IDF algorithm from *Chapter 5, Sentiment Lexicons and Vector Space Models* when building the training set; max_iter sets an upper bound on the number of iterations the SVM algorithm should carry out – for our examples, the scores tend to converge by 2,000 steps, so we generally use that as the limit):

```
def __init__(self, train, args={"useDF":True}):
    self.readTrainingData(train, args=args)
    # Make an sklearn SVM
    self.clsf = sklearn.svm.LinearSVC(max_iter=2000)
    # Get it to learn from the data
    self.clsf.fit(self.matrix, self.values)
```

This is exactly like the constructor for NBCLASSIFIERS – just use readTrainingData to get the data into the right format and then use the sklearn implementation to construct the SVM.

As usual, we start by applying this to our standard datasets:

	Precision	Recall	micro F1	macro F1	Jaccard
SEM4-EN	**0.916**	**0.916**	**0.916**	**0.916**	**0.845**
SEM11-EN	0.620	0.260	0.366	0.372	0.224
WASSA-EN	**0.870**	**0.870**	**0.870**	**0.870**	**0.770**
CARER-EN	0.870	0.870	0.870	0.870	0.770
IMDB-EN	0.848	0.848	0.848	0.848	0.736
SEM4-AR	**0.679**	**0.679**	**0.679**	**0.679**	**0.514**
SEM11-AR	0.586	0.255	0.356	0.367	0.216
KWT.M-AR	0.781	0.767	0.774	0.778	0.631
SEM4-ES	0.592	0.574	0.583	0.494	0.412
SEM11-ES	0.493	0.295	0.369	0.372	0.226

Figure 7.12 – SVM applied to the standard datasets

The basic SVM gets us the best scores we have seen so far for the WASSA and two of the SEM4 datasets, with scores for most of the other datasets that are close to the best we have obtained so far. As with the previous algorithms, if we use it with the standard settings, it does very poorly on the multi-label problems, simply because an algorithm that returns exactly one label will fail to cope with datasets where items can have zero or more than one label.

Training an SVM takes significantly longer than training any of the classifiers we have looked at so far. Therefore, it is worth looking briefly at how accuracy and training time for CARER vary as we vary the size of the training data – if we find that having more data has little effect on accuracy but makes training take much longer, we may decide that getting more data is not worth the bother.

When we plot accuracy (because there is no empty class, the values of recall and macro- and micro-F measure are all the same) and Jaccard score for CARER against the size of the training set, we see that we do not need the entire dataset – these two measures converge fairly rapidly, and if anything, performance starts to go down after a while:

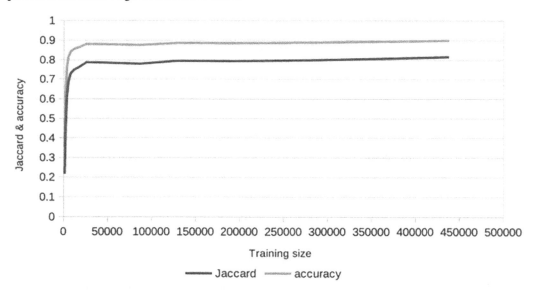

Figure 7.13 – Accuracy versus training data size for SVMs

The decrease in performance after about 30K tweets could just be noise or it could be the result of over-training – as machine learning algorithms see more and more data, they can start to pick up on things that are specific to the training data and are not present in the test data. Either way, the performance is substantially better than anything we saw in *Chapters 5* and *6* and appears to have leveled out at around 0.89 accuracy and 0.80 Jaccard.

We also plotted training time against data size to see whether it would be feasible to run it with more data if we could get it, and the time went up more or less linearly with the data size (this is commonly reported for this kind of problem). However, since the accuracy has already leveled off by about 40K, it seems unlikely that adding more data would make any difference anyway:

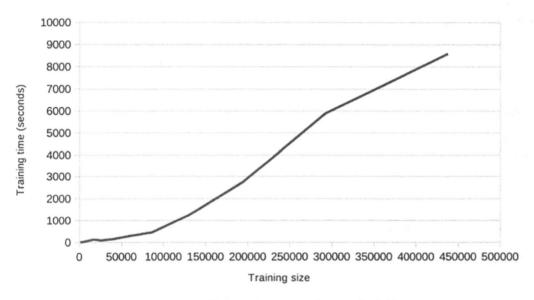

Figure 7.14 – Training time versus data size for SVMs

> **Note**
>
> The accuracy that's obtained by any classifier with any amount of data must level off before reaching 1. Most of the curves that can easily be fitted to plots such as the one shown here (for example, polynomial curves) continue increasing as the X-value increases, so they can only be approximations to the real curve, but they do let you get an impression of whether increasing the amount of training data is worthwhile.

Experiments with datasets with tweets with no labels and tweets with multiple labels

Why is the behavior of the standard SVM so much worse for the multi-label datasets than for most of the others?

SVMs, like any other standard classifier, are designed for assigning each item to a single class. Each point in the training set is given a set of features and a label and the learning algorithm works out how the features and labels are connected. It is fairly straightforward to adapt this to include data where some points have no label, simply by saying that there is an extra label, called something such as neutral, or none of the above, or something like that, to be used when a point has not been given a label. This is a slightly artificial way to proceed because it means that the classifier finds words that are associated with having no emotion, whereas the real situation is that such points simply don't have any words that carry emotional weight. However, it usually works reasonably well and can be assimilated into the standard SVM training algorithm (the definition of `onehot2value` shown in *Chapter 6*, *Naive Bayes*, allows for exactly this kind of situation).

The SEM11 and KWT.M-AR examples belong to a harder, and arguably more realistic, class of problem, where a single tweet may express zero *or more* emotions. The second tweet in the test set for SEM11-EN, *I'm doing all this to make sure you smiling down on me bro*, expresses all three of joy, love, and optimism, and the second to last, *# ThingsIveLearned The wise # shepherd never trusts his flock to a # smiling wolf. # TeamFollowBack # fact # wisewords*, has no emotion linked to it.

It is easy enough to encode these as vectors, given the possible set of emotions ['anger', 'anticipation', 'disgust', 'fear', 'joy', 'love', 'optimism', 'pessimism', 'sadness', 'surprise', 'trust']: we use [0, 0, 0, 0, 1, 1, 1, 0, 0, 0, 0] for joy, love, and optimism and [0, 0, 0, 0, 1, 0, 1, 0, 0, 0, 0] for no emotion. *But these are not one-hot encodings*, and `onehot2value` will not deal with them properly. In particular, it will interpret [0, 0, 0, 0, 1, 1, 1, 0, 0, 0, 0] as joy since that is the first non-zero item it encounters.

There is no simple way around this – SEM11 data has multiple emotions, and SVMs expect single emotions. This has two consequences. During training, only one of the emotions associated with a tweet will be used – if the preceding example had occurred during training, it would have led to the words *smiling* and *bro* (which are the only low document frequency words in this tweet) being associated with joy but not with love and optimism, which could lead to lower precision and lower recall; and if it occurred during testing, then it would inevitably have led to a loss of recall because only one of the three could be returned. This is borne out by the results shown previously, where SEM11-EN in particular has quite good precision but very poor recall, in contrast to the best of the results in *Chapter 6*, *Naive Bayes* where it has good recall but poor precision.

The illustration earlier in this chapter of how SVMs work showed a two-class problem – Rs and Bs. There are two obvious ways of coping with the extension to multiclass problems (such as the CARER and WASSA datasets). Suppose we had Rs, Bs, and Gs. We could train three two-class classifiers, one for R versus B, one for R versus G, and one for B versus G (**one versus one**), and combine the results; alternatively, we could train a different set of two-class classifiers, one for R versus (B or G), one for B versus (R or G), and one for G versus (R or B) (**one versus many**). Both give similar results, but when there are a lot of classes, you have to train $N*(N+1)/2$ classifiers (N for the first class versus each of the rest + N-1 for the second class versus each of the rest + ...) for one versus one but only N for one versus many. For CARER, for instance, where there are six classes, we would have to train 21 classifiers and combine their results for one versus one, whereas for one versus many, we would only have to train six classifiers and combine their results.

We need to follow one of these strategies for all our datasets since they all have several possible outcomes. Fortunately, `sklearn.svm.LinearSVC` does this automatically (using one versus many) for problems where there are a range of possible labels. This by itself, however, will not solve the problem of multi-label datasets – there is a difference between having an outcome consisting of one label drawn from several options and an outcome having an unknown number of labels drawn from several options. The standard multiple-classifiers, which are combined as one versus one or one versus many, will solve the first of these problems but not the second.

There are two ways we can adapt our SVM classifier to deal with this problem:

- We can follow the same strategy as with the Naive Bayes classifier of taking the real-valued scores for each emotion and using a threshold to determine whether or not a tweet satisfies each emotion.

- We can train several classifiers, one versus many style, and simply accept the results from each of them. In the preceding example, if the R versus (B or G) classifier says R, then we accept R as one of the labels for a test case; if B versus (R or G) says B, then we accept that *as well*.

We will look at each of these in turn in the next two sections.

Using a standard SVM with a threshold

To use Naive Bayes with multi-label datasets, we changed `applyToTweet` like so:

```
def applyToTweet(self, tweet):
    tweet = tweets.tweet2sparse(tweet, self)
    # use predict_log_proba
    p = self.clsf.predict_log_proba(tweet)[0]
    # compare to previously defined threshold
    threshold = numpy.log(self.threshold)
    return [1 if i > threshold else 0 for i in p]
```

The preceding code used the fact that `predict_log_proba` returns a value for every label. In the standard version of Naive Bayes, we just pick the highest scoring label for each case, but using a threshold allows us to pick any number of labels, starting from 0.

This won't quite work for SVMs because they do not have a method called `predict_log_proba`. What they do have is a method called `decision_function`, which produces a score for each label. Rather than changing the definition of `applyToTweet` to use `decision_function` instead of `predict_log_proba`, we simply set the value of `predict_log_proba` to be `decision_function` in the constructor for SVMs, and then use `applyToTweet`, as we did previously. So, we must adapt the constructor for SVMs, as shown here:

```
def __init__(self, train, args={}):
    self.readTrainingData(train, args=args)
```

```
# Make an sklearn SVM
self.clsf = sklearn.svm.LinearSVC(max_iter=2000)
# Get it to learn from the data
self.clsf.fit(self.matrix, self.values)
# Set its version of predict_proba to be its decision_function
self.clsf.predict_proba = self.clsf.decision_function
# and set its version of weights to be its coefficients
self.weights = self.clsf.coef_
```

In other words, once we have made the underlying SVM, we must set a couple of standard properties that we will find useful and that do not have the same names in all the `sklearn` classifiers. The results of this for the multi-label cases are as follows:

	Precision	Recall	micro F1	macro F1	Jaccard
SEM11-EN	0.511	0.328	0.399	0.387	0.249
SEM11-AR	0.521	0.290	0.373	0.361	0.229
KWT.M-AR	0.135	0.694	0.227	0.131	0.128
SEM11-ES	0.434	0.338	0.380	0.361	0.235

Figure 7.15 – SVMs using thresholds to deal with multi-label problems

The SEM11 cases are better than those for the simple SVM that we looked at earlier but are not better than the scores we obtained using the earlier algorithms, and the scores for KWT.M-AR are worse than with the simple SVMs. Just using the values that the decision function for the SVM assigns to each label does not solve the problem of multi-label datasets. We will refer to SVMs that use the set of values for each label plus a threshold as SVM (multi) classifiers.

Making multiple SVMs

The second option is to make a set of one versus rest classifiers and accept every label for which the relevant classifier succeeds. The key is to take each label in turn and `squeeze` the N labels in the training data into two – one for the target label and one for all the others. Consider a tweet labeled as joy. The representation of this as a vector would be $[0, 0, 0, 0, 1, 0, 0, 0, 0, 0, 0]$ – that is, with 1 in the column for joy. If we squeeze this to be joy versus the rest, then it will come out as $[1, 0]$ – that is, with a 1 in the new column for joy and a 0 in the column for not-joy. If we squeeze it to be angry versus not-angry, then it would be $[0, 1]$, with a 0 in the new column for anger and a 1 in not-angry. If it had been labeled as joy and love, then the vector would have been $[0, 0, 0, 0, 1, 1, 0, 0, 0, 0, 0]$ and the squeezed version would have been $[1, 1]$: 1 in the first column because it does express joy and 1 in the second because it *also* expresses something else.

Suppose we have a vector, gs, that represents the emotions for a multi-label tweet and we want to squeeze it on the I column. The first column is easy – we just set it to gs[i]. To get the second, which represents whether some column other than I is non-zero, we use numpy.sign(sum(gs[:i]+gs[i+1:]): gs[:i] and gs[i+1:] are the other columns. Taking their sum will be greater than 0 if at least one of them is non-zero while taking the sign of that will be 0 if the sum was 0 and 1 if it was greater than zero. Note that it is possible for both gs[i] and numpy.sign(sum(gs[:i]+gs[i+1:]) to be 0 and for both of them to be 1:

```
def squeeze(train, i):
# Collapse the Gold Standard for each tweet so that we just
# have two columns, one for emotion[i] in the original and
# one for the rest.
    l = []
    for tweet in train.tweets:
        # now squeeze the Gold Standard value
        gs = tweet.GS
        scores=[gs[i], numpy.sign(sum(gs[:i]+gs[i+1:]))]
        tweet = tweets.TWEET(id=tweet.id, src=tweet.src,
                         text=tweet.text, tf=tweet.tf,
                         scores=scores,
                         tokens=tweet.tokens,
                         args=tweet.ARGS)
        l.append(tweet)
    emotion = train.emotions[i]
    emotions = [emotion, "not %s"%(emotion)]
    return tweets.DATASET(emotions, l, train.df,
                      train.idf, train.ARGS)
```

The constructor for MULTISVMCLASSIFIER is straightforward – just make one standard SVMCLASSIFIER for each emotion. To apply one to a tweet, we must apply each of the standard ones and gather the positive results. So, if the classifier that has been trained on joy versus not-joy says some tweet expresses joy, then we mark the tweet as satisfying joy, but we ignore what it says about not-joy since a positive score on not-joy simply tells us that the tweet also expresses some other emotion, and we are allowing tweets to express more than one emotion:

```
def applyToTweet(self, tweet):
    k = [0 for i in self.train.emotions]
    for i in self.classifiers:
        c = self.classifiers[i]
        p = c.clsf.predict(tweets.tweet2sparse(tweet, self))[0]
        """
        if classifier i says that this tweet expresses
        the classifier's emotion (i.e. if the underlying
        SVM returns 0) then set the ith column of the
```

```
main classifier to 1
"""
if p == 0:
    k[i] = 1
return k
```

This is pretty much the standard one versus many approach to training an SVM with multiple labels. The key difference is in the way that the results of the individual X versus not-X classifiers are combined – we accept *all* the positive results, whereas the standard approach just accepts one.

The following table is a repeat of the table for the multi-label problems using SVM (multi) for comparison:

	Precision	Recall	micro F1	macro F1	Jaccard
SEM11-EN	0.511	0.328	0.399	0.387	0.249
SEM11-AR	0.521	0.290	0.373	0.361	0.229
KWT.M-AR	0.135	0.694	0.227	0.131	0.128
SEM11-ES	0.434	0.338	0.380	0.361	0.235

Figure 7.16 – Multi-label datasets, SVM (multi)

When we use multiple SVMs, one per label, we get an improvement in each case, with the score for SEM11-EN being the best so far:

	Precision	Recall	micro F1	macro F1	Jaccard
SEM11-EN	**0.580**	**0.535**	**0.556**	**0.529**	**0.385**
SEM11-AR	0.531	0.485	0.507	0.478	0.340
KWT.M-AR	0.648	0.419	0.509	0.340	0.341
SEM11-ES	0.498	0.368	0.423	0.378	0.268

Figure 7.17 – Multi-label datasets, multiple SVMs

This is better than the results for the SVM (multi) case and is the best so far for SEM11-EN. The improvement over the SVM for the SEM11 datasets comes from the huge improvement in recall. Remember that the standard SVM can only return one result per datapoint, so its recall *must* be poor in cases where the Gold Standard contains more than one emotion – if a tweet has three emotions associated with it and the classifier reports just one, then the recall for that tweet is 1/3. The improvement for KWT.M-AR comes from the improvement in precision – if a tweet has zero emotions associated with it, as is common in this dataset, then the standard SVM must produce a false positive for it.

Numerous tweaks can be applied to `sklearn.svm.LinearSVC`, and we can also try the tweaks from *Chapter 5, Sentiment Lexicons and Vector Space Models* – using IDF to get the feature values, for instance, produces a small improvement across the board. These are worth trying once you have reasonable results with the default values, but it is easy to get carried away trying variations to try to gain a few percentage points on a given dataset. For now, we will simply note that even the default values provide good results in cases where the dataset has exactly one emotion per tweet, with the multi-SVM providing the best results yet for some of the more difficult cases.

Using an SVM can easily be seen as yet another way of extracting a lexicon with weights from a corpus. The dimensions of the SVMs that were used in this chapter are just the words in the lexicon, and we can play the same games with that as in *Chapter 5, Sentiment Lexicons and Vector Space Models* – using different tokenizers, stemming, and eliminating uncommon words. We will not repeat these variations here: we know from *Chapter 5, Sentiment Lexicons and Vector Space Models* that different combinations suit different datasets, and simply running through all the variations will not tell us anything new. It is, however, worth reflecting on exactly how SVMs use the weights that they assign to individual words.

The SVM for the CARER dataset, for instance, has an array of six rows by 74,902 columns as its coefficients: six rows because there are six emotions in this dataset, and 75K columns because there are 75K distinct words. If we pick several words more or less at random, some of which are associated with some emotion and some that have very little emotional significance, we will see that their weights for the various emotions reflect our intuition:

	anger	fear	joy	love	sadness	surprise
sorrow	-0.033	-0.233	0.014	0.026	0.119	0.068
scared	-0.508	1.392	-1.039	-0.474	-0.701	-0.290
disgust	1.115	-0.293	-0.973	-0.185	-0.855	-0.121
happy	-0.239	-0.267	0.546	-0.210	-0.432	-0.080
adores	0.000	0.000	0.412	-0.060	-0.059	-0.000
and	-0.027	-0.008	0.001	-0.008	-0.020	-0.004
the	0.001	-0.012	-0.004	0.001	-0.002	-0.002

Figure 7.18 – Associations between words and emotions, SVM as the classifier, with the CARER dataset

sorrow is strongly linked to **sadness**, *scared* is strongly linked to **fear**, *disgust* is strongly linked to **anger**, *happy* is strongly linked to **joy**, and *adores* is strongly linked to **joy** (but not, interestingly, to **love**: words always throw up surprises); and neutral words are not strongly linked to any particular emotion. The main thing that is different from the lexicons in *Chapter 6, Naive Bayes* is that some words also vote very strongly *against* some emotions – if you are *scared*, then you are not joyous, and if you are *happy*, then you are not angry, fearful, or sad.

The way that SVMs use these weights for classification is the same as in *Chapter 6, Naive Bayes* – if you are given a vector of values, V = [v0, v1, ..., vn], and a set of coefficients, C = [w0, w1, ..., wn], then checking whether `V.dot(C)` is greater than some threshold is exactly what we did with the weights in *Chapter 6, Naive Bayes* (given that V and C are sparse arrays in `sklearn.svm.LinearSVC`, this may be a fairly fast way to do this sum, but it is the same sum). The only differences lie in the way that SVMs obtain the weights and the fact that an SVM can assign negative weights to words. We will return to ways of handling multi-label datasets in *Chapter 10, Multiclassifiers*. For now, we will just note that SVMs and the simple lexicon-based approaches end up using the same decision function on the same features, but that the way that SVMs arrive at the weights for those features is generally better, and in some cases much better.

Summary

Figure 7.17 shows the best classifiers that we have seen so far, with Jaccard scores, for each of the datasets:

	LEX	CP (unstemmed)	CP (stemmed)	NB (single)	NB (multi)	SVM (single)	SVM (multi)	MULTI-SVM
SEM4-EN	0.497	0.593	0.593	0.775	0.778	*0.845*	0.836	
SEM11-EN	0.348	0.352	0.353	0.227	0.267	0.224	0.249	*0.385*
WASSA-EN	0.437	0.512	0.505	0.709	0.707	*0.770*	0.749	
CARER-EN	0.350	0.414	0.395	0.776	0.774	0.770	*0.796*	
IMDB-EN	0.667	0.721	0.722	0.738	*0.740*	0.736	0.736	
SEM4-AR	0.509	0.493	0.513	0.531	*0.532*	0.514	0.494	
SEM11-AR	*0.386*	0.370	0.382	0.236	0.274	0.216	0.229	0.340
KWT.M-AR	0.663	*0.684*	0.666	0.494	0.507	0.631	0.128	0.341
SEM4-ES	*0.420*	0.191	0.177	0.360	0.331	0.412	0.336	
SEM11-ES	0.271	0.276	*0.278*	0.230	0.255	0.226	0.235	0.268

Figure 7.19 – Best classifier for each dataset

As we can see, different classifiers work well with different datasets. The major lesson here is that you should not just accept that there is a single best classification algorithm: do experiments, try out variations, and see for yourself what works best with your data. It is also worth noting that the multi-label datasets (SEM11-EN, SEM11-AR, SEM11-ES, and KWT.M-AR) score very poorly with simple SVMs, and the only one where the multi-SVM wins is SEM11-EN, with simple algorithms from *Chapter 5, Sentiment Lexicons and Vector-Space Models*, still producing the best scores for the other cases.

References

To learn more about the topics that were covered in this chapter, take a look at the following resources:

- Bennett, K. P., & Bredensteiner, E. J. (2000). *Duality and Geometry in SVM Classifiers*. Proceedings of the Seventeenth International Conference on Machine Learning, 57–64.

- Boser, B. E., Guyon, I. M., & Vapnik, V. N. (1992). *A Training Algorithm for Optimal Margin Classifiers*. Proceedings of the Fifth Annual Workshop on Computational Learning Theory, 144–152. https://doi.org/10.1145/130385.130401.

- Graham, R. L. (1972). *An efficient algorithm for determining the convex hull of a finite planar set*. Information Processing Letters, 1(4), 132–133. https://doi.org/10.1016/0020-0190(72)90045-2.

8

Neural Networks and Deep Neural Networks

In *Chapter 7, Support Vector Machines*, we saw that **support vector machines (SVMs)** can be used to classify tweets for emotions based on the words that they contain. Is there anything else that we can use that simply looks at the words that are present? In this chapter, we will consider the use of neural networks for this purpose. Neural networks are a way of carrying out computations by assigning weights to a network of nodes and propagating an initial set of values through the network until the output nodes are reached. The values of the output nodes will then be a representation of the result of the computation. When neural networks were introduced in the 1940s, they were intended as a model of the way that the human brain carries out computations (Hebb, 1949) (McCulloch & Pitts, 1943). This kind of network is no longer taken seriously as a model of the human brain, but the results that can sometimes be achieved this way can be very impressive, particularly when the relationship between the inputs and outputs is hard to determine. A typical neural network has an **input layer** of nodes, a set of **hidden layers**, and an **output layer**, with connections usually linking nodes in one layer with nodes in either the same layer or the next.

We will start by looking at the use of simple neural networks with no hidden layers, and we will investigate the effect of varying several relevant parameters. As with the algorithms from *Chapters 6 and 7*, the standard application of neural networks aims to produce a single value for each input set of features; however, as with the Naïve Bayes algorithm from *Chapter 6, Naive Bayes* it does this by assigning a score to each potential output label, and hence we can easily adapt it to the case where a tweet can have any number of labels. By the end of this chapter, you'll have a clear understanding of how neural networks carry out computations and how adding hidden layers to a network allows it to compute functions that cannot be computed with a single hidden layer. You will also understand how they can be used to assign labels to tweets in our datasets.

In this chapter, we'll cover the following topics:

- Single-layer neural networks and their use as classifiers
- Multi-layer neural networks and their use as classifiers

Single-layer neural networks

A neural network, in general, consists of a set of nodes, organized in layers, with connections between them. A **simple neural network** (**SNN**) simply has an input layer that corresponds to the features that the classification is to be based on, and an output layer that corresponds to the possible outcomes. In the simplest case, where we just want to know whether something belongs to a specified category, there will be just one output node, but in our case, where we have multiple possible outcomes, we will have multiple output nodes. An SNN looks something like the following:

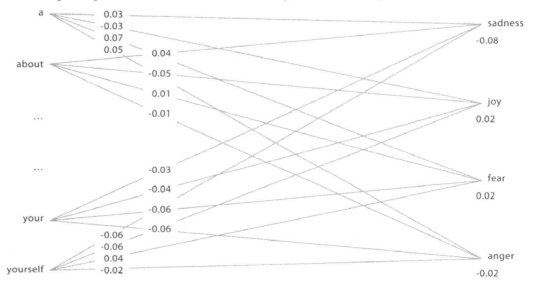

Figure 8.1 – A single-layer neural network where the inputs are words and the outputs are emotions

The links between nodes each have a weight and every node that's not in the input layer has a bias. The weights and the bias are essentially the same as the weights and the constant term in the $A1 * x1 + A2 * x2 + ... + An * xn + B = 0$ equation, which we used to define the separating hyperplane in *Chapter 7, Support Vector Machines.*

Applying such a network to a tweet that needs to be classified is very simple: just multiply the weights associated with each word in the tweet (each **active input node**), take the sum of those, and add it to the bias for the connected node: if this is positive, then set it as the activation for the connected node; otherwise, set the activation to 0. Training a network of this kind is more challenging. The basic idea is that you look at the output nodes. If an output node is doing what the training data says it should, then there is nothing to be done (after all, if all the output nodes did what they should on all the training data, then the classifier would be trained as well as possible). If it is not, then there must be something wrong with the connections leading into it. There are two possibilities: the node is on when it should be off, or it is off when it should be on. Suppose it is on when it should be off. The only reason for it to be on is if the sum of the weights on the links from active nodes that lead into it is greater than its threshold, so to stop it from turning on, the weights on those links should all be decreased slightly.

Similarly, if a node is off when it should be on, then the weights on active nodes that lead into it should be increased slightly. Note that in both cases, it is the links from active nodes that are adjusted – inactive nodes cannot contribute to turning a node that they are connected to on, so changing the weights on the links from them has no effect. Exactly how much the weights should be increased or decreased, and when this should happen, has substantial effects on the accuracy of the results and the time taken to get them. If you change the weights too much, the process may fail to converge or it may converge on a sub-optimal configuration; if you change them too little, then convergence can take a very long time. This process of gradually changing the weights to drive the network to reproduce the training data is known as **gradient descent**, reflecting the fact that the aim is to move the network downhill in the space of weights and thresholds to obtain the minimum overall error.

In the original presentations of neural networks, this process was **back-propagated** through the network so that the weights on connections leading into the layer before the output layer were also adjusted per their overall contribution to the output, and the weights on the layer before that, and so on until the input layer was reached (Rumelhart et al., 1986). Doing this could be very slow with networks with many hidden layers, with very small changes – sometimes vanishingly small changes – happening in the early layers. The use of neural networks was therefore restricted to quite shallow networks until it was realized that you could train a network with *N* hidden layers by training one with N-1 layers and adding another layer and fine-tuning the resulting network (Hinton et al., 2006). This meant that you could train a network with, say, three hidden layers by training one with no hidden layers and then adding a new layer just before the output layer and retraining this network (which has one hidden layer), then adding another new layer just before the output layers and retraining this network (which has two hidden layers), and then adding another new layer, retraining with this one (which has three hidden layers). This strategy makes it feasible to train complex networks based on the assumption that the generalizations captured by the early layers are robust so that errors in later ones will not have a major effect on the early ones.

There are numerous strategies for implementing the training algorithm (there is only one way to do the actual application once a network has been trained), and numerous implementations of the training algorithm and the machinery for applying a trained network to a task. For very large datasets, using an implementation that can run in parallel can be a good idea, but the sparse nature of our data means that the `sklearn.neural_network.MLPClassifier` implementation runs in a reasonable amount of time. We will not try out every possible combination of features for every dataset. As with SVMs (but more so), there are countless settings and parameters to play with, and it is easy to get diverted into trying variations in the hope of getting a few percentage points of improvement. We will look at the effect of some of the more significant choices, but we will concentrate mainly on considering the way that features are used rather than on the minutiae of the training regime. We will start by considering an SNN – that is, a neural network with just an input layer and an output layer, as in *Figure 8.1*.

An SNN is just a **deep neural network** (**DNN**) with no hidden layers. We start by specifying the class of DNNCLASSIFIER as a subclass of SVMCLASSIFIER (they have several shared properties, which we can exploit by doing this). If we specify that the default is that DNNCLASSIFIER should have no hidden layers, then we have a constructor for SNNs. The initialization code follows the same pattern as for the other SKLEARNCLASSIFIER (including SVMCLASSIFIER) – use readTrainingData to read the training data and put it into the standard format and then invoke the sklearn implementation of the classification algorithm and fit it to the training data:

```
class DNNCLASSIFIER(svmclassifier.SVMCLASSIFIER):

    def __init__(self, train=None,
                 args={"hiddenlayers":()}):
        args0 = ARGS({"N":500, "wthreshold":5,
                      "useDF": False,
                      "max_iter":sys.maxsize,
                      "solver":"sgd", "alpha": 1e-5})
        for k in args:
            args0[k] = args[k]
        self.readTrainingData(train, N=args0["N"])
        # making a multi-layer classifier requires a
        # lot of parameters to be set
        self.clsf = MLPClassifier(solver=args["solver"],
                    alpha=args["alpha"],
                    max_iter=args["max_iter"],
                    hidden_layer_sizes=args["hiddenlayers"],
                    random_state=1)
        self.clsf.fit(self.matrix, self.values)
```

We are using the sklearn.neural_network.MLPClassifier package from sklearn. This package takes a large number of parameters that control the shape of the network and the ways that the weights are calculated and used. As ever, we are not going to carry out experiments to see how varying these parameters affects performance on our tasks. Our goal is to see how well the basic algorithm works for us, so we will largely use the default values for these parameters. Once we have ascertained how well the algorithm works in general, it may be worth tweaking the parameters, but since, as with all these algorithms, the performance depends to a large extent on the nature of the dataset, this is something that can be left for later.

As with all the classifiers so far, the constructor trains the model: with the sklearn-based ones, this always involves using readTrainingData to convert the data into its standard form, making a model of the specified type, and calling self.clsf.fit(self.matrix, self.values) to train it. Applying the trained model involves applying the applyToTweets method, which is inherited from the abstract BASECLASSIFIER class from *Chapter 5, Sentiment Lexicons and Vector-Space Models*.

Trying it out on our datasets, we get the following. (The results for CARER were obtained by training on 70K of the full 440K available. Training neural networks is considerably slower than other algorithms. We will look at the relationships between training size, accuracy, and time later, but for now, just note that the accuracy on the CARER dataset seems to have started to level off after about 70K, so we can use that for comparison with the other algorithms):

	Precision	Recall	Micro F1	Macro F1	Jaccard
SEM4-EN	0.902	0.902	0.902	0.902	0.822
SEM11-EN	0.648	0.275	0.386	0.388	0.239
WASSA-EN	**0.837**	**0.837**	**0.837**	**0.837**	**0.720**
CARER-EN	**0.901**	**0.901**	**0.901**	**0.901**	**0.820**
IMDB-EN	0.885	0.885	0.885	0.885	0.793
SEM4-AR	0.670	0.670	0.670	0.670	0.504
SEM11-AR	0.596	0.260	0.362	0.370	0.221
KWT.M-AR	0.035	0.126	0.055	0.034	0.028
SEM4-ES	0.541	0.472	0.504	0.409	0.337
SEM11-ES	0.484	0.290	0.362	0.361	0.221

Figure 8.2 – Simple neural network applied to the standard datasets

The scores in the preceding table for the two big datasets are the best so far, but the others are all slightly worse than what we achieved using Naïve Bayes and SVMs. The obvious way to improve the performance of this algorithm is to use a DNN. DNNs have been shown to have better performance than SNNs on many tasks, and it is reasonable to expect that they will help here. There are, however, a huge number of options to choose from when you start using networks with hidden layers, and it is worth looking at what the non-hidden layer version is doing with the data it was supplied with before trying to add hidden layers. Do we want one hidden layer that is half the size of the input layer? Do we want 50 hidden layers, each of which is of size 15? Given that training a neural network with hidden layers can be very slow, it is a good idea to think about what we want the hidden layers to do before we start doing any experiments.

We will start by looking at the effects of varying parameters, such as the size of the training data, the number of input features, and the number of iterations. Training even a no-hidden- layers neural network can be quite slow (see *Figure 8.3*), and it is worth looking at how changes to the training data affect the time for training and the accuracy: if we find that there is a way of reducing training time while maintaining a reasonable level of performance, then it may be worth using that rather than the full unrestricted training set.

There are three obvious things we can look at:

- How does the accuracy and training time vary with the size of the training set?

- How does the accuracy and training time vary with the number of input features (that is, words)?

- How does the accuracy and training time vary with the number of iterations?

We will start by looking at how accuracy (reported as Jaccard score) and training time vary with the size of the training set. The following graph plots these for the CARER dataset (which is the largest of our datasets) with the other factors held constant (only use the 10K most frequent words, do at most 1K iterations):

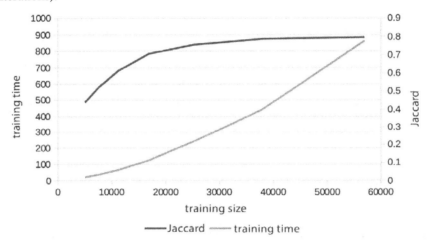

Figure 8.3 – Jaccard score and training time in seconds versus training size with the CARER-EN dataset

It is clear that the Jaccard score levels off after about 40K tweets, while the training time seems to be on an upward trend. It is not easy to fit a curve to the Jaccard plot – a polynomial one will inevitably begin to trend downwards, and a logarithmic one will inevitably increase to above 1 at some point – however, a simple inspection should give you a reasonable idea of the point at which adding extra data will stop producing useful increases in performance.

The next thing to vary is the size of the dictionary. Since the input layer consists of the words that appear in the tweets, removing infrequent words may speed things up without having too much effect on accuracy:

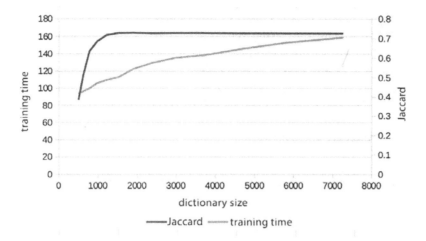

Figure 8.4 – Jaccard score and training time in seconds versus dictionary size with the CARER-EN dataset

The CARER-EN dataset contains 16.7K words, but the Jaccard score flattens out at somewhere between 1K and 2K. Since training time does increase more or less linearly as the number of input features increases, it is worth checking for the point at which adding new words has little effect on the accuracy.

The third thing that we can vary is the number of iterations. Neural network training involves making a series of adjustments to the weights and thresholds until no further improvement is achievable. The more iterations that we carry out, the longer training takes, but the accuracy tends to start to flatten out before the best possible result is found. The following chart shows how the training time and the Jaccard score vary as the number of iterations increases for SEM4-EN. There were no further improvements after 1,800 iterations for this dataset, so we stopped the plot at this point. Unsurprisingly, the training time goes up linearly with the number of iterations, whereas the Jaccard score starts to level off at around 1,400 iterations:

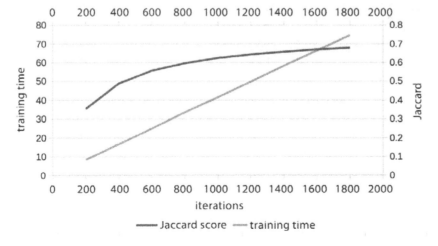

Figure 8.5 – Jaccard score and training time versus iterations with the SEM4-EN dataset

Varying the size of the training data, the number of input features, and the number of iterations affects the scores and the training time. While you are developing a model and are trying out different combinations of parameters, settings, and preprocessing steps, it is certainly worth doing some preliminary investigations to find a set of values for these factors at which the Jaccard score appears to be leveling off. But in the end, you just have to grit your teeth and train the model using a large amount of training data, a large dictionary, and a large number of iterations.

Multi-layer neural networks

We have seen that if we are prepared to wait, using an SNN can produce, at least in some cases, better results than any of the previous algorithms. For a lot of problems, adding extra hidden layers can produce better results than networks with just an input layer and an output layer. Will this help with our current task?

SNNs compute very similar information to that calculated by Naïve Bayes and SVMs. The links between input and output nodes carry information about how strongly the input nodes (that is, words) are correlated to the output nodes (that is, emotions) and how the biases roughly carry information about how likely the given output is. The following tables show the links between several common words and emotions after training on the CARER dataset:

	anger	fear	joy	love	sadness	surprise
the	-0.036	-0.065	0.031	0.046	-0.015	0.036
sorrow	0.002	-0.028	-0.098	0.098	0.063	0.020
scared	-0.356	1.792	-0.683	-0.283	-0.562	0.057
happy	-0.090	-0.161	0.936	-0.332	-0.191	-0.156
disgusting	0.048	-0.014	-0.031	-0.045	0.020	-0.000
and	-0.001	-0.033	0.014	0.015	-0.031	0.022
adoring	-0.054	-0.034	-0.110	0.218	-0.085	0.007
irritated	1.727	-0.249	-0.558	-0.183	-0.621	-0.124
kisses	-0.004	-0.041	-0.041	0.120	-0.038	-0.001

Figure 8.6 – Links between words and emotions in the CARER-EN dataset

The following table displays the words with the strongest and weakest connections to the emotions:

anger	offended, greedy, rushed, resentful, selfish … passionate, supporting, strange, amazing, weird
fear	unsure, reluctant, shaky, insecure, vulnerable … shocked, supporting, sweet, stressed
joy	smug, sincere, invigorated, joyful, positive … helpless, agitated, weird, strange, overwhelmed
love	horny, sympathetic, gentle, naughty, liked … amazing, overwhelmed, hated, strange, weird
sadness	burdened, homesick, disturbed, rotten, guilty … sweet, agitated, weird, strange
surprise	impressed, shocked, amazed, surprised, curious … feelings, don, very, being, or

Figure 8.7 – Strongest and weakest words for each emotion in the CARER-EN dataset

Given a set of input words (a tweet!), the neural network calculates the sum of the links from those words to each emotion and compares it with the threshold (different implementations of neural networks carry out slightly different calculations: the one used here, **rectified linear activation** (Fukushima, 1969), calculates the weighted sum of the inputs and the bias but then sets it to zero if it is negative). This is very similar to what all the other algorithms do – SVMs also calculate a weighted sum of the inputs but do not reset negative outcomes to zero; the lexicon-based algorithms also just calculate a weighted sum but since none of the weights are negative, the total cannot be less than zero, so there is no need to reset them. Naïve Bayes combines the conditional probabilities of the various observed events to produce an overall probability. What they all have in common is that a single word *always* makes the same contribution to the total. This may not always be true:

- There are words whose sole job is to change the meaning of other words. Consider the word *happy*. This word is linked to **joy** rather than to any of the other emotions:

	anger	**fear**	**joy**	**sadness**
happy	-0.077	-0.159	0.320	-0.048

Figure 8.8 – Links between happy and the four emotions from SEM4-EN

Tweets where *happy* appears next to *not*, however, do not express joy:

This is kind of screwed up , but my brother is about to join the police academy . . . . and I ' m not happy about . And I 'm not the only one.

Yay bmth canceled Melbourne show fanpoxytastic just lost a days pay and hotel fees not happy atm # sad # angry

I was just put on hold for 20 minutes till I hung up . # not happy # terribleservice # unhappy @ virginmedia I should have stayed . . .

The presence of *not* changes the meaning of these tweets so that they express something other than joy.

Not all words that affect the meanings of other words are as easy to identify as *not*, particularly in informal texts where abbreviations such as *don't* and *can't* are very common, but there are certainly others that do something like this. It is also important to note that the word whose meaning is being affected by the modifying term may not be adjacent to it.

- Some words form compounds that express meanings that are not straightforwardly related to the meanings of the individual words in isolation. We saw this with Chinese compounds earlier, but even English words can do this. Using pointwise mutual information to find compounds (as in *Chapter 5, Sentiment Lexicons and Vector Space Models*), we find that *supporting cast* and *sweet potatoes* occur more often in the CARER-EN dataset than you would expect given the distributions of the individual words – that is, these terms may be viewed as compounds. The weights for the individual words are given in the following table, with *supporting* and *sweet* both having strong links to **love** and slightly weaker links to **joy**. Neither of the compound words would be expected to have these links – there is nothing particularly lovely or joyous about sweet potatoes! It is not possible to capture the fact that these words make a different contribution to the overall emotional charge of the texts containing them when they co-occur with *cast* and *potatoes* using an SNN or indeed any of the earlier algorithms:

	anger	fear	joy	love	sadness	surprise
supporting	-0.183	-0.154	0.220	0.515	-0.319	-0.043
cast	-0.015	0.017	-0.012	0.003	0.006	-0.009
sweet	-0.177	-0.187	0.207	0.553	-0.371	-0.079
potatoes	-0.009	0.003	0.004	0.003	-0.020	-0.019

Figure 8.8 – Weights for individual words that can occur as compounds

- Some words are simply ambiguous, with one interpretation carrying one emotional charge and another carrying a different one (or none). It is extremely difficult to detect that a word is ambiguous simply by looking at texts that contain it, and even more difficult to detect how many interpretations it has, and even if you do know how many interpretations a word has, you still have to decide which one is intended in a given text. So, inferring what emotional charge each interpretation has and then deciding which interpretation is intended is more or less impossible. However, in some cases, we can see, as with the cases of compounds previously, that two words are cooccurring unexpectedly often, and in such cases, we can be reasonably sure that the same interpretations are intended in each case. *Feel like* and *looks like*, for instance, occur more often in the SEM4-EN data than they should: both of these could be ambiguous, with the different meanings carrying different emotional charges. But it seems very likely that in each occurrence of *feel like* the same interpretations of *feel* and *like* are intended – as it happens, the interpretation of *like* in these phrases is not the one that is closely linked to **love**.

All the algorithms that we have seen so far, including SNNs, treat the contributions made by individual words atomistically – they all compute a score for each word for each emotion, and they then combine the scores using some fairly simple arithmetical calculation. Therefore, they *cannot* be sensitive to the issues raised here.

Adding extra layers to our neural network will enable us to handle these phenomena. The simplest demonstration of how adding layers will allow a neural network to compute something that cannot be dealt with by an SNN involves the XOR function, where we have two inputs and we want to get a response if one, but not both, of the inputs is on.

This cannot be done with an SNN. We will explore the reasons for this and the way that DNNs overcome this limitation by considering a set of made-up tweets consisting solely of the words *love*, *like*, *hate*, and *shock* and the emotions *anger*, *joy*, and *surprise*, as shown in *Figure 8.9*:

ID	tweet	joy	anger	surprise
1	love	1	0	0
2	like	1	0	0
3	love like	1	0	0
4	hate	0	1	0
5	shock	0	0	1
6	love	1	0	0
7	like	1	0	0
8	love like	1	1	0
9	hate	0	1	0
10	shock	0	0	1

Figure 8.9 – Straightforward training data

If we train an SNN on this data, we will get the following network:

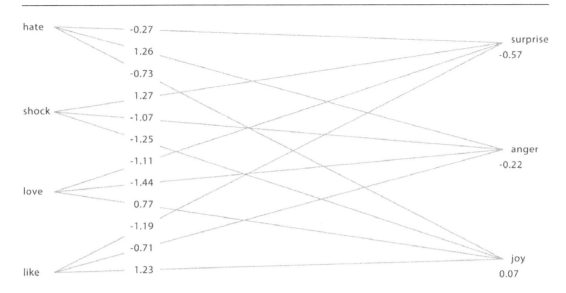

Figure 8.10 – An SNN for surprise, anger, and joy, with straightforward training data

The strongest link from *hate* is to **anger**, the strongest link from *shock* is to **surprise**, and the strongest links from *love* and *like* are to **joy**. So, if a tweet consists of one of these words, it will trigger the appropriate emotion. If a tweet contains both *love* and *like*, it will also trigger **joy**, but the training data says nothing about what should happen if a tweet consists of, for instance, *shock* and *like* or *shock* and *hate*. Looking at the network, we can see that *hate* votes quite strongly for **anger** and *shock* votes by about the same amount for **surprise**, but that *shock* votes much more strongly *against* **anger** than *hate* does against **surprise**. So, overall, *shock* and *hate* vote for **surprise**. There is nothing meaningful going on here: the network is initialized with random values, and these spill over into random decisions about configurations of features that have not been seen in the training data.

As noted previously, our SNN carries out essentially the same operations as an SVM: if the weights on the connections between a set of input nodes, $N_1, …, N_k$, and an output node, O, are $w(N_1, O), …, w(N_k, O)$ and the bias for the output node is $b(O)$, then if the input values for $N_1, …, N_k$ are $v(N_1), …, v(N_k)$, then the excitation of the output node is determined by $v(N_1) \times w(N_1, O) + … + v(N_k) \times w(N_k, O) + b(O)$ – the excitation of the output node will be 0 if this sum is negative and on to some degree if it is positive. $v(N_1) \times w(N_1, O) + … + v(N_k) \times w(N_k, O) + b(O)$ determines a hyperplane that divides points into two classes, O or $not(O)$, just like the coefficients in SVMs.

But that means that an SNN cannot classify if the classes are *not* linearly separable. The classic example here is the XOR function – that is, examples where each of two features in isolation denotes a specific class but the two together do not – that is, *XOR(0, 0)=0, XOR(0, 1)=1, XOR(1, 0)=1*, and *XOR(1, 1)=0*. It is easy enough to draw this function and show that it looks as though no line separates the 0 and 1 cases. In *Figure 8.11*, the red circles (at (0, 0) and (1, 1)) represent the cases where XOR is 0, and the blue diamonds (at (1, 0) and (0, 1)) represent where XOR is 1:

Figure 8.11 – XOR – the blue diamonds and red circles cannot be separated by a straight line

It looks as though it would be impossible to draw a line that divides the blue diamonds and red circles – that is, these two classes look as though they are not linearly separable.

For formal proof of this, assume that there is such a line. It will have an equation such as $A \times x + B \times y + C = 0$ where, for any point that is above the line, $A \times x + B \times y + C > 0$, and for any point below the line, $A \times x + B \times y + C < 0$ (if B is positive and vice versa if B is negative).

Given our four points, let's assume that the red circles are both below the line and the blue diamonds are above it and B is positive. Then, for the red circle at $(0, 0)$, we would have $C < 0$, since putting 0 for each of x and y would give us $A \times 0 + B \times 0 + C < 0)$, which makes C<0. Similarly, for the red circle at $(1, 1)$, substituting 1 for each of x and y would give us $A + B + C < 0$, for the blue diamond at $(1, 0)$ substituting 1 for x and 0 for y would give us $A + C > 0$, and for the blue diamond at $(1, 0)$, we would get $B + C > 0$.

From $C < 0$ and $A + C > 0$, we get $A > 0$, and likewise from $C < 0$ and $B + C > 0$, we get $B > 0$. But then $A + B + C > A + B + 2 \times C$, so since $(A + C) + (B + C) > 0$, then $A + B + C > 0$, contradicting the observation that $A + B + C < 0$ for the point $(1, 1)$. We do have to consider the possibility that the blue diamonds are both above the line and the red circles are below, or that B is negative, but an exactly parallel argument rules these out in the same way – there is no way to draw a straight line that separates the blue diamonds and red circles.

What does this mean for our task? Suppose we adjust our made-up data as follows:

ID	tweet	joy	anger	Surprise
1	love	1	0	0
2	like	1	0	0
3	love like	0	1	0
4	hate	0	1	0
5	shock	0	0	1
6	love	1	0	0
7	like	1	0	0
8	love like	0	1	0
9	hate	0	1	0

Figure 8.12 – Difficult training data

The only change we have made is that we have made the tweets that contain *love* and *like* express **anger** rather than **joy**. This is much like the situation with XOR previously, where two features express one emotion when they appear in isolation and a different one when they appear together. There is no exact parallel to the (0, 0) point from XOR, but in the cases where neither was present, then the target is either **anger** (if the tweet was just the word *hate*) or **surprise** (if the tweet was just the word *shock*) – that is, when neither *love* nor *like* is present, then the tweets do not express **joy**.

When we train on this data, we will find that the SNN cannot be relied on to find weights that assign the right emotions. Sometimes it does, sometimes not. The problem is not that there is no set of weights that will assign the correct labels. Over a run of 10 folds of 90% training/10% testing, weights that split the data correctly were found in two cases, but in eight cases, the classifier assigned the wrong emotion to tweets containing both *like* and *love*.

In the incorrectly trained network shown here, the scores for joy, anger, and surprise for tweets containing both these words were 0.35, -0.25, and -3.99, with joy the clear winner. The data *is* linearly separable since the correctly trained classifier does separate the data into the right classes by using hyperplanes defined by the connection weights and biases; however, the gradient descent process can easily get stuck in local minima, doing the best it can with the single-word tweets but unable to find the correct weights for the compound ones:

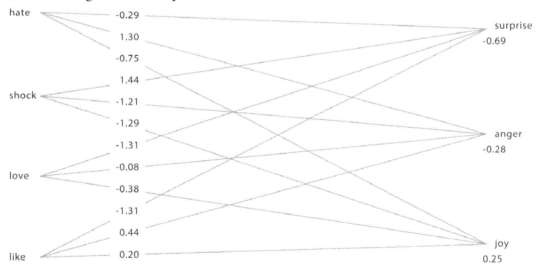

Figure 8.13 – Correctly trained network

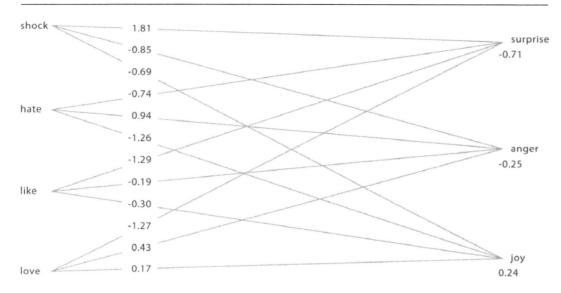

Figure 8.14 – Incorrectly trained SNN

Therefore, we have two kinds of problems:

- If the data is not linearly separable, then no SNN can classify it correctly

- Even if it can be divided by a set of hyperplanes, SNNs can easily get stuck in local minima, doing the best they can with most of the data but unable to find the right weights for cases where words have a different effect when they occur together from the effect they would have in isolation

We can solve the first problem by adding extra layers. In order, for instance, to calculate XOR, you need a node in the network that is turned on when both the input nodes are on and has a negative link to the output. A simple feedforward network should have the nodes in the input layer connected to nodes in the first hidden layer and then nodes in the first hidden layer connected to nodes in the second hidden layer and so on until the nodes in the last hidden layer are connected to nodes in the output layer. You need at least one hidden layer with at least three nodes in it. However, as we have seen, networks can quite easily get stuck in local minima, and the smallest configuration that can be reliably trained to recognize XOR has a single hidden layer with five nodes:

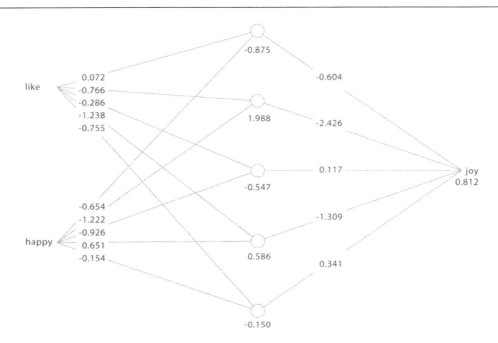

Figure 8.15 – DNN trained to classify tweets with either happy or like, but not both, as joy

If *like* is on but *happy* is off, then the second hidden node will be on with a score of 1.22 (i.e. -0.766+1.988), which will propagate through to the output node as -2.96 (1.22*-2.46). This will then be added to the bias of the output node to produce -2.15. If *happy* is on but *like* is not, then the second and fourth hidden nodes will be on, with scores of 0.76 and 1.23, which will propagate through to the output node as -0.766*0.76 (for the second hidden node) + -1.309*1.23, which when added to the bias for the output node becomes -2.66. If both the input nodes are on, then none of the hidden nodes will be, so the score at the output node is just its own bias – that is, 0.81. For networks with just one output, the standard logistic function used for interpreting the final score treats negative numbers as being on and positive ones as off, so this network classifies tweets that contain just *like* or *happy* as expressing joy and ones that contain both as not expressing it.

Adding hidden units will let the network recognize significant combinations of input features as being non-compositional, in that the effect of the combination is not just the cumulative effect of the features themselves. We can also see that if you do not have enough hidden features, then the training process can get stuck in local minima – although you *can* compute XOR using just three features in the hidden layer, it is very difficult to train such a network for this task (see (Minsky & Papert, 1969) for further discussion of this issue). This is not just a matter of not having enough data, or of not allowing the network to train for long enough. Networks with hidden layers with three nodes converge very quickly (after about 10 or 12 epochs) and ones with four just take a few hundred. We can also add extra layers – networks with two hidden layers with four and three nodes each can also solve this problem and typically converge slightly more quickly than ones with one hidden layer with five nodes:

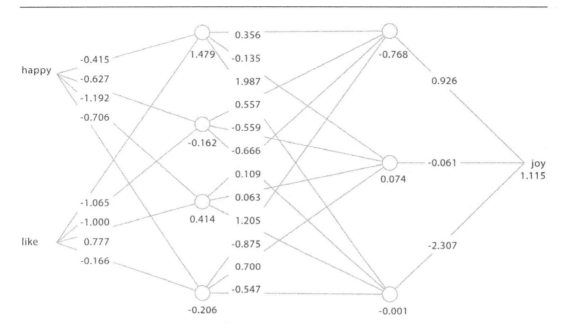

Figure 8.16 – Network with two hidden layers for solving XOR

The problem is that setting the initial weights and biases at random in small networks nearly always leaves you in an area of the search space where you will end up in a local minimum. Using larger networks, on the other hand, nearly always produces networks that can solve the problem since there will be nodes that are in the right part of the search space that can be given increasing significance, but they take much longer to train. So, the key task is to find the appropriate number of hidden units.

The role of a hidden unit is to find words that feed differently into the output nodes when they occur in isolation and when they occur in combinations with other words. The two key parameters here seem likely to be the number of input features (that is, the number of distinct words in the data) and the number of output classes (that is, the number of emotions). If there are more words in the lexicon, then there are more possible combinations of words, which might mean that having more words requires more hidden nodes. If there are more output classes, then there are more places where having combinations of words might be helpful.

Given that there are many thousands of words in the lexicons for our datasets, but only four to eleven emotions, it seems sensible to start by investigating the effect of relating the number of hidden nodes to the number of emotions. *Figure 8.17* shows what happens when we have a hidden layer with 0.5 times as many nodes as there are emotions, 1 times as many, or 1.5 times as many:

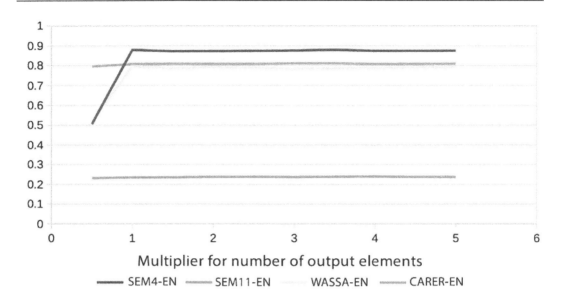

Figure 8.17 – Jaccard score versus the number of hidden nodes = F*number of emotions, F from 0.5 to 5

For the three datasets for which we obtained quite good results with an SNN, the effect of adding a hidden layer with a moderate number of nodes is substantial. The original scores have been repeated here for ease of reference:

	Precision	**Recall**	**Micro F1**	**Macro F1**	**Jaccard**
SEM4-EN	0.902	0.902	0.902	0.902	0.822
SEM11-EN	0.648	0.275	0.386	0.388	0.239
WASSA-EN	0.837	0.837	0.837	0.837	0.720
CARER-EN	0.901	0.901	0.901	0.901	0.820

Figure 8.18 – Simple neural network applied to the standard English datasets

The original Jaccard score for CARER-EN was 0.77, which is equivalent to around 0.87 accuracy; when we add a hidden layer with half as many nodes as the number of emotions in CARER (that is, with just three nodes in the hidden layer since CARER has six emotions), we get a better score (Jaccard 0.79, accuracy 0.89) than in the original, and then as we increase the number of hidden nodes to 6, 9, 12, we get a very gradual improvement, up to the point where the score seems to have flattened out and maybe even started to overtrain.

A similar, but more marked, pattern occurs with SEM4-EN and WASSA-EN. In these cases, the score starts fairly low when we only have half as many nodes in the hidden layer as we have emotions (that is, just two for both of these), but then leaps up considerably higher than the original scores as soon as we have as many nodes in the hidden layer as we have emotions and then flattens out at around Jaccard 0.875 (accuracy 0.93) for SEM4-EN and Jaccard 0.81 (accuracy 0.9) for WASSA-EN. In general, it looks as though adding a hidden layer with a modest number of nodes produces some improvement over the basic neural network with no hidden units, but experiments with more hidden layers or a single hidden layer with more nodes suggest that these improvements are fairly limited. This is likely to be because hidden layers look for non-compositional combinations of words. There are two possible reasons why this has limited effects:

- There simply are not all that many cases of words whose emotional weight changes when they co-occur with specific partners
- Where there are such combinations, their frequency in the data is not enough to override their normal interpretation

It may be that using much more training data makes using networks with multiple or large hidden layers more effective, but with modest-sized datasets, doing so has comparatively little effect.

Summary

In this chapter, we looked at using neural networks for our task of identifying the emotions expressed in informal communications such as tweets. We examined the way that the lexicon for the datasets is used as the nodes in the input layer and looked at how the weights associated with individual words reflect the emotional significance of those words. We considered simple neural networks with no hidden layers and also slightly deeper ones with a single hidden layer with slightly more nodes than the set of output nodes – the performance of the neural network flattened out once the hidden layer contained 1.5 to 2 times as many nodes as the output layer, so there seemed little point.

The highest-scoring algorithms for the various datasets are now as follows:

	LEX (unstemmed)	LEX (stemmed)	CP (stemmed)	NB (multi)	SVM (single)	MULTI-SVM	SNN (single)	DNN
SEM4-EN	0.503	0.497	0.593	0.778	0.845		0.829	*0.847*
SEM11-EN	0.347	0.348	0.353	0.267	0.224	*0.385*	0.242	0.246
WASSA-EN	0.445	0.437	0.505	0.707	*0.770*		0.737	0.752
CARER-EN	0.350	0.350	0.395	0.774	0.770		*0.820*	0.804
IMDB-EN	0.722	0.667	0.722	0.740	0.736		*0.793*	*0.793*
SEM4-AR	0.506	0.509	0.513	*0.532*	0.514		0.504	0.444
SEM11-AR	0.378	*0.386*	0.382	0.274	0.216	0.340	0.221	0.207
KWT.M-AR	*0.687*	0.663	0.666	0.507	0.631	0.341	0.028	0.026
SEM4-ES	*0.425*	0.420	0.177	0.331	0.412		0.337	0.343
SEM11-ES	0.269	0.271	*0.278*	0.255	0.226	0.268	0.221	0.222

Figure 8.19 – Scores for the best algorithms so far

Neural networks produced the best results in 4 of the 10 datasets, but the simple lexical algorithms are still the best for the multi-label datasets. The general lesson remains the same as it was at the end of *Chapter 7, Support Vector Machines* – you shouldn't just accept that there is a single best classification algorithm: do experiments, try out variations, and see for yourself what works best with your data.

References

To learn more about the topics that were covered in this chapter, take a look at the following resources:

- Fukushima, K. (1969). *Visual Feature Extraction by a Multilayered Network of Analog Threshold Elements*. IEEE Transactions on Systems Science and Cybernetics, 5(4), 322–333. https://doi.org/10.1109/TSSC.1969.300225.

- Hebb, D. O. (1949). *The organization of behavior: A neuropsychological theory*. Wiley.

- Hinton, G. E., Osindero, S., & Teh, Y.-W. (2006). *A Fast Learning Algorithm for Deep Belief Nets*. Neural Comput., 18(7), 1527–1554. https://doi.org/10.1162/neco.2006.18.7.1527.

- McCulloch, W. S., & Pitts, W. (1943). *A logical calculus of the ideas immanent in nervous activity*. The Bulletin of Mathematical Biophysics, 5(4), 115–133. https://doi.org/10.1007/BF02478259.

- Minsky, M., & Papert, S. (1969). *Perceptrons*. MIT Press.

- Rumelhart, D. E., Hinton, G. E., & Williams, R. J. (1986). *Learning representations by back-propagating errors*. Nature, 323(6088), 533–536. https://doi.org/10.1038/323533a0.

9

Exploring Transformers

Transformers are a new type of machine learning model that has completely revolutionized the way human language is processed and understood. These models can analyze huge amounts of data, find and understand complex patterns with hitherto unmatched accuracy, and produce insights that would otherwise be impossible for humans to obtain on tasks such as translation, text summarization, and text generation.

Transformers are powerful because they can handle large amounts of data, and learn from previous examples to make better predictions. They have totally "transformed" (pun intended) **NLP** and have outperformed traditional methods in many NLP tasks, quickly becoming state of the art.

In this chapter, we will introduce transformers, discuss how they work, and look at some of their key components. We will then present Hugging Face and see how it helps in our task before introducing some useful existing transformer models. We'll also show how we can use Hugging Face to implement two models using transformers.

This chapter will demonstrate how to build transformer models while taking you through important steps such as linking Google Colab to Google Drive so that files can be persisted, preparing the data, using auto classes, and ultimately building models that can be used for classification.

We will cover the following topics:

- Introduction to transformers
- How data flows through the transformer
- Hugging Face
- Existing models
- Transformers for classification
- Implementing transformers

Let's begin by having a closer look at transformers, who invented them, and how they work.

Introduction to transformers

In this chapter, we will briefly introduce transformers. In language and NLP tasks, context plays a crucial role – that is, to know what a word means, knowledge about the situation (that is, the context) must also be taken into account. Before transformers came along, sequence-to-sequence models were used for many NLP tasks. These are models that generate an output sequence by predicting a single word at a time and encode the source text to gain knowledge about the context. However, the problem with languages is that they are complex, fluid, and difficult to turn into a rigid rule-based structure. The context itself is also hard to track as it is often found far away (that is, many words, sentences, or even paragraphs) from where it is required. To address this problem, sequence-to-sequence models work by using neural networks, which have some limited form of memory:

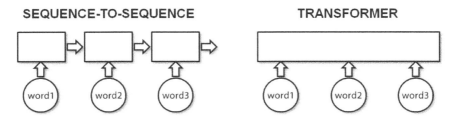

Figure 9.1 – Sequence-to-sequence model versus transformer

The ubiquitous paper on transformers, *Attention Is All You Need*, was published by Vaswani et al., in 2017. They presented a new type of neural network architecture, known as **transformers**, which could be used for NLP tasks. Transformers have several components, as can be seen in *Figure 9.2*, with an "encoder" (on the left), a "decoder" (on the right), and a block of attention and feed-forward components that repeat *N* times:

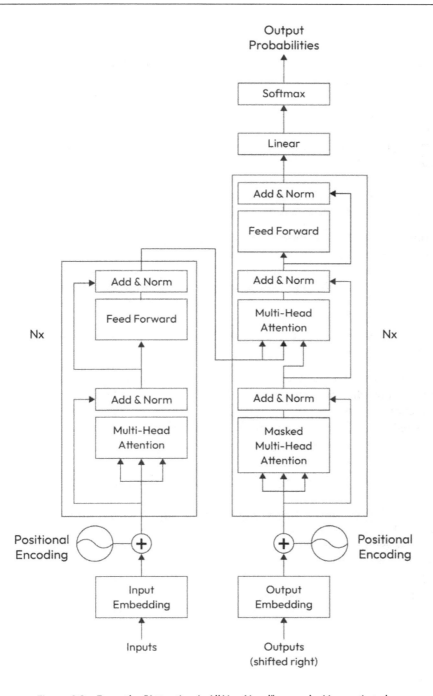

Figure 9.2 – From the "Attention Is All You Need" paper by Vaswani et al.

The transformer consists of encoder and decoder layers; each usually has more than one identical instance (for example, six as in the original research paper), and each has its own set of weights. On the left-hand side, the encoder's job is to convert a sequence of inputs into a set of continuous representations. On the right-hand side, the decoder uses the output from the encoder as well as the output from the previous time step to produce a sequence of outputs. The first encoder and decoder in each stack of the architecture has an embedding layer and positional encoding as inputs. Each encoder contains a self-attention layer that calculates the relationships between different words and a feed-forward layer. Each decoder also contains a feed-forward layer, but it has two self-attention layers. The output from the last encoder is used as the input to the first decoder. These components combine to make the transformer architecture faster and more efficient and allow it to handle much longer sequences, making the separation between words irrelevant. Consequently, the architecture can outperform other, more traditional, methods.

The transformer architecture described by Vaswani et al. was created with the goal of translation. The encoder is fed inputs (that is, sentences) in one language (for example, English) during training, while the decoder is fed the same inputs (that is, sentences) in the intended target language (for example, French). The attention layers in the encoder make use of each word in an input sentence, but the encoder operates sequentially and can only focus on the words in the translated text (that is, only the words before the word that is currently being generated). For example, if the first N words of the translated target have been predicted, these are input to the decoder, which uses all the inputs of the encoder to predict the word at $N+1$.

The decoder is supplied with the entire target sentence but is constrained from using forthcoming words. Consequently, when predicting a word, the decoder cannot refer to any words beyond it in the target sentence. For instance, while predicting the *Nth* word, only the words in positions *1* to *N-1* can be considered by the attention layer. This constraint is crucial to guarantee that the task remains suitably demanding for the model to acquire knowledge competently.

How data flows through the transformer model

In this section, we will take a closer look at how data flows through the transformer model. Understanding how data flows through a transformer, and the steps that transform raw input into meaningful output, is crucial to understanding its power and potential. The transformer enables efficient and effective modeling of long-range dependencies in data, making it highly capable of capturing context and semantics. By exploring these inner mechanisms of data flow within the transformer, we will gain a deeper understanding of its ability to process and understand language. We will look at input embeddings first.

Input embeddings

Starting on the left-hand side, the inputs into the encoder are word tokens from the source text. This textual data has to be converted into a numeric representation (of size 512 according to the authors) using methods such as GloVe or Word2Vec, among others.

Positional encoding

A positional element is then added to these embeddings. This is important as it allows the transformer to discover information about the distances between words and the order of the words. This information is then passed to the self-attention layer of the first encoder block.

> **Note**
> Positional encodings do not alter the vector dimensions.

Encoders

Each encoder has several sub-layers within it:

- **Multi-headed attention**: This allows the transformer to attend to different parts of the input sequence at the same time, thus improving its input processing abilities, and allowing it to obtain more context and make much better-informed decisions. It is the most important part of the architecture and is also the most computationally expensive. When working on words in the input, self-attention relates every word in the input to every other word. It is interesting to consider how the transformer decides which set of weights will yield the best results. The aim is that the attention value should be large for words that are somehow related in a sentence, and vice versa. For example, let's look at the sentence *The weather was very sunny.*

  The words *weather* and *sunny* are related and hence should generate a high attention value; conversely, the attention value for *The* and *was* should be small. As described earlier, transformers are trained on embeddings. Consequently, the transformer will learn from them and be able to produce the vectors required so that words produce attention values that correspond to the relatedness of the words. Furthermore, instead of just considering individual meanings, the self-attention mechanism weighs the input words differently according to their importance and their relationships with other words. This allows it to be able to handle the aforementioned long-distance context problems and hence achieve much better performance on NLP tasks. Briefly, the attention value is computed using three matrices, with each row in each matrix representing an input word. It is important to note that the values in these rows are learned by the model so that the desired outputs are generated. Let's take a look at each of these important matrices in turn:

  - **Query**: Each row corresponds to the embeddings of an input word. In other words, the query word is the specific word for which an attention value is being calculated.

  - **Key**: Each word in the input text that the model is comparing the query to – that is, the word that is being paid attention to – to calculate its importance to the query word.

  - **Value**: The information that the model is trying to generate based on the comparison between the query and key matrices. The key and value matrices can be the same.

Given these matrices, the attention value is obtained by calculating the dot product of the query and key matrices. These are then used to weigh the value matrix, hence effectively allowing the model to "learn" which words in the input text should be focused upon.

- **Add and norm**: These layers comprise a residual connection layer followed by a normalization layer. For our purposes, it is enough to know that they help address the vanishing gradient problem and improve the model's performance.

- **Feed-forward neural network**: This is a neural network that processes the attention vector inputs and transforms them into a form, of the same dimensions as the input, that can be input into the next layer. These attention vectors are independent of each other; consequently, parallelization can be used in this stage, rather than processing them sequentially as in the sequence-to-sequence architecture.

Let's now move on to decoders.

Decoders

The output from the encoder is used as the input to the second layer of each decoder in the decoder stack.

Similar to the encoder, masked multi-headed attention takes an output embedding and a positional embedding. The target for the transformer is to learn how to generate the output, given both the input and the required output.

> **Note**
> During training, the required output (for example, a translation) is provided to the decoder.

Some of the words are masked so that the model can learn how to predict them. These are changed during each iteration. The decoders process this along with the encoded representation from the encoders to produce a target sequence.

However, during prediction, an empty sequence (with a special **start of sentence** (<SOS>) token) is used. This is converted into an embedding; positional encoding is added and is used as input to the decoder. The decoder and other layers work as before but the last word from the output sequence is used to fill in the first blank of the input sequence, hence the input is now the <SOS> and the first predicted word. This is, again, fed into the decoder and the process is repeated until the end of the sentence.

Linear layer

The output from the decoder is used as input to this linear layer, a simple fully connected neural network that generates the vectors for the next layer.

Softmax layer

The softmax layer transforms the input into a probability distribution – that is, it takes a set of numbers and turns them into positive numbers that sum up to 1, applying higher importance to higher values and less importance to smaller values.

Output probabilities

Finally, the output probabilities are the word tokens for the target. The transformer compares this output with the target sequence that came from the training data and uses it to improve the results via back-propagation.

Now that we've learned how transformers work, in the next section, we will have a very brief look at how one organization has made the process of implementing and experimenting with transformer-based models easy, making it accessible to all.

Hugging Face

Transformers need a *lot* of data to be effective and produce good results. Furthermore, a huge amount of computing power and time is also needed; the best models are usually trained using multiple GPUs and can take days (or even longer) to complete training. Consequently, not everyone can afford to train such models and usually, this is done by the big players such as Google, Facebook, and OpenAI. Luckily, there are pretrained models available.

The name Hugging Face (named after the emoji with a smiling face and open hands) is synonymous with transformers, models, and NLP. Hugging Face (https://huggingface.co) provides a repository for pretrained transformer (and other) models to be published. These can then be easily downloaded, free of charge, and used for a wide range of NLP tasks. Furthermore, if the task involves a domain that has unique nomenclature, terminology, and domain-specific language, then models can be "fine-tuned" to improve the model's performance. Fine-tuning is a process that uses the weights from a pretrained model as a starting point and uses new domain-specific data to update them so that the model becomes better at the domain-specific task. As well as publishing models, Hugging Face also provides services that allow models to be fine-tuned, trained, and much more.

Hugging Face also provides a Python library that provides a high-level interface for NLP tasks. The library offers a wide range of state-of-the-art pretrained models, including BERT, GPT, RoBERTa, T5, and many others (see the next section). It can be installed using the following command:

```
pip install transformers
```

Apart from downloading pretrained models, the library can also be used to download tokenizers. Both of these can then be used with your datasets to fine-tune tasks such as classification to create state-of-the-art NLP systems.

In summary, the Hugging Face `transformers` library is a powerful tool for working with NLP models, making it easy to work with transformer models. It has an intuitive design and extensive model selection and is well worth a look.

Existing models

Driven by boosts in computing, storage, and data capacity, transformers have taken the world by storm. Some of the more famous pretrained models include the following:

- **Bidirectional Encoder Representations from Transformers (BERT)**: Created by the Google AI team, and trained on a huge corpus of text data, BERT takes the context from both the left and right sides of each word into account.

- **Efficiently Learning an Encoder that Classifies Token Accurately (ELECTRA)**: ELECTRA uses a generator-discriminator model to distinguish between generated and real text. The generator is trained to generate text that is similar to real text, while the discriminator is trained to distinguish between real and generated text.

- **Generative Pre-trained Transformer 3 (GPT-3)**: Developed by OpenAI and pretrained on a huge range of internet text, GPT-3 has 175 billion parameters and is one of the largest models available to date.

- **Megatron (a large transformer model trained by NVIDIA)**: Developed by NVIDIA, Megatron is scalable and can be trained on hundreds of GPUs, so it can use much larger models.

- **Robustly Optimized BERT (RoBERTa)**: Based on BERT, RoBERTa is designed to improve upon BERT by using a larger training corpus and more training steps to learn more robust representations of text.

- **Text-to-Text Transfer Transformer (T5)**: Developed by Google, T5 treats NLP problems as "text-to-text" problems. It is trained on unlabeled and labeled data and then fine-tunes it individually for a variety of tasks.

- **Transformer with extra-long context (Transformer-XL)**: This model introduces a memory module that allows the model to handle and understand long-term dependencies much better.

- **XLNet (generalized autoregressive pretraining)**: Developed by Google, XLNet takes the best bits from Transformer-XL and BERT and models dependencies between all input words.

In the next section, we look will look closer at how transformers are trained for the task we are interested in: classification. Inspiration for this section came from the Hugging Face pages.

Transformers for classification

Transformer models are trained as language models. These are a type of algorithm that has been trained by analyzing patterns of human language to understand and produce human language.

They have knowledge of grammar, syntax, and semantics, and can discern patterns and connections among words and phrases. Moreover, they can detect named entities, such as individuals, locations, and establishments, and interpret the context in which they are referenced. Essentially, a transformer model is a computer program that uses statistical models to analyze and generate language.

Language models are trained in a self-supervised manner on large amounts of text data, such as books, articles, and online content, to learn patterns and relationships between words and phrases. Some of the popular datasets used for pretraining transformers include Common Crawl, Wikipedia, and BooksCorpus. For example, BERT was trained using around 3.5 billion words in total with around 2.5 billion from Wikipedia and around 1 billion from BooksCorpus. This allows the model to predict the likelihood of a certain word or phrase occurring after a given sequence of words. The outputs of a pretrained large language model typically involve predictions based on the input text. The model may output probabilities of certain words or phrases being used next in a sentence, make predictions of the most likely word to follow a given input word, or generate an entire sentence or paragraph based on the input text. The output can be used for various purposes, such as text generation, translation, sentiment analysis, and more.

Self-supervised learning is a type of machine learning where the model learns to extract useful information from unlabeled data without requiring any explicit labels or supervision. Instead, the model is trained on a task such as predicting the missing part of an image or reconstructing a corrupted sentence. Consequently, this type of model builds an understanding of the language it has been trained on – but only from a statistical point of view. However, this approach lacks practicality for everyday tasks, and therefore, a generalized **pretrained** model must be customized through supervised **fine-tuning** using human-annotated labels specific to the task at hand.

Pretraining (that is, training a model from scratch) requires huge amounts of data, and hence the process can take weeks or months. Fine-tuning is then performed *on* the pretrained model, so a pretrained language model is required to do the fine-tuning. Essentially, fine-tuning is a further training step with a dataset that suits the task.

Fine-tuning a model typically adjusts the weights of the model's pretrained layers to better fit a new dataset or task. The process of fine-tuning involves initializing the weights of the pretrained layers, and then training the entire model on the new dataset or task. During training, the weights of the pretrained layers are updated along with the weights of the newly added layers, allowing the model to learn more nuanced features from the new dataset while preserving the knowledge learned from the pretrained model. The degree to which the weights of the pretrained layers are updated during fine-tuning depends on the specifics of the new task and the amount of available data. In some cases, only the weights of the newly added layers are updated, while in others, the weights of the pretrained layers may be updated significantly. Another option is to keep all layers fixed apart from the final layer, whose weights are then modified during training. Consequently, fixing the layers with these techniques, and using a smaller learning rate, during the fine-tuning process, often yields a performance improvement. Sometimes, this goes hand in hand with adding new layers on top of the old architecture, thus persisting the old fixed weights and only allowing the weights of new layers to be changed.

But what exactly happens when fine-tuning? There are various techniques, but the general thought is that early layers learn generic patterns that are irrelevant to the actual task (for example, classification), while later layers learn the patterns that are relevant to the task. This intuition has been verified by various research teams.

> **Note**
> During the gradient descent calculation, the size of the step that's taken in each iteration is determined by the learning rate, with the overall goal being to locate the minimum of a loss function.

In practical terms, for classification, we would download a model such as **BertForSequenceClassification** – a BERT model with a linear layer for sentence classification. So, the final layer produces a probability vector that indicates the probability of each potential class label for the input sequence.

In short, fine-tuning a model enables it to adapt features it has learned to a new task or dataset, which can result in improved performance.

We looked at the individual bits of the model earlier in this chapter and saw how the model has encoder and decoder blocks. Depending on the task, each of these parts can be utilized separately. For the classification task, an encoder-only model is recommended. For more details, there are some great Packt books available, such as *Transformers for Natural Language Processing*, by Denis Rothman.

In the next section, we will fine-tune a model using a training dataset, make some predictions on a test dataset, and evaluate the results.

Implementing transformers

In this section, we will work through the code for implementing transformers for both single-emotion and multi-emotion datasets. We will be using **Google Colaboratory** (**Colab**) as it simplifies the implementation of transformers by providing a powerful cloud-based environment with pre-installed libraries and resources. So, let's begin by looking at that.

Google Colab

Google Colab is a free notebook environment service that runs in the cloud (https://colab.research.google.com). There are many benefits of using Colab; for example, it allows developers to start programming rapidly without having to worry about setup, it allows code to be shared with people who do not have the correct software installed locally, and it also integrates well with GitHub. However, one of the biggest advantages is that Google provides free access to GPUs. Machine learning, at its core, involves lots and lots of mathematical operations – something that GPUs are good at. In practical terms, even for simple models with small training datasets, the time-saving between GPU and non-GPU-powered systems can be many hours (for example, 10 minutes compared to 10 hours).

A few words of warning, though. Colab is ephemeral – in other words, files (for example, data files) uploaded to a session or generated by a session (for example, results) will eventually disappear. The workaround for this is to upload files to Google Drive and give permission for Colab to access them.

Debugging on Colab is also a little more cumbersome than, say, via VS Code. It involves installing and importing the `ipdb` (IPython-enabled Python Debugger) package:

```
!pip install -Uqq ipdb
import ipdb
```

Breakpoints are useful for developers and these can be set via code to cause the debugger to stop:

```
ipdb.set_trace()
```

We can use command-line arguments to control the debugger, such as the following:

- `c`: Continue execution
- `n`: Move to the next line
- `r`: Continue execution until the current function returns

Debugging can be globally turned off using the following command:

```
%pdb off
```

Debugging can also be globally turned on using the following command:

```
%pdb on
```

Now that we know what a transformer is, how it works, and how to implement it, let's implement a transformer in Python using Colab to classify the datasets introduced in the previous chapters.

Single-emotion datasets

We will implement two transformers to cater to the two different types of datasets. Let's start with the single-emotion task. Broadly, we will be following these steps:

1. Install the necessary libraries.
2. Import the necessary libraries.
3. Provide access to Google Drive.
4. Create dataset and model variables.
5. Load and prepare the datasets.
6. Tokenize the datasets.
7. Load a model for classification.

8. Set up trainer arguments.

9. Train the model.

10. Use the trained model to predict.

11. Evaluate.

Classifying the single-emotion tweets is a somewhat easier task, so let's being with this.

Let's begin by installing some libraries:

```
!pip install datasets
!pip install evaluate
!pip install transformers
```

These libraries are used to easily access datasets, evaluate the results of a model, and access the pretrained models available from Hugging Face, respectively. We can now import these into our code:

```
import datasets
from datasets import load_dataset
from enum import Enum
import evaluate
from evaluate import evaluator
import numpy as np
from sklearn.metrics import jaccard_score
from transformers import (
    AutoModelForSequenceClassification,
    AutoTokenizer,
    Pipeline,
    Trainer,
    TrainingArguments
)
import pandas as pd
from pathlib import Path

from google.colab import drive
```

As mentioned previously, we want to upload our training and test files once and access them on-demand whenever we need them, so let's give Colab access to our Google Drive, which is where the files are uploaded. In reality, some of these files are already available via the datasets library, but for now, let's assume we want to access them from our repository:

```
drive.mount("/content/gdrive/", force_remount=True)
BASE_PATH = "/content/gdrive/MyDrive/PacktBook/Data/C9"
```

> **Note**
> You should replace `BASE_PATH` with your own path.

We should now set up a few things to make our task easier for us. Different datasets need different parameters, so enum can be used to control the execution flow of the code. We must name our files so that the names contain the language code of the tweets within the file (that is, AR, ES, and EN), and then use enum and the filename to set variables that are useful in the code:

```
class Dataset(Enum):
  SEM4_EN=1
  WASSA_EN=2
  CARER_EN=3
  SEM4_AR=4
  SEM4_ES=5
  IMDB_EN=6
```

For now, we will also set a variable such as `NUM_LABELS` to tell the model how many labels there are. Later, we will see that we don't need to do this:

```
# set the required dataset here
ds = Dataset.SEM4_EN
NUM_LABELS = 4
COLS = 'ID', 'tweet', 'label'
```

Now, we can use enum to set some dataset-specific variables. This way, when we want to try other datasets, we only need to modify the `ds` variable:

```
if (ds == Dataset.SEM4_EN):
  training_file = "SEM4_EN_train.csv"
  test_file = "SEM4_EN_dev.csv"
elif (ds == Dataset.WASSA_EN):
  training_file = "WASSA_train.csv"
  test_file = "WASSA_dev.csv"
elif(ds == Dataset.CARER_EN):
  training_file = "CARER_EN_train.csv"
  test_file = "CARER_EN_dev.csv"
  NUM_LABELS = 6
elif(ds == Dataset.SEM4_ES):
  training_file = "SEM4_ES_train.csv"
  test_file = "SEM4_ES_dev.csv"
  NUM_LABELS = 5
elif(ds == Dataset.SEM4_AR):
  training_file = "SEM4_AR_train.csv"
  test_file = "SEM4_AR_dev.csv"
```

```
elif(ds == Dataset.IMDB_EN):
  NUM_LABELS = 2
  training_file = "IMDB_EN_train.csv"
  test_file = "IMDB_EN_dev.csv"
```

We must also set `model_name` to tell the program which language-specific model to use:

```
# select a model
if "_AR_" in training_file:
  model_name = "asafaya/bert-base-arabic"
elif "_EN_" in training_file:
  model_name = "bert-base-cased"
elif "_ES_" in training_file:
  model_name = "dccuchile/bert-base-spanish-wwm-cased"
```

Then, we can set various file path variables:

```
# add the base path
training_file = f"{BASE_PATH}/{training_file}"
test_file = f"{BASE_PATH}/{test_file}"
```

Finally, we must set a variable called `stub`, which we will use to save our model:

```
# get file name for saving
stub = (Path(training_file).stem)
```

The Hugging Face `transformers` library works well with the `datasets` library. So, next, we will load the data files, remove any unwanted columns, and create a `DatasetDict` object that will be used in subsequent parts of the pipeline:

```
def get_tweets_dataset():
  data_files = {"train": training_file, "test": test_file}
  ds = datasets.load_dataset("csv", data_files=data_files,
                             delimiter=",",
                             encoding='utf-8')
  ds_columns = ds['train'].column_names
  drop_columns = [x for x in ds_columns if x not in COLS]
  ds = ds.remove_columns(drop_columns)

  dd = datasets.DatasetDict({"train":ds["train"],
                             "test":ds["test"]})

  return dd

dataset = get_tweets_dataset()
```

Next, we must create a function that tokenizes the tweets from the training and test datasets that are held in the `dataset` variable. Simply put, the job of the tokenizer is to prepare the data, making it ready for input to a model. It does this by splitting sentences into words (tokens) and then splitting words into pieces (for example, *flyfishing* would be split into *fly*, *fish*, and *ing*). These tokens are then split into IDs (numbers) via a lookup table. Typically, you would use the tokenizer associated with the model that you are using. For example, for the `bert-base-cased` model, you would use `BertTokenizer`. However, in the following code, we have used something called `AutoTokenizer`. `AutoTokenizer` is a generic tokenizer auto class that automatically fetches the correct tokenizer class from the Hugging Face tokenizers library, as well as the data associated with the model's tokenizer. An auto class is a generic class that simplifies the coding process by automatically finding the architecture of a pretrained model based on its name. All we need to do is choose the appropriate `AutoModel` for our task. Essentially, they are more flexible and make the programming somewhat simpler:

```
tokenizer = AutoTokenizer.from_pretrained(model_name)

def tokenise_function(tweets):
    return tokenizer(tweets["tweet"],
                     padding="max_length",
                     truncation=True,
                     max_length = 512)

tokenised_datasets = dataset.map(tokenise_function, batched=True)
```

Now comes the interesting part! We need to load a model for classification. As before, we could have used a specific BERT model that has been trained for sentence classification, such as `BertForSequenceClassification`. However, we have chosen to use an auto class to obtain the text classification model. In this case, since we are classifying text, we used `AutoModelForSequenceClassification` as `AutoModel`. We just supplied the name of the model and the number of labels that we are dealing with – the library takes care of the rest:

```
model = AutoModelForSequenceClassification.from_pretrained(
    model_name,
    num_labels=NUM_LABELS)
training_args = TrainingArguments(output_dir=f"{stub}")
```

We are now ready to train the model, but first, we need to set up some arguments specifying what we want the trainer to do. We can do this by simply creating a `TrainingArguments` instance telling it where to save our model and that we want it to evaluate at the end of each epoch. The arguments are passed to `Trainer`, along with the model and the training and test datasets. Now, it is a simple matter of invoking the training and waiting for the results. Note how we save the resultant model:

```
training_args = TrainingArguments(
    output_dir=f"{stub}",
    evaluation_strategy="epoch")
```

```
trainer = Trainer(
    model=model,
    args=training_args,
    train_dataset=tokenised_datasets["train"],
    eval_dataset=tokenised_datasets["test"],
)

trainer.train()
trainer.save_model(stub)
```

If all went well, you should see something like this (truncated):

```
The following columns in the training set don't have a corresponding
argument in `BertForSequenceClassification.forward` and have
been ignored: ID, tweet. If ID, tweet are not expected by
`BertForSequenceClassification.forward`,  you can safely ignore this
message.
/usr/local/lib/python3.8/dist-packages/transformers/optimization.
py:306: FutureWarning: This implementation of AdamW is deprecated and
will be removed in a future version. Use the PyTorch implementation
torch.optim.AdamW instead, or set `no_deprecation_warning=True` to
disable this warning
  warnings.warn(
***** Running training *****
  Num examples = 3860
  Num Epochs = 3
  Instantaneous batch size per device = 8
  Total train batch size (w. parallel, distributed & accumulation) = 8
  Gradient Accumulation steps = 1
  Total optimization steps = 1449
  Number of trainable parameters = 108313348
  [1449/1449 19:47, Epoch 3/3]
Epoch  Training Loss  Validation Loss
1  No log  0.240059
2  0.555900  0.210987
3  0.208900  0.179072


Training completed. Do not forget to share your model on huggingface.
co/models =)

Saving model checkpoint to SEM4_EN_train
Configuration saved in SEM4_EN_train/config.json
Model weights saved in SEM4_EN_train/pytorch_model.bin
```

> **Note**
>
> The algorithms and programs used in this chapter all randomize aspects of the data, particularly the initial assignments of weights to internal nodes of the network, and hence the results that you obtain by running the same scripts on the same data may vary slightly from the results in the text.

Now that we have a model fine-tuned on our dataset, we can see whether it does a good job on our test dataset:

```
predictions = trainer.predict(tokenized_datasets["test"])
```

Finally, we can set up a dictionary of measures and iterate through them, computing and printing as we go:

```
model_predictions = np.argmax(predictions.predictions,
    axis=1)
model_predictions = model_predictions.tolist()
model_references = tokenised_datasets["test"]["label"]
measures = [
                ["precision" , "macro"],
                ["recall" , "macro"],
                ["f1" , "micro"],
                ["f1" , "macro"],
                ["jaccard" , "macro"],
                ["accuracy" , None],
            ]


for measure in measures:
  measure_name = measure[0]
  average = measure[1]
  if measure_name = = "jaccard":
    results = get_jaccard_score(references = model_references,
    predictions = model_predictions,average = average)
  else:
    metric = evaluate.load(measure_name)
    if measure_name=="accuracy":
      results = metric.compute(references = model_references,
      predictions = model_predictions)
    else:
      results = metric.compute(references = model_references,
        predictions = model_predictions, average = average)

  print(measure_name, average, results[measure_name])
```

This will generate something like this:

```
precision macro 0.9577305808563304
recall macro 0.9592563645499727
f1 micro 0.9576446280991735
f1 macro 0.9576513771741846
jaccard macro 0.9192365565992706
accuracy None 0.9576446280991735
```

The results from the model are summarized in the following table:

Dataset	Precision	Recall	micro F1	macro F1	Jaccard
SEM4-EN	**0.962**	**0.964**	**0.962**	**0.962**	**0.927**
WASSA-EN	0.855	0.861	0.855	0.856	0.753
CARER-EN	0.881	0.921	0.927	0.896	0.816
SEM4-AR	**0.817**	**0.837**	**0.843**	**0.825**	**0.710**
SEM4-ES	**0.791**	**0.786**	**0.807**	**0.787**	**0.663**
IMDB-EN	**0.905**	**0.905**	**0.905**	**0.905**	**0.826**

Table 9.1 – Scores for transformer-based models for the single-label datasets

Most of the scores here are better than the scores that we obtained using the classifiers earlier in this book, though the best classifier for WASSA-EN and CARER-EN remains the single-class SVM. The scores for SEM4-AR and SEM4-ES are both significantly better than the previous scores, possibly because the pretrained models do a better job of finding roots, and maybe even doing disambiguation, than the simple stemmers we used in the earlier chapters. It is very hard to extract intermediate results from a complex DNN such as a transformer, so it is even more difficult than was the case in previous chapters to analyze why one classifier of this kind does better than another, but it seems likely that this is a key factor in these cases.

Multi-emotion datasets

Now, let's build a transformer model to classify multi-label tweets. Much of the code is similar, so we won't reproduce that, concentrating instead on the interesting bits of the multi-classification problem. We will be following these steps:

1. Install the necessary libraries.
2. Import the necessary libraries.
3. Provide access to Google Drive.
4. Create dataset variables.
5. Convert datasets into `DatasetDict`.

6. Load and prepare the datasets.

7. Tokenize the datasets.

8. Load a model for classification.

9. Define metric functions.

10. Set up trainer arguments.

11. Train the model.

12. Evaluate.

Let's begin!

We must install and import the libraries as before, and also allow access to Google Drive as before. Now, let's get the data files from the online repository. However, the KWT files are in Google Drive, so we need some code to load and convert these into a DatasetDict object:

```
def get_kwt_tweets_dataset(code):
  if code == "KWTM":
    training_file = "train-KWT-M.csv"
    test_file = "test-KWT-M.csv"
  else:
    training_file = "train-KWT-U.csv"
    test_file = "test-KWT-U.csv"

  # add the base path
  training_file = f"{BASE_PATH}/{training_file}"
  test_file = f"{BASE_PATH}/{test_file}"

  data_files = {"train": training_file, "validation": test_file}
  ds = datasets.load_dataset("csv", data_files=data_files,
      delimiter=",",encoding='utf-8')

  dd = datasets.DatasetDict(
                          {"train":ds["train"],
                           "validation":ds["validation"]
                          })
  return dd
```

Our Dataset enum now also reflects the fact that we are working with different files, so let's use enum to get the right data files and set the model:

```
class Dataset(Enum):
  SEM11_AR=1
  SEM11_EN=2
```

```
  SEM11_ES=3
  KWT_M_AR=4
  KWT_U_AR=5

ds = Dataset.SEM11_EN

if (ds == Dataset.SEM11_AR):
  dataset = load_dataset("sem_eval_2018_task_1",
    "subtask5.arabic")
  model_name = "asafaya/bert-base-arabic"
elif (ds == Dataset.SEM11_EN):
  dataset = load_dataset("sem_eval_2018_task_1",
    "subtask5.english")
  model_name = "bert-base-cased"
elif(ds == Dataset.SEM11_ES):
  dataset = load_dataset("sem_eval_2018_task_1",
    "subtask5.spanish")
  model_name = "dccuchile/bert-base-spanish-wwm-cased"
elif(ds == Dataset.KWT_M_AR):
  dataset = get_tweets_dataset("KWTM")
  model_name = "asafaya/bert-base-arabic"
elif(ds == Dataset.KWT_U_AR):
  dataset = get_tweets_dataset("KWTU")
  model_name = "asafaya/bert-base-arabic"
```

There are three types of datasets: train, test, and validation. We will use the train and validation datasets:

```
DatasetDict({
    train: Dataset({
        features: ['ID', 'Tweet', 'anger', 'anticipation',
        'disgust', 'fear', 'joy', 'love', 'optimism',
        'pessimism', 'sadness', 'surprise', 'trust'],
        num_rows: 6838
    })
    test: Dataset({
        features: ['ID', 'Tweet', 'anger', 'anticipation',
        'disgust', 'fear', 'joy', 'love', 'optimism',
        'pessimism', 'sadness', 'surprise', 'trust'],
        num_rows: 3259
    })
    validation: Dataset({
        features: ['ID', 'Tweet', 'anger', 'anticipation',
        'disgust', 'fear', 'joy', 'love', 'optimism',
        'pessimism', 'sadness', 'surprise', 'trust'],
```

```
        num_rows: 886
    })
})
```

Note how in the first example, we had to set NUM_LABELS and we had no idea of what the actual labels were. Here, we are going to dynamically work out the labels and also create some lookup tables that allow us to easily go from an emotion to a label and vice versa:

```
Labels = [label for label in dataset[ 'train'].features.keys() if
label not in ['ID', 'Tweet']]
id2label = {idx:label for idx, label in enumerate(labels)}
label2id = {label:idx for idx, label in enumerate(labels)}
```

The following output clarifies what each of these looks like:

```
['anger', 'anticipation', 'disgust', 'fear', 'joy', 'love',
'optimism', 'pessimism', 'sadness', 'surprise', 'trust']
{0: 'anger', 1: 'anticipation', 2: 'disgust', 3: 'fear', 4: 'joy', 5:
'love', 6: 'optimism', 7: 'pessimism', 8: 'sadness', 9: 'surprise',
10: 'trust'}
{'anger': 0, 'anticipation': 1, 'disgust': 2, 'fear': 3, 'joy': 4,
'love': 5, 'optimism': 6, 'pessimism': 7, 'sadness': 8, 'surprise': 9,
'trust': 10}
```

Now, we need to tokenize the datasets, as we did previously. The task is slightly more complicated here as we have multiple labels for each tweet, and the labels are loaded as True and False, whereas we need 0 and 1 for our model. The tokenize_function takes 1,000 tweets at a time, tokenizes the tweet text as before, and converts the labels into an array of 1s and 0s:

```
tokenizer = AutoTokenizer.from_pretrained(model_name)

def tokenise_function(tweets):
  text = tweets["Tweet"]
 encoding = tokenizer(text,
                     padding="max_length",
                     truncation=True,
                     max_length=512)
  labels_batch = {k: tweets[k] for k in tweets.keys() if k in labels}
  labels_matrix = np.zeros((len(text), len(labels)))
  for idx, label in enumerate(labels):
    labels_matrix[:, idx] = labels_batch[label]
  encoding["labels"] = labels_matrix.tolist()

  return encoding

encoded_dataset = dataset.map(tokenise_function,
```

```
        batched=True,
        remove_columns = dataset['train'].column_names)
```

We are using pytorch in this example, so we need to set the format of the dataset so that it's compatible:

```
encoded_dataset.set_format("torch")
```

Now, we can instantiate an auto class, as we did previously. Note how we have to set problem_type and also pass in the id-label and label-id mapping objects:

```
model = AutoModelForSequenceClassification.from_pretrained(
    model_name,
    problem_type="multi_label_classification",
    num_labels=len(labels),
    id2label=id2label,
    label2id=label2id
    )
```

Next, we need to define some functions to calculate some metrics for us. Because we have multi-labels, we are dealing with probabilities. Consequently, we need a threshold to distinguish between a 0 and a 1 for the emotion – we have arbitrarily set this to 0.5 for now. In practice, this would need to be carefully determined. These probabilities are turned into 0s and 1s using the threshold and, as before, we piggyback on scikit-learn functions to do the heavy lifting for us:

```
def compute_multi_label_metrics(predictions,
        labels, threshold=0.5):
    sigmoid = torch.nn.Sigmoid()
    probs = sigmoid(torch.Tensor(predictions))
    y_pred = np.zeros(probs.shape)
    y_pred[np.where(probs >= threshold)] = 1
    y_true = labels
    f1_macro_average = f1_score(y_true=y_true,
                                y_pred=y_pred,
                                average='macro')
    f1_micro_average = f1_score(y_true=y_true,
                                y_pred=y_pred,
                                average='micro')
    accuracy = accuracy_score(y_true, y_pred)
    precision = precision_score(y_true, y_pred,
        average = 'macro')
    recall = recall_score(y_true, y_pred,
        average = 'macro')
    jaccard = jaccard_score(y_true, y_pred,
        average='macro')
    metrics = {
```

```
                'precision': precision,
                'recall': recall,
                'f1_micro_average': f1_micro_average,
                'f1_macro_average': f1_macro_average,
                'jaccard': jaccard,
                'accuracy': accuracy
            }

    return metrics

def compute_metrics(p: EvalPrediction):
    if isinstance(p.predictions, tuple):
      preds = p.predictions[0]
    else:
      preds = p.predictions

    result = compute_multi_label_metrics(predictions=preds,
                                    labels=p.label_ids)
    return result
```

We can now set up some `TrainingArguments` and train the model:

```
metric_name = "jaccard"
training_args = TrainingArguments(
    model_name,
    evaluation_strategy = "epoch",
    save_strategy = "epoch",
    num_train_epochs = 3,
    load_best_model_at_end = True,
    metric_for_best_model = metric_name,
)
trainer = Trainer(
    model,
    training_args,
    train_dataset=encoded_dataset["train"],
    eval_dataset=encoded_dataset["validation"],
    tokenizer=tokenizer,
    compute_metrics=compute_metrics
)
trainer.train()
```

The final step is to evaluate the results using our metric functions. Notice how we pass the name of the `compute_metrics` function as a parameter. This function, in turn, calls `compute_multi_label_metrics` to calculate the various metrics:

```
trainer.evaluate()
```

The final results should look something like this:

```
{'eval_loss': 0.3063639998435974,
 'eval_precision': 0.6944130688122799,
 'eval_recall': 0.4961206747689895,
 'eval_f1_micro_average': 0.7107381546134663,
 'eval_f1_macro_average': 0.539464842236441,
 'eval_jaccard': 0.4181996269238169,
 'eval_accuracy': 0.30242437923250563,
 'eval_runtime': 26.6373,
 'eval_samples_per_second': 33.262,
 'eval_steps_per_second': 4.167,
 'epoch': 3.0}
```

The results from the model are summarized in the following table:

Dataset	Precision	Recall	micro F1	macro F1	Jaccard
SEM11-EN	**0.694**	**0.496**	**0.710**	**0.539**	**0.418**
SEM11-AR	0.552	0.441	0.658	0.462	0.359
KWT.M-AR	0.132	0.074	0.224	0.092	0.053
SEM11-ES	**0.594**	**0.399**	**0.597**	**0.463**	**0.340**

Table 9.2 – Scores for transformer-based models for the multi-class datasets

Again, the transformer-based models work better for some, but not all, datasets. It is worth noting that the previous best classifier for SEM11-AR was the stemmed version of the simple lexical model from *Chapter 5, Sentiment Lexicons and Vector-Space Models*, with a Jaccard score of 0.386. For SEM11-ES, it was the stemmed version of the conditional probability model, also from *Chapter 5, Sentiment Lexicons and Vector Space Models*, with a Jaccard score of 0.278. As with the single-class datasets, it seems likely that using the pretrained models may have helped us with identifying and disambiguating tokens, but this time, the underlying model is less good at handling multi-class cases. The score for the KWT.M-AR dataset is particularly poor: using transformers of the kind described here does not seem to be a good way to handle datasets with large numbers of tweets with no emotion ascribed to them.

In several cases, using transformers produced better results than the classifiers from previous chapters. The following table shows the scores for a range of classifiers on our datasets (given the number of classifiers we have looked at now, this table only includes ones that were the best on at least one dataset):

	LEX (unstemmed)	LEX (stemmed)	SVM (single)	SNN (single)	Transformers
SEM4-EN	0.503	0.497	0.845	0.829	**0.927**
SEM11-EN	0.347	0.348	0.224	0.242	**0.418**
WASSA-EN	0.445	0.437	**0.770**	0.737	0.753
CARER-EN	0.350	0.350	0.770	**0.820**	0.816
IMDB-EN	0.722	0.667	0.736	0.793	**0.826**
SEM4-AR	0.506	0.509	0.514	0.504	**0.710**
SEM11-AR	0.378	**0.386**	0.216	0.221	0.359
KWT.M-AR	**0.687**	0.663	0.631	0.028	0.053
SEM4-ES	0.425	0.420	0.412	0.337	**0.663**
SEM11-ES	0.269	0.271	0.226	0.221	**0.340**

Table 9.3 – Best scores to date for the standard datasets – Jaccard scores

The results of using transformers are better than any of the previous classifiers for 6 of our 10 datasets, though surprisingly, the very simple lexicon-based classifiers from *Chapter 5, Sentiment Lexicons and Vector Space Models* still produce the best results for the multi-class Arabic datasets!

It remains the case that there is a drop-off in performance between the single-emotion datasets and the multi-emotion datasets. As before, this is likely to be due to a combination of factors. The fact that the multi-class datasets have more labels than the others also makes the task harder, simply because there is more scope for mistakes. However, we know that multi-emotion classification is much more difficult than single-emotion classification because it involves working out how many emotions a text expresses, from zero upward, rather than just choosing the one with the highest scores. We will look at ways of dealing with this kind of data in more detail in *Chapter 10, Multiclassifiers*.

An interesting, natural question here is, why do transformers perform better than other methods? We have already seen how the self-attention mechanism allows transformers to focus on different parts of the input sequence when making predictions, hence allowing them to capture important long-range dependencies and contextual information. This is important for robust classification. Furthermore, we have also seen how transformers use multi-head attention, which allows them to attend to different parts of the input sequence simultaneously, thus making them more effective at capturing the different types of information that may be important for robust classification. Transformers also handle long input sequences without losing important information, and this may also be more useful in classification than other tasks. Finally, as we have seen, transformers are pretrained on huge datasets. Hence, even before fine-tuning, they already know general representations of language. These concepts can be combined in a highly effective way to create a mechanism that can generate good results.

Now, let's summarize what we've learned in this chapter.

Summary

Transformers have proved to be very successful in a range of natural language tasks, with numerous recently released chatbots outperforming existing models in their ability to understand and manipulate human language. In this chapter, we looked at how transformers can be used for the task of assigning emotions to informal texts and investigated how well they perform on this task with a range of datasets. We started by taking a brief look at transformers, focusing on the individual components of a transformer, and how data flows through them. Transformers need a lot of data to be effective and produce good results, and a huge amount of computing power and time is also needed. Then, we introduced Hugging Face, discussed why it was useful, and introduced some of the more common pretrained models that are available on the Hugging Face platform, before moving on to discussing how transformers are used for classification. Finally, we showed how to code classifiers using transformers for single-emotion datasets and multi-emotion datasets before rounding off this chapter by discussing the results. In the next chapter, we will look at multiclassifiers.

References

To learn more about the topics that were covered in this chapter, take a look at the following resources:

- Vaswani, A., Shazeer, N., Parmar, N., Uszkoreit, J., Jones, L., Gomez, A. N., Kaiser, Ł. and Polosukhin, I., 2017. *Attention Is All You Need.* Advances in neural information processing systems, 30.

- Rothman, D., 2021. *Transformers for Natural Language Processing: Build innovative deep neural network architectures for NLP with Python, PyTorch, TensorFlow, BERT, RoBERTa, and more.* Packt Publishing Ltd.

- Devlin, J., Chang, M. W., Lee, K., and Toutanova, K., 2018. *Bert: Pre-training of deep bidirectional transformers for language understanding.* arXiv preprint arXiv:1810.04805.

- Clark, K., Luong, M. T., Le, Q. V. and Manning, C. D., 2020. *Electra: Pre-training text encoders as discriminators rather than generators.* arXiv preprint arXiv:2003.10555.

- Brown, T., Mann, B., Ryder, N., Subbiah, M., Kaplan, J. D., Dhariwal, P., Neelakantan, A., Shyam, P., Sastry, G., Askell, A., and Agarwal, S., 2020. *Language models are few-shot learners.* Advances in neural information processing systems, 33, pp.1877-1901.

- Shoeybi, M., Patwary, M., Puri, R., LeGresley, P., Casper, J., and Catanzaro, B., 2019. *Megatron-lm: Training multi-billion parameter language models using model parallelism.* arXiv preprint arXiv:1909.08053.

- Liu, Y., Ott, M., Goyal, N., Du, J., Joshi, M., Chen, D., Levy, O., Lewis, M., Zettlemoyer, L., and Stoyanov, V., 2019. *RoBERTa: A Robustly Optimized BERT Pretraining Approach.* arXiv preprint arXiv:1907.11692.

- Raffel, C., Shazeer, N., Roberts, A., Lee, K., Narang, S., Matena, M., Zhou, Y., Li, W., and Liu, P. J., 2020. *Exploring the limits of transfer learning with a unified text-to-text transformer.* J. Mach. Learn. Res., 21(140), pp.1-67.

- Dai, Z., Yang, Z., Yang, Y., Carbonell, J., Le, Q. V., and Salakhutdinov, R., 2019. *Transformer-xl: Attentive language models beyond a fixed-length context.* arXiv preprint arXiv:1901.02860.

- Yang, Z., Dai, Z., Yang, Y., Carbonell, J., Salakhutdinov, R. R., and Le, Q. V., 2019. *XLNet: Generalized autoregressive pretraining for language understanding.* Advances in neural information processing systems, 32.

Multiclassifiers

In the preceding chapters, we saw that multi-label datasets, where a tweet may have zero, one, or more labels, are considerably harder to deal with than simple multi-class datasets where each tweet has exactly one label, albeit drawn from a set of more than one option. In this chapter, we will investigate ways of dealing with these cases, looking in particular at the use of **neutral** as a label for handling cases where a tweet is allowed to have zero labels; at using varying thresholds to enable standard classifiers to return a variable number of labels; and at training multiple classifiers, one per label, and allowing them each to make a decision about the label they were trained for. The conclusion, as ever, will be that there is no single "silver bullet" that provides the best solution in every case, but in general, the use of multiple classifiers tends to be better than the other approaches.

In this chapter, we'll cover the following topics:

- Using confusion matrices to analyze the behavior of classifiers on complex data
- Using **neutral** as a label to deal with tweets that have no label assigned to them
- Varying thresholds to handle multi-label datasets
- Training multiple classifiers to handle multi-label datasets

By the end of this chapter, you will understand how to implement several strategies for dealing with muti-label datasets and will have an appreciation of the effectiveness of these strategies for different kinds of data.

Multilabel datasets are hard to work with

We will start by looking at the performance of a selection of classifiers from previous chapters on the main datasets. We have said several times that multi-label datasets are particularly challenging, but it is worth bringing together the results from the best-performing algorithms to see exactly how challenging they are. *Figure 10.1* includes all the major classifiers that we have looked at so far. The multi-label datasets are highlighted in gray, and the best-performing classifier for each row is marked in bold/asterisks:

	LEX	CP	NB	SVM	SNN	DNN	Transformers
SEM4-EN	0.497	0.593	0.775	0.845	0.829	0.847	* **0.927** *
SEM11-EN	0.348	0.353	0.227	0.224	0.242	0.246	* **0.418** *
WASSA-EN	0.437	0.505	0.709	* **0.770** *	0.737	0.752	0.753
CARER-EN	0.350	0.395	0.776	0.770	* **0.820** *	0.804	0.816
IMDB-EN	0.667	0.722	0.738	0.736	0.793	0.793	* **0.826** *
SEM4-AR	0.509	0.513	0.531	0.514	0.504	0.444	* **0.710** *
SEM11-AR	* **0.386** *	0.382	0.236	0.216	0.221	0.207	0.359
KWT.M-AR	0.663	* **0.666** *	0.494	0.631	0.028	0.026	0.053
SEM4-ES	0.420	0.177	0.360	0.412	0.337	0.343	* **0.663** *
SEM11-ES	0.271	0.278	0.230	0.226	0.221	0.222	* **0.340** *

Figure 10.1 – Selected Jaccard scores for the standard datasets (multi-label datasets in gray)

Two things stand out from this table:

- For most of the entries in this table, LEX is the worst classifier, with NB coming next, and then the others generally scoring fairly similarly. For the multi-label cases, however, LEX or CP are always better than anything else except transformers, and in a couple of cases, they are better than transformers as well. Given that these seem to be the most realistic datasets, since plenty of tweets express no emotion and a fair number express more than one, it is worth looking in more detail at what is going on in these cases.

- The multi-label cases also score significantly worse overall – while LEX and CP score better than most other classifiers on these cases, they do generally score worse on them than on the other cases, and for all the other classifiers, the gap between these cases and the one emotion/ tweet cases is substantial.

These cases seem likely to be the most useful in practice since most tweets do not express any sentiment and a fair number express more than one, so algorithms that do not deal well with these cases may not be the most suitable for this task.

In the *Confusion matrices* section, we will look at what the various algorithms do with the two kinds of datasets. Once we have a clearer idea of why multi-label datasets are so much more difficult to handle than single-label ones, and we have seen the specific problems that they cause for particular algorithms, we will look at ways of dealing with this kind of dataset. We will not carry out these experiments with transformer-based models, partly because the time it takes to train a transformer makes this infeasible, but more importantly because we need to look inside the models to understand what is going on – this is all but impossible with transformer-based models.

Confusion matrices

It can be very difficult to see what kinds of mistakes a classifier makes just by looking at the raw output. **Confusion matrices** allow us to visualize a classifier's behavior, making it possible to see when two classes are being systematically confused or when a given class is being assigned too few or too many items. Consider the following dataset, where each item is classified as A, B, or C by the Gold Standard (G) and also has a predicted value (P):

G	C	C	A	B	C	B	C	B	B	B	A	A	B	B	C	C	B	C	B	B	C	A	B	A	A	C	C	C	A	A	A	C	B	C	A	A	B	A
P	C	B	B	B	C	A	A	B	B	A	A	A	C	B	A	B	B	C	B	C	C	A	B	B	B	C	B	B	B	A	B	C	B	B	A	A	B	A

Figure 10.2 – Gold Standard and predicted values for the example data

It is hard to see any pattern in this table. Simply counting how many cases have the same value for G and P gives us 22 out of 38 – that is, an accuracy of 0.58 – but it is very hard to see what kinds of things it gets right and what kinds of things it gets wrong. Converting this into a confusion table can help with this. We do this by counting the number of times that an item that ought to be assigned C1 as its value is predicted to have C2, producing a table of correct versus predicted assignments. The confusion matrix in *Figure 10.3*, for instance, shows that seven things that should have been assigned the label A were indeed assigned that label but five were assigned B, and that six things that should have been assigned C were assigned C but five were assigned B. This suggests that there is something about the properties of Bs that makes it easy to assign things to this class when they should be assigned to A or C, which might lead to a line of inquiry about which properties of Bs were leading to this problem:

	A	B	C
A	7	5	0
B	2	9	2
C	2	5	6

Figure 10.3 – Confusion matrix for the data in Figure 10.2

If gs and p are the Gold Standard values for a set of points, then confusion will calculate the confusion matrix: c is a table with an entry for each label in gs, where the value for a label is the set of counts of each time a label has been predicted for it:

```
def confusion(gs, p):
    c = {}
    for x, y in zip(gs, p):
        if not x in c:
            c[x] = counter()
        c[x].add(y)
```

Confusion matrices can provide a considerable amount of information about what a classifier is doing. We do, however, have a slight problem with constructing confusion matrices when the Gold Standard and the prediction can each contain a varying number of emotions. Suppose, for instance, that the Gold Standard for some tweets is **love+joy** and the prediction is **love+sad+angry**. We want to acknowledge that the classifier was right when it predicted **love**, but what do we do about the fact that it missed **joy** (that is, there is a false negative) and predicted **sad** and **angry** (two false positives)?

There is no right answer to this question. We adapt the standard way of constructing a confusion matrix as follows, where C[e1][e2] is the score for *e1* in the Gold Standard and *e2* in the prediction. We need to add a row and a column for "no emotion assigned" (we will use -- for this class):

- For every case where the Golden Standard and the prediction contain a given emotion, *e*, add 1 to *C[e][e]* and remove *e* from both the Golden Standard and the prediction.

- If the Golden Standard is now empty, then every *e* left in the prediction must be a false positive, so add 1 to *C[--][e]* for each remaining e.

- If the prediction is empty, then every *e* left in the Golden Standard must be a false negative, so add 1 to *C[e][--]*.

- If neither of them is empty after removing the shared cases, it is hard to see what to do. Consider the preceding example. After removing **love**, we are left with **joy** in the Golden Standard and **sad+angry** in the prediction. Is **joy** a mistake for **sad**, with **angry** as a false positive? Is **joy** a mistake for **angry**, with **sad** as a false positive? Is **joy** a false negative and **sad** and **angry** both false positives? This last suggestion does not seem right. Suppose we had one case where **joy** was matched with **sad+angry**, another where it was matched with **sad+fear**, and another where it was matched with just **sad**. If we marked all of these as cases where **joy** was a false negative and **sad** was a false positive, we would miss the fact that there appears to be a connection between **joy** and **sad**.

We deal with this as follows. Suppose there are **G** items left in the Gold Standard and **P** items left in the prediction after the labels that appear on both have been removed. Here, for each **g** in the Gold Standard and each **p** in the prediction, we add *1/P* to *C[p][g]*. Doing this adds a total of **G** to the confusion matrix, thus acknowledging that the number of emotions in the Gold Standard has not been matched, with each item in the prediction seen being as equally likely to be the one that should be substituted for **g**.

The machinery for calculating modified confusion matrices is fairly intricate, and including it here would add very little to the preceding explanation. The code for this can be found in this book's GitHub repository – for now, it is probably best just to note that when an item can be assigned multiple labels, the confusion matrix has to take account of situations where the Gold Standard and the prediction both assign multiple labels, with the sets being assigned being of different sizes and where some labels are common to both, some only appear in the Gold Standard and some only appear in the prediction.

The way we do this is not symmetric between the Gold Standard and the prediction, but it does provide confusion matrices that tell us something useful about what a given classifier is doing. For cases where there is exactly one item in the Gold Standard and one in the prediction, it collapses to the standard version, and where there are differing numbers in each, it does provide a picture of what is going on.

We will start by looking at the confusion matrix for CARER-EN using SVM as the classifier (the scores for SVMs and DNNs are very similar, and the confusion matrices are also very similar, so for convenience, we will use SVMs for the explorations here). The following matrix was obtained using a version of SVM which simply picks the most likely emotion for each tweet instead of using a threshold to try to work out whether there are any that are likely enough for them to be counted and if so, whether there are several that could count:

	anger	fear	joy	love	sadness	surprise	
anger	124	0	1	0	1	0	
fear	1	128	0	0	0	1	
joy	0	0	337	1	0	0	
love	0	0	1	73	0	0	
sadness	0	1	1	0	293	0	
surprise	0	0	0	0	0	37	

Figure 10.4 – Confusion matrix for CARER-EN, one emotion per tweet, with SVM as the classifier

This is what you expect a confusion matrix to look like – the largest scores down the diagonal with a scattering of other assignments, with the biggest confusion being between **love** and **joy**. When we use the same algorithm for SEM11-EN, we get a very different picture:

	ange	anti	disg	fear	joy	love	opti	pess	sadn	surp	trus	--
anger	311	2	0	1	2	0	0	0	0	0	1	1
antici	8	65	1	2	1	0	0	0	0	0	0	12
disgus	10	3	36	1	3	0	0	0	0	0	1	182
fear	9	0	0	46	0	0	0	0	0	0	0	34
joy	11	2	1	1	186	0	0	0	0	0	1	39
love	0	1	0	0	0	4	0	0	0	0	0	40
optimi	7	1	0	2	2	0	20	1	0	0	0	119
pessim	0	1	0	0	0	0	0	19	0	0	0	26
sadnes	9	3	1	1	3	0	0	1	16	0	0	119
surpri	4	1	0	0	0	0	0	0	0	1	0	16
trust	2	1	0	1	0	0	0	0	0	0	1	15
--	2	0	0	0	0	0	0	0	0	0	21	0

Figure 10.5 – Confusion matrix for SEM11-EN, one emotion per tweet, with SVM as the classifier

We get several false positives (places where nothing was expected but something was predicted – that is, the row headed with --: two of these have **anger** assigned and 21 **trust**). This happens because we have forced the classifier to choose something even in cases where the Gold Standard doesn't expect anything. We also have a much larger number of places where there are false negatives (the column headed with --), where something was expected but nothing was found, generally because the Gold Standard had multiple labels and there was only one prediction. And there are numerous cases where the assignment is just wrong, with an awful lot of things being labeled as **anger** when they should be something else.

The problem is that if the classifier is forced to assign exactly one emotion per tweet, then it cannot help producing false positives (if the Gold Standard says that nothing should be assigned) and false negatives (if the Gold Standard says that more than one emotion should be assigned). If we look at the test set in detail, we will see that there are 23 tweets with no emotion assigned, which show up as false positives, and 645 tweets with more than one emotion assigned, which show up as 1,065 false negatives (because some of them have three or more emotions assigned). *There is nothing that can be done about this if our classifier assumes that there is one emotion per tweet.*

Suppose that we have N tweets, X of which have no emotion assigned to them and Y have more than one. In this case, there must be at least X false positives (one for each tweet that should have no labels assigned but the classifier assigns one) and at least Y false negatives (one for each tweet that should have more than one label assigned but the classifier only assigns one), meaning that the best possible Jaccard score is $(N-X)/((N-X)+X+Y)$. For the set of 772 tweets in SEM11-EN, this comes out as $(772-23)/(772-23+(1065+23)) = 0.41$ (the number of false negatives is very high because of the preponderance of tweets that should be given more than two labels – this equation assumed that tweets were assigned zero, one, or two labels). This is a strict upper bound. No classifier that assigns exactly one label to each tweet can achieve a higher Jaccard score than 0.41 on this dataset.

The position is worse than that. Careful inspection of the diagonal shows that several emotions have good scores on the diagonal (**anger**, **joy**), while others have very poor scores on the diagonal and a lot of false negatives (**disgust**, **love**, **optimism**), with several emotions being confused with **anger**.

When we look at the KWT.M-AR dataset, we will see an output that is in some ways similar and is no more encouraging:

	ange	diss	fear	joy	love	opti	pess	reje	trus	--
anger	5	0	0	0	0	0	0	0	7	0
dissat	0	21	0	0	0	0	0	0	31	1
fear	0	0	2	0	0	0	0	0	1	0
joy	0	0	0	11	0	0	0	0	12	0
love	0	0	0	0	50	0	0	0	44	3
optimi	0	0	0	0	0	22	0	0	17	0
pessim	0	0	0	0	0	0	1	0	2	2
reject	0	0	0	0	0	0	0	0	1	0
trust	0	0	0	0	0	0	0	0	14	0
--	0	1	0	0	8	3	0	0	751	0

Figure 10.6 – Confusion matrix for KWT.M-AR, one emotion per tweet, with SVM as the classifier

This time, there are a massive number of false positives, reflecting the fact that these datasets have a very high proportion of cases where no emotion is assigned in the Gold Standard (763 out of 1,000 in the test set used here, with a maximum attainable F1-score of around 0.42). Again, this is inevitable – if a tweet should have no emotions assigned to it and the classifier is forced to assign one, then we will get a false positive. It is also worth noting that while there are non-trivial entries on the diagonal, a surprising number of cases have the correct assignment replaced by **trust**. The key here is that emotions such as **anger** and **joy** have words that are strongly associated with them (angry: 2.38, fuming: 2.32, annoying: 2.31, revenge: 2.26, … for **anger**, for instance, and positivity: 1.82, 😊: 1.75, rejoice: 1.74, gift: 1.72, laughing: 1.70 for

joy), and that are used for identifying them in tweets. **trust**, on the other hand, does not have such clear identifiers – the top few words for **trust** when training on SEM11-EN with an SVM are `flat: 1.25, com: 1.19, cup: 1.06, need: 1.05, major: 1.05`. These are not words that are obviously associated with trust, and indeed the links between them and this emotion are not strong. So, when the classifier is forced to choose an emotion for a tweet that does not contain any words that are linked to specific emotions, it is likely to resort to choosing the one for which no such words are expected anyway.

If, as suggested previously, large numbers of tweets express either no emotion or several emotions, then we have to deal with these issues. There are several things we can try:

- We can include an explicit "none-of-the-above" or "neutral" class to represent the fact that a tweet does not carry any emotional weight. This is the easiest thing to do for "zero emotion" cases, though it will not be ideal in cases where more than one emotion is assigned to a tweet.

- We can use the fact that some of the classifiers calculate a score for each emotion. We will look at this in more detail shortly.

- We can train a set of binary classifiers – **joy** versus **not-joy**, **anger** versus **not-anger**, and so on. This will potentially deal with both kinds of cases: if each of these classifiers returns the negative version, we will get an overall zero assignment, and if more than one returns the positive version, we will get multiple assignments.

For the remainder of this chapter, we will concentrate on the SEM-11 and KWT datasets since these are the only ones with variable numbers of labels. If your training data assigns exactly one emotion to each tweet, and you want to have exactly one emotion assigned when running the classifier on live data, then one of the others will generally provide the best solution – LEXCLASSIFIER usually provides reasonably accurate results with very little training time, Transformers usually provide the best results but take a lot of training, and SVMs and DNNs come somewhere in between for both accuracy and training time.

Using "neutral" as a label

We can introduce **neutral** as a label simply by looking at the labels assigned by the Gold Standard and assigning **neutral** if no other emotion is assigned. This does not affect the CARER-EN set: nothing is assigned **neutral** in the training data, so no words are found to be associated with this label, so, in turn, nothing is assigned to it by the classifier. The effect on the SEM11-EN data is more interesting:

	ange	anti	disg	fear	joy	love	opti	pess	sadn	surp	trus	neut	--
anger	311	2	0	1	2	0	0	0	0	0	0	1	1
antici	8	65	1	2	1	0	0	0	0	0	0	1	12
disgus	10	3	36	1	3	0	0	0	0	0	0	1	182
fear	9	0	0	46	0	0	0	0	0	0	0	0	34
joy	11	2	1	1	186	0	0	0	0	0	0	1	39
love	0	1	0	0	0	4	0	0	0	0	0	0	40
optimi	7	1	0	2	2	0	20	1	0	0	0	1	118
pessim	0	1	0	0	0	0	0	19	0	0	0	0	26
sadnes	9	3	1	1	3	0	0	1	16	0	0	0	119
surpri	4	1	0	0	0	0	0	0	0	1	0	0	16
trust	2	1	0	1	0	0	0	0	0	0	0	1	15
neutra	2	0	0	0	0	0	0	0	0	0	0	21	0

Figure 10.7 – Confusion matrix for SEM11-EN, one emotion per tweet,
with SVM as the classifier, and neutral as a label

There is very little change down the diagonal – that is, the classifier gets the same actual emotions right with or without **neutral** as a label; most things that ought to be classified as neutral are indeed labeled as such, with a couple mislabeled as **anger**; a few things are labeled as **neutral** when they should not be; and there are still a lot of false negatives because there were a lot of tweets that ought to have been given more than one label. These can't be labeled **neutral** by the classifier since it can only assign one label to each tweet, so any tweet that ought to have more than one will contribute to the set of false negatives.

The situation with the KWT examples is intriguing. These have large numbers of tweets with no emotion assigned to them, so we expect a lot of false positives if the classifier is set to assign one emotion per tweet. The confusion matrices for KWT.M-AR without and with **neutral** as a label are given here:

	ange	diss	fear	joy	love	opti	pess	reje	trus	--
anger	7	0	0	0	0	0	0	0	5	0
dissat	0	19	0	0	0	0	0	0	17	4
fear	0	0	3	0	0	0	0	0	1	1
joy	0	0	0	11	0	0	0	0	23	2
love	0	0	0	0	82	0	0	0	47	1
optimi	0	0	0	0	0	37	0	0	18	2
pessim	0	0	0	0	0	0	1	0	2	0
reject	0	0	0	0	0	0	0	1	2	0
trust	0	0	0	0	0	0	0	0	12	1
--	0	2	0	3	13	2	0	0	697	0

Figure 10.8 – Confusion matrix for KWT.M-AR, one emotion per tweet,
with SVM as the classifier, and neutral not included

As before, most of the scores on the diagonal are quite good – that is, most of the time, the classifier assigns the right label where there is a label to be assigned. Inevitably, there are a large number of false positives, nearly all of which are assigned to **trust**. As before, in almost every case where the Gold Standard says there should be no label, the classifier has chosen **trust**, rather than distributing the false positives evenly. Again, what seems to be happening is that the classifier does not associate any words particularly strongly with **trust**, so when it is given a tweet without any very significant words in it, it decides it cannot be any of the other classes, for which there are stronger clues, so it chooses **trust**.

When we allow **neutral** as a label, the situation changes quite dramatically. Now, nearly all the false positives are assigned to **neutral**, which is the most reasonable outcome. There is a smattering of false negatives because this dataset contains tweets with multiple labels, but the diagonal is much clearer – most emotions are assigned correctly and most cases with no emotion are assigned to **neutral**:

	ange	diss	fear	joy	love	opti	pess	reje	trus	neut	--
anger	7	0	0	0	0	0	0	0	0	5	0
dissat	0	19	0	0	0	0	0	0	0	17	4
fear	0	0	3	0	0	0	0	0	0	1	1
joy	0	0	0	11	0	0	0	0	0	24	1

	ange	diss	fear	joy	love	opti	pess	reje	trus	neut	--
love	0	0	0	0	81	0	0	0	0	48	1
optimi	0	0	0	0	0	37	0	0	0	18	2
pessim	0	0	0	0	0	0	1	0	0	2	0
reject	0	0	0	0	0	0	0	1	0	2	0
trust	0	0	0	0	0	0	0	0	7	5	1
neutra	0	2	0	2	14	2	0	0	0	697	0

Figure 10.9 – Confusion matrix for KWT.M-AR, one emotion per
tweet, with SVM as the classifier, and neutral included

So, using **neutral** as a label provides a partial solution to the problems of none and multiple labels, but it *cannot* provide a complete one. Even if a classifier were 100% accurate when it assigned labels to tweets that ought to have exactly one label and when it assigned **neutral** to ones that ought to have no labels, it must introduce false negatives for cases where there ought to be more than one label.

Now is a good time to introduce a new measure of performance. The fact that most of the cases that are neither classified as **neutral** nor given no label at all lie on the diagonal suggests that the gross classification assigned to a set of tweets might be useful for gauging opinion, even if the assignments to individual tweets are unreliable. In particular, false negatives may not matter too much when you're trying to spot general trends, so long as the cases where the classifier does assign a label are consistent with the underlying reality.

It is, of course, not possible to spot whether something is a false negative or is a genuine instance of a neutral assignment, and then ask what the assignment for the false negatives should have been. If we could do that, then we would have trained the classifier to do it in the first place, and likewise with false positives. The best we can do is assess just how much we would be led astray if we accepted all the assignments that the classifier made at face value. So, we define the **proportionality** of the classifier as the cosine distance between the proportion of concrete tweets assigned to each emotion in the Gold Standard and the predictions (that is, ignoring tweets that are assigned to **neutral** or were not given any labels at all). The nearer to 1 this is, the more we can expect our classifier to give us a reliable overall picture, even if some of the individual assignments were wrong.

To take a simple example, suppose that we had a dataset with the 11 emotions from the SEM11 data, with the same number of tweets assigned to **pessimism** and **sadness**, and that it got everything right except that it labeled exactly half the tweets that should be labeled as pessimistic as sad and exactly half the tweets that should be labeled as sad as pessimistic. In this case, proportionality would be perfect, and you could safely use the classifier to make judgments about the overall picture, even though you could not rely on it to tell you whether a given tweet was sad or pessimistic. Similarly, if half the tweets in every category were assigned no emotion, then proportionality would be perfect, whereas if half the tweets in the most common category were assigned neutral but no others were, then it would be fairly poor.

From now on, we will do this for all the classifiers that are generated by the folds that we perform the training on, because the test sets associated with the individual folds are comparatively small (which is why we do cross-fold validation in the first place) and we lose quite a lot of instances by ignoring neutral and unassigned tweets. To calculate the proportionality, we can just count the number of tweets whose predicted/Gold Standard includes each emotion, *ignoring neutral and unassigned*, and normalize the result:

```
def proportions(clsfs, emotions, which=lambda x: x.predicted,
ignore=["neutral", "--"]):
    conf = numpy.zeros(len(emotions))
    for clsf in clsfs:
        for t in clsf.test.tweets:
            for i, k in enumerate(which(t)):
                if not emotions[i] in ignore:
                    if k == 1:
                        conf[i] += 1
    return conf/sum(conf)
```

Now, we can do this for the prediction and the Gold Standard and use cosine similarity to calculate the similarity between the two:

```
def scoreproportions(clsfs):
    ignore = ["neutral", "--"]
    emotions = clsfs[0].train.emotions
    predictedproportions = proportions(clsfs, emotions, ignore)
    gsproportions = proportions(clsfs, emotions, ignore,
                                which=lambda x: x.GS)
    return cosine_similarity(predictedproportions.reshape(1, -1),
                             gsproportions.reshape(1, -1))[0][0]
```

For SEM11-EN, allowing an arbitrary number of emotions per tweet and using LEX as a classifier and neutral as a label, for instance, the proportions of the tweets that have each of the labels assigned in the prediction and the Gold Standard are anger: 0.30, anticipation: 0.00, disgust: 0.31, fear: 0.02, joy: 0.25, love: 0.00, optimism: 0.04, pessimism: 0.00, sadness: 0.06, surprise: 0.00, trust: 0.00 and anger: 0.18, anticipation: 0.06, disgust: 0.17, fear: 0.06, joy: 0.15, love: 0.04, optimism: 0.12, pessimism: 0.04, sadness: 0.12, surprise: 0.02, trust: 0.02, respectively, for a proportionality score of 0.89. If we use the same classifier with neutral as a label but allow exactly one label per tweet, the proportionality drops to 0.87.

If we apply this to the KWT.M-AR dataset, we get `anger: 0.03`, `dissatisfaction: 0.07`, `fear: 0.00`, `joy: 0.07`, `love: 0.69`, `optimism: 0.10`, `pessimism: 0.00`, `rejection: 0.02`, `trust: 0.02` for the predictions and `anger: 0.04`, `dissatisfaction: 0.16`, `fear: 0.02`, `joy: 0.10`, `love: 0.43`, `optimism: 0.18`, `pessimism: 0.01`, `rejection: 0.01`, `trust: 0.05` for the Gold Standard, for a proportionality score of 0.94. If we had not ignored the neutral/unassigned cases, the score would have been much higher, at 0.99, because of the huge preponderance of cases that are neutral in this dataset. So, we have a useful single number that gives us a handle on how reliable a classifier is for providing an overall picture, even if it fails to assign a concrete label to every tweet (that is, if some are either not assigned anything at all or are assigned **neutral**).

This score will typically be quite high since, in most cases, most of the concrete scores lie on the diagonal. What matters is whether the distribution of neutral/unassigned cases follows the general distribution of the concrete cases – if it does, then the classifier will be useful for assessing general trends, even if it does sometimes fail to assign concrete labels when it should. So, we will use this measure in addition to Jaccard to assess the classifiers in the remainder of this chapter. The tables in *Figures 10.10* and *10.12* show what happens to the proportionality for various classifiers when we add **neutral** as a label, sticking to assigning exactly one label per tweet. As a reference point, we will start by looking at what happens if we specify that each classifier returns without using **neutral**. As before, the classifier with the best Jaccard score is marked in bold:

	LEX	NB	SVM	DNN
SEM11-EN	0.224 (0.813)	0.229 (0.690)	0.223 (0.771)	* **0.242 (0.677)** *
SEM11-AR	* **0.247 (0.824)** *	0.216 (0.667)	0.204 (0.736)	0.207 (0.613)
SEM11-ES	0.225 (0.799)	* **0.226 (0.788)** *	0.215 (0.888)	0.222 (0.774)
KWT.M-AR	* **0.208 (0.973)** *	0.108 (0.352)	0.078 (0.207)	0.026 (0.148)

Figure 10.10 – Jaccard and proportionality (in brackets), one label per tweet, neutral not included

Figure 10.10 shows that if we simply use the original classifiers unchanged – that is, with one emotion per tweet and without **neutral** as a label – we get fairly poor Jaccard scores, but the proportionality scores for LEX range from reasonable to pretty good, with the other classifiers generally doing worse on this metric. The proportionality score for LEX on the KWT.M-AR dataset in particular is massively better than the same score for any of the other classifiers on this dataset. The key here is that NB, SVM, and DNN assign nearly all the cases that should have been labeled as **neutral** to **trust** because these cases lack any of the distinguishing words that are common in the more clearly marked emotions, whereas LEX distributes them more closely in line with the marked cases. It is worth noting that the classifier with the best score for a given dataset does not always produce the best proportionality for that set:

	ange	diss	fear	joy	love	opti	pess	reje	trus	--	
anger	9	19	0	0	11	2	0	0	0	14	
dissat	4	133	0	2	71	1	0	0	0	0	
fear	0	3	2	0	12	2	0	0	0	2	
joy	1	6	0	53	50	8	0	0	1	18	
love	0	7	0	8	548	12	0	0	0	0	
optimi	0	5	0	1	44	180	0	0	1	2	
pessim	0	4	0	0	7	2	2	0	1	1	
reject	0	2	0	0	3	0	0	3	0	2	
trust	1	9	0	2	28	8	0	0	13	3	
--	30	880	4	159	2008	577	2	1	61	0	

Figure 10.11 – Confusion matrix for KWT.M-AR, one label per tweet,
with LEX as the classifier, and neutral not included

When we allow **neutral** as a label, NB and SVM can choose this as the class with the least distinctive terms and hence assign cases that should be **neutral** to it, leading to a massive improvement in both Jaccard and proportionality for these classifiers:

	LEX	NB	SVM	DNN
SEM11-EN	0.222 (0.813)	0.227 (0.690)	0.222 (0.768)	* 0.239 (0.677) *
SEM11-AR	* 0.246 (0.824) *	0.216 (0.666)	0.204 (0.736)	0.207 (0.615)
SEM11-ES	0.221 (0.800)	* 0.222 (0.787) *	0.211 (0.885)	0.216 (0.774)
KWT.M-AR	0.608 (0.984)	0.510 (0.986)	* 0.632 (0.992) *	0.595 (0.905)

Figure 10.12 – Jaccard and proportionality, one label per tweet, and neutral included

So, we can see that using proportionality as a metric allows us to spot general trends. Most of our classifiers work better on multi-label datasets if we allow **neutral** as a label, particularly when looking at proportionality, but LEX performs quite well even without **neutral** as a label.

Thresholds and local thresholds

The next option to be explored is the use of thresholds. As we have seen, most of our classifiers provide scores for every option for each tweet, with the default setting being to choose the option with the highest score. In *Chapter 6, Naive Bayes*, we saw that assuming that our classifier will assign exactly one label to each tweet puts quite a tight upper bound on how well it can perform and that instead of doing that, we can set a threshold and say that everything that exceeds that threshold should be accepted as a label.

Consider the following tweet: *"Hi guys ! I now do lessons via Skype ! Contact me for more info . # skype # lesson # basslessons # teacher # free lesson # music # groove # rock # blues."*

The Gold Standard assigns this the scores ('anger', 0), ('anticipation', 1), ('disgust', 0), ('fear', 0), ('joy', 1), ('love', 0), ('optimism', 0), ('pessimism', 0), ('sadness', 0), ('surprise', 0), ('trust', 0), so it should be labeled as **anticipation+joy**.

Naive Bayes assigns this tweet the scores ('anger', '0.00'), ('anticipation', '0.88'), ('disgust', '0.00'), ('fear', '0.00'), ('joy', '0.11'), ('love', '0.00'), ('optimism', '0.00'), ('pessimism', '0.00'), ('sadness', '0.00'), ('surprise', '0.00'), ('trust', '0.00'), so if we set the threshold at 0.1, we would get **anticipation+joy**, if we set it at 0.2, we would just get **anticipation**, and if we set it at 0.9, we would get nothing.

For the same tweet, SVM assigns ('anger', '-0.77'), ('anticipation', '0.65'), ('disgust', '-2.64'), ('fear', '-1.67'), ('joy', '-0.99'), ('love', '-1.93'), ('optimism', '-3.52'), ('pessimism', '-1.61'), ('sadness', '-2.58'), ('surprise', '-1.47'), ('trust', '-3.86'). So, this time, if we set the threshold to -1, we would get **anger+anticipation+joy**, if we set it to 0, we would just get **anticipation**, and if we set it to 1, we would get nothing.

So, using a threshold will let us generate zero or more labels. We have to optimize the threshold, but we can do that simply by finding the smallest and greatest values that are assigned to any label in any tweet and incrementing evenly between these. The `bestThreshold` function, which was provided in *Chapter 5, Sentiment Lexicons and Vector-Space Models*, will work just as well with the raw scores produced by Naive Bayes, SVMs, and DNNs as it did there.

If we contrast the scores that were obtained previously by requiring a single label and the ones we obtained using a threshold to allow zero or more labels on the crucial datasets, we will see that, overall, the latter produces better results:

	LEX	NB	SVM	DNN
SEM11-EN	* 0.347 (0.898) *	0.270 (0.764)	0.250 (0.828)	0.273 (0.729)
SEM11-AR	* 0.377 (0.940) *	0.257 (0.761)	0.224 (0.798)	0.246 (0.731)
SEM11-ES	* 0.266 (0.890) *	0.250 (0.837)	0.228 (0.924)	0.238 (0.791)
KWT.M-AR	* 0.691 (0.990) *	0.522 (0.988)	0.631 (0.998)	0.604 (0.935)

Figure 10.13 – Zero or more emotions per tweet, with optimal global thresholds

The scores here are much better than they were with the simple classifiers, with the proportionality scores all but perfect in some cases. There is, however, still some way to go if we want to get the labels for individual tweets right, rather than just getting a good overall picture. The next move is to set a threshold for each label, rather than for the dataset as a whole. We will adapt bestThreshold from *Chapter 5, Sentiment Lexicons and Vector Space Models* so that we can assign individual thresholds to labels. We will make two changes to the original definition:

- We will split it into two cases – one for calculating a global threshold (a single threshold for all cases) and another for calculating a local threshold for each label.

- In the original version, we looked at every column in the data, finding the minimum and maximum values that occur anywhere, and then looked at the predicted values for every column to calculate the Jaccard scores for each potential threshold. To calculate local thresholds, we just want to look at one column at a time. We can deal with both cases if we specify a range of columns, from start to end, to look at. For the global case, we must set start=0 and end=sys. maxsize; for the case where we want to choose the best threshold for the i column, we must set start=i and end=i+1. This lets us use the same machinery for calculating both types of thresholds. The major changes to the original are highlighted in the following updated version:

```
def bestThreshold(self, bestthreshold, start=0, end=sys.
maxsize):
    train = self.train.tweets[:len(self.test.tweets)]
    self.applyToTweets(train, threshold=0, probs=True)
    if bestthreshold == "global":
        predicted = [t.predicted for t in train]
        # select the required columns from the prediction
        predicted = numpy.array(predicted)[start:end, :]
        lowest = threshold = numpy.min(predicted)
        highest = numpy.max(predicted)
        step = (highest-lowest)/20
        best = []
        GS = numpy.array([t.GS for t in train])[:,
start:end]
```

```
                    for i in range(20):
                        l = self.applyToTweets(train,
threshold=threshold)
                        l = numpy.array(l)[:, start:end]
                        m = metrics.getmetrics(GS, l, show=False)
                        (macroF, tp, tn, fp, fn) = m
                        j = tp/(tp+fp+fn)
                        best = max(best, [j, threshold])
                        if show:
                            print("%.2f %.3f"%(threshold, j))
                        threshold += step
                    return best[1]
            elif bestthreshold == "local":
                    # do the global version, but just for each column in
turn
                    localthresholds = []
                    for i in range(len(self.train.emotions)):
                        localthreshold = self.bestThreshold("global",
                                                    start=i,
end=i+1)
                        localthresholds.append(localthreshold)
                    return localthresholds
            else:
                    raise Exception("%s unexpected value for
bestthreshold"%(bestthreshold))
```

The results of allowing the classifiers to choose different thresholds for different labels are shown here:

	LEX	NB	SVM	DNN
SEM11-EN	* **0.371 (0.987)** *	0.271 (0.827)	0.270 (0.809)	0.277 (0.811)
SEM11-AR	0.371 (0.965)	0.255 (0.854)	0.236 (0.809)	0.238 (0.795)
SEM11-ES	* **0.267 (0.962)** *	0.192 (0.674)	0.222 (0.983)	0.202 (0.852)
KWT.M-AR	0.681 (0.989)	0.217 (0.163)	0.615 (0.987)	0.226 (0.167)

Figure 10.14 – Zero or more emotions per tweet, with optimal local thresholds

The proportionality scores for LEX have all improved, with LEX now easily giving the best proportionality score for SEM11-EN and Naive Bayes now reverting to choosing neutral/unassigned for nearly everything for KWT.U-AR and most of the other scores decreasing slightly, though the Jaccard scores have only improved for SEM11-EN and SEM11-ES. Yet again, different classifiers are better suited to different datasets and different tasks.

Multiple independent classifiers

Using either LEX with optimal local thresholds or Naïve Bayes or SVM with an optimal global threshold with **neutral** as a label seems to be the best way so far of dealing with multilabel datasets. Our final strategy for these datasets is to train a set of classifiers via the one-versus-the-rest strategy, using one of our existing classifiers for training each member of the set. For this, we will adapt the MULTICLASSIFIER class from *Chapter 7, Support Vector Machines*, to allow different kinds of classifiers to be used at the lower level. The key change here from the original is that we specify what classifier to use in the set of optional arguments, rather than assuming that we will be using SVMCLASSIFIER:

```
def __init__(self, train, showprogress=True, args={}):
    self.train = train
    T = time.time()
    self.datasets = {}
    self.classifiers = {}
    self.args = args
    # Find what kind of classifier to use for the individual
emotions
    subclassifier = args["subclassifiers"]
    for i in range(len(self.train.emotions)):
        squeezed = self.squeeze(i)
        if squeezed:
            self.datasets[i] = squeezed
            self.classifiers[i] = subclassifier(self.datasets[i],
args=args)
```

This will make two-way classifiers for **anger** versus **not-anger**, **love** versus **not-love**, and so on using the specified kind of sub-classifier. For the individual classifiers, there is no point in allowing more than one label since while a tweet can satisfy both **love** and **joy**, or both **anger** and **fear**, it does not make any sense to allow a tweet to satisfy **anger** and **not-anger**. We can still get multiple labels overall if, for instance, both **love** versus **not-love** and **joy** versus **not-joy** are satisfied, and we can still get zero labels if all the negative labels are chosen, but it makes no sense to allow the individual classifiers to assign zero or more than one label.

As ever, there is a wide range of settings for the various subclassifiers. The main multiclassifier just combines the results of the individual subclassifiers and hence has no significant parameters beyond the choice of what to use as the subclassifiers, but the individual subclassifiers have the usual range of options. The following tables report the scores using just one label per subclassifier but varying whether or not neutral is allowed as a label:

	MULTI-LEX	MULTI-NB	MULTI-SVM	MULTI-DNN
SEM11-EN	0.348 (0.868)	*0.441 (0.996) *	0.385 (1.000)	0.422 (0.991)
SEM11-AR	0.363 (0.878)	0.376 (0.996)	0.314 (0.997)	0.333 (0.956)
SEM11-ES	0.260 (0.852)	* 0.296 (0.993) *	0.256 (0.995)	0.236 (0.936)
KWT.M-AR	0.304 (0.979)	0.236 (0.989)	0.294 (0.996)	0.182 (0.938)

Figure 10.15 (a) – 0 or more emotions per tweet, multiple classifiers, -neutral

	MULTI-LEX	MULTI-NB	MULTI-SVM	MULTI-DNN
SEM11-EN	0.342 (0.861)	0.438 (0.996)	0.381 (1.000)	0.419 (0.991)
SEM11-AR	0.363 (0.879)	0.376 (0.996)	0.313 (0.997)	0.333 (0.956)
SEM11-ES	0.256 (0.836)	0.290 (0.993)	0.250 (0.995)	0.234 (0.938)
KWT.M-AR	0.665 (0.984)	0.546 (0.989)	0.617 (0.996)	0.599 (0.950)

Figure 10.15 (b) – 0 or more emotions per tweet, multiple classifiers, +neutral

The overall picture here is that using multiple independent classifiers to decide whether a tweet should have a given label produces the best proportionality results yet for zero-to-many datasets. Although the Jaccard scores are only improved for SEM11-EN and SEM11-ES, there is considerable variation between the performance of the different classifiers under this regime. All four classifiers do marginally better on the SEM11 cases when we do not allow **neutral** as a label, but they all do substantially better on the KWT.M-AR dataset when we do allow **neutral**. This is slightly surprising, given that the individual classifiers are allowed to choose not to assign their labels, so it is perfectly possible to get a "no label assigned" outcome for a given tweet, even without allowing **neutral**. *Figure 10.16* shows how scores vary as we look at the +/-neutral classifiers for KWT.M-AR:

	Precision	Recall	Micro F1	Macro F1	Jaccard	Proportionality
MULTI-LEX, -NEUTRAL	0.400	0.559	0.467	0.319	0.304	0.979
MULTI-LEX, +NEUTRAL	0.731	0.881	0.799	0.817	0.665	0.984
MULTI-NB, -NEUTRAL	0.338	0.441	0.383	0.247	0.236	0.989

	Precision	Recall	Micro F1	Macro F1	Jaccard	Proportionality
MULTI-NB, +NEUTRAL	0.645	0.781	0.707	0.714	0.546	0.989
MULTI-SVM, -NEUTRAL	0.598	0.367	0.455	0.294	0.294	0.996
MULTI-SVM, +NEUTRAL	0.764	0.763	0.763	0.747	0.617	0.996
MULTI-DNN, -NEUTRAL	0.255	0.389	0.308	0.194	0.182	0.938
MULTI-DNN, +NEUTRAL	0.725	0.776	0.750	0.758	0.599	0.950

Figure 10.16 – KWT.M-AR, multiple classifiers, without and with neutral

In every case, both recall and precision go up when we allow neutral as a label.

Looking at the confusion matrices for Naive Bayes (the others are very similar, but Naive Bayes gives the best overall results and hence is the most interesting) is revealing:

	ange	diss	fear	joy	love	opti	pess	reje	trus	--
anger	31	7	0	0	1	0	0	0	0	23
dissat	0	111	0	0	15	0	0	0	0	94
fear	0	2	3	0	1	0	0	0	0	15
joy	0	6	0	56	12	6	0	0	0	66
love	0	2	0	4	327	4	0	0	0	155
optimi	0	2	0	3	0	123	0	0	0	70
pessim	1	2	0	0	1	0	2	0	0	15
reject	0	1	0	0	1	0	0	0	0	6
trust	0	4	0	1	2	0	0	0	26	50
--	65	329	5	182	527	318	6	3	67	0

Figure 10.17 (a) – Confusion matrix, multiclassifiers with NB as a subclassifier, KWT.M-AR, -neutral

	ange	diss	fear	joy	love	opti	pess	reje	trus	neut	--
anger	35	3	0	0	1	0	0	0	0	23	4
dissat	0	118	0	0	12	0	0	0	0	92	4
fear	0	1	3	0	1	0	0	0	0	13	3
joy	0	3	0	58	12	3	0	0	0	67	8
love	0	2	0	2	343	2	0	0	1	138	11
optimi	0	1	0	1	0	126	0	0	0	67	3
pessim	0	2	0	0	0	0	2	0	0	18	0
reject	0	0	0	0	1	0	0	0	0	7	0
trust	0	2	0	0	1	0	0	0	27	54	0
neutra	2	14	0	15	162	64	0	0	5	3521	0
--	60	333	5	165	398	273	6	3	63	378	0

Figure 10.17 (b) – Confusion matrix, multiclassifiers with NB as a subclassifier, KWT.M-AR, -neutral

There are small differences between the scores in the main sections of the two tables – slightly better scores on the diagonal and slightly lower confusion between other labels – but the crucial difference is that, as before, when we do not have **neutral** as a label, we get a large number of false positives. Using **neutral** as a label reduces the number of false positives, even when we have multiple independent classifiers that each make their recommendations without looking at the results of the other classifiers.

Summary

Over the past few chapters, we have looked at a wide range of classifiers and compared their performance on a range of datasets. Now, it is time to reflect on what we have learned. Our final table of the best classifiers for the datasets we have looked at is as follows:

	SVM	SNN	Transformers	MULTI-NB	LEX, MULTI
SEM4-EN	0.845	0.829	* **0.927**		
SEM11-EN	0.224	0.242	0.418	* **0.438**	0.347
WASSA-EN	* **0.770**	0.737	0.753		
CARER-EN	0.770	* **0.820**	0.816		
IMDB-EN	0.736	0.793	* **0.826**		
SEM4-AR	0.514	0.504	* **0.710**		
SEM11-AR	0.216	0.221	0.359	* **0.412**	0.377
KWT.M-AR	0.631	0.028	0.053	0.537	* **0.691**
SEM4-ES	0.412	0.337	* **0.663**		
SEM11-ES	0.226	0.221	* **0.340**	0.294	0.266

Figure 10.18 – Overall best classifiers

Given what we have seen, there are several general observations we can make:

- The difference in performance of the various algorithms is not huge. For each dataset and each configuration of settings, the performances of the best classifiers are very similar, so it may be sensible to take training time as well as scores on the various measures into account when choosing a classifier. In particular, no classifier is the best in every case, and sometimes, the very simple algorithms (LEX and Naive Bayes) are as good as or even better than the more complex ones.

- Datasets where an individual tweet can be assigned zero, one, or more labels are considerably more challenging than ones where each tweet is given exactly one label. There is, in fact, a clear upper bound to the performance of classifiers that do assign exactly one label per tweet to these datasets, and the best results are obtained by reconsidering the way that the classifiers are used. Some classifiers are more suitable than others for this kind of task, and this must be taken into account when you're choosing a classifier for datasets of this kind. Again, it is worth considering training time when choosing this: training a single classifier and then setting N individual thresholds is considerably quicker than training N classifiers, and in at least some cases, the difference in performance is quite small.

- We also investigated a variety of preprocessing steps, including the use of different tokenizers and stemmers, and we looked at using algorithms that can suggest "similar" words to replace words in the target tweets that do not appear in the training data. All these tweaks pay off in some situations and not in others.

We cannot overstate this: **there is no silver bullet**. Different tasks require different classifiers, and you should always investigate a range of classifiers before deciding which one you want to use. In particular, if you are working with a multi-label dataset, you should consider one of the algorithms from this chapter.

When training a classifier, it is a good idea to look at the confusion matrix for the labels that it assigns. Several classifiers, particularly for the datasets with large numbers of zero assignments, produce quite good F1 and Jaccard scores simply by choosing the most common class (that is, **neutral!**) in every case. And when choosing between classifiers, it is a good idea to consider the end task that the classifier is needed for. If what you want is to get a feel for an opinion on some topic, without worrying too much about what individual tweets say about it, then using proportionality as a metric can be a helpful tool. We will use this in the next chapter, where we will look at the link between emotions expressed in tweets and real-life events over a certain period.

Part 4:
Case Study

Part 3 discussed a range of approaches to the task of EA and compared their effectiveness on a set of standard datasets. In this final part, we investigate how well these approaches work on real-world data that is not connected to the standard sets, looking at how changes in the emotions expressed in tweets reflect key real-world events. We also examine how robust the various approaches are when applied to novel data, showing how approaches that work well when the test data is drawn from the same population as the training data can be fragile when applied to novel data.

This part has the following chapter:

- *Chapter 11, Case Study – The Qatar Blockade*

11

Case Study – The Qatar Blockade

In this chapter, we will look at what happens when we apply one of our classifiers to real data that has not been carefully curated, that we don't have a Gold Standard for, and that was not the data that we trained the classifier on. This is a real-life situation. You've trained a classifier; now, you want to use it. How well do the classifiers that we have looked at so far work in this situation? In this chapter, we will compare the output of a classifier on data collected over an extended period with events in an ongoing news story to see whether changes in the pattern of emotions can be linked to developments in the story and whether it is possible to detect long-term changes in public attitudes as well as immediate responses to key events. This analysis will be divided into three parts:

- We will look at how specific events give rise to short-term changes in the pattern of emotions expressed in tweets
- We will investigate whether it is possible to detect long-term changes in public attitudes by tracking trends in the way emotions change over time
- We will look at the proportionality scores for several classifiers over the period to see whether proportionality is a good metric – if the proportionality scores for all our classifiers show the same trends, then it is likely to be safe to use this as a metric when looking for spikes and long-term trends in the emotions expressed by tweets

By the end of this chapter, you will have an appreciation of the extent to which emotion analysis tools can tell you interesting things about public attitudes, even when the data they have been trained on is not closely aligned with the data they are being applied to.

In the previous chapters, we have seen that it is possible to use machine learning techniques to train tools that can assign emotions to tweets. These algorithms can perform well on data where one emotion is assigned to each tweet, with comparatively little variation in performance on this kind of data, but have more difficulty with datasets where zero or more labels can be assigned to a tweet. In the previous chapter, we suggested that proportionality might provide a useful metric for assessing whether a classifier provided a reliable overall view of a set of tweets even when there were large numbers of tweets with zero or multiple labels. Using multiple classifiers with either LEX or Naive Bayes for the base-level classifiers, and using **neutral** as an explicit label, gave acceptable F1 scores and quite high proportionality scores for the key datasets.

However, this analysis was carried out on carefully curated datasets, where all the tweets were rigorously labeled and the training and test sets were drawn from the same overall collection split into sets of 10 separate 90:10 folds. The labels were assigned by multiple annotators, with a label assigned to a tweet if either all the annotators for that tweet agreed or the majority did. The folds were carefully constructed so that the tweets were randomly shuffled before being split into training and test sets, with no overlap between the training and test sets for a given fold and with every tweet appearing exactly once in a test set. Therefore, the results were as reliable as they could be for the relevant data.

They do not, however, tell us how reliable the classifiers will be when applied to data other than the given training and test sets. It is almost inevitable that data collected using other criteria will have different characteristics. The overall distribution of emotions is likely to vary – after all, the obvious application of this technology is to analyze how attitudes to some event vary over time, which will affect, for instance, the prior probabilities used by Naive Bayes and hence is likely to affect the assignment of various labels. Suppose, for instance, that 10% of the tweets in the training set have the label **anger**, but that on some specific day, there is an upswell of anger over some issue and 50% of the tweets that day are angry. Consider some tweets containing the words $T1, ..., Tn$. The formula for Naive Bayes says that $p(anger \mid T1\ \&\ ...\ \&\ Tn) = p(T1 \mid anger) \times ... \times p(Tn \mid anger) \times p(anger)/p(T1) \times ... \times p(Tn)$. The term $p(anger)$ here will come from the original data, where only 10% of the tweets express anger; but on the day in question, 50% do, so this part of the formula will lead to considerable underestimates for this emotion. If $T1, ... Tn$ are words that are linked to **anger**, $p(T1), ..., P(Tn)$ will also probably be underestimates of their frequency on this day, which may to some degree compensate for the error in $p(anger)$, but it is not reasonable to assume that they will exactly compensate for it.

The other algorithms are likely to suffer from similar issues, though it is less easy to see exactly how this will play out for other cases. It is clear, however, that performance on test data extracted from one collection cannot be assumed to carry over to data collected from another.

It is also not feasible to annotate all the new data to check the accuracy of a classifier. The whole point of building a classifier is that we want to collect information from new data that we do not have the resources to label by hand – if we could afford to label it by hand, then we would almost certainly get better results than can be achieved by any classifier since assigning labels to tweets is an essentially subjective task.

The case study

To investigate the links between emotions expressed in texts and real-world events, we needed a set of tweets collected over an extended period, along with a picture of the major events that occurred during that period that could reasonably be expected to affect public opinion. We had two goals here:

- To see whether emotions expressed in tweets could be matched to events that would be likely to affect public opinion

- To see whether classification algorithms that perform well on carefully curated datasets (where the test sets are drawn from the same collection of tweets as the training sets) continue to give good results on brand-new data

So, we carried out a longitudinal test on historic data to see how variations in the daily pattern of assignments matched real-world events. This provides a test of the utility of the overall strategy. If a classifier detects that labels corresponding to some emotion show variations that are explicable in terms of real-world events, then it is reasonable to use it for that kind of task, irrespective of how it performs on the data that it was originally trained and tested on. A classifier that performs well on test data but does not find changes in data collected as events unfold is less useful than one that does not do so well on the tests but does detect changes corresponding to real-world events.

For our test set, we collected around 160,000 Arabic tweets that originated from Qatar between June 2017 and March 2018. This was a period during which Qatar was subject to a blockade by neighboring countries, with decisions made by the Qatari governments and those of its neighbors leading to substantial rapid changes in public opinion. We applied a version of LEX with a tokenizer and stemmer for Arabic and the standard set of 11 emotions (**sadness, anger, fear, disgust, pessimism, love, joy, anticipation, trust, surprise,** and **optimism**) to this data and looked at how the distribution changed in response to these decisions. The results revealed that the residents of Qatar experienced an emotional rollercoaster during the first 9 months of the blockade, with opinions as expressed in tweets following very rapidly after public events. This provides some validation of the use of a classifier trained on a specific dataset as a tool for extracting information from data that may be linguistically different from the training data (the training data for the classifier was general Gulf Arabic, which is not identical to Qatari dialect, even for Modern Standard Arabic) and where the distribution of emotions may be quite different from that in the training data.

Short-term changes

The first thing to look for is correlations between spikes in the various emotions and events in the real world. Even if the actual distribution of labels is less than 100% accurate, if divergences from the baseline scores can be shown to correspond to real-world events, then the tool can be used to track public opinion. Being able to tell that people are angrier or more fearful today than they were yesterday is probably as useful as knowing that 56.7% of today's tweets are angry where the level is usually 43.6% – messages on social media are, after all, not an accurate picture of public opinion in general. Twitter and similar outlets are echo chambers that tend to overestimate the strength of feeling in the general population. If 56.7% of tweets about some topic are angry, about 5% of the general population are likely mildly annoyed about it. But if twice as many tweets are angry about it today compared to yesterday, then the general population may well be twice as angry about it today than it was yesterday.

Due to this, we looked for spikes in positive and negative sentiments and mapped them to the most relevant news in Qatar on that day. To identify the most relevant news, we looked at Google News (news.google.com) and used Google's sorting feature to identify the most important blockade event of the day based on news relevance. We also looked at Al Jazeera's dedicated page (https://www.aljazeera.com/news/2018/8/2/qatar-gulf-crisis-all-the-latest-updates) on events related to the blockade to identify the main events of the day. Our results showed that the spikes in sentiments that our algorithm identified from the collected tweets corresponded to significant blockade-related events, simultaneously confirming that the results that were obtained by controlled testing in the SemEval experiments transfer effectively to real-world scenarios for at least some classifiers and allowing us to probe the way that people reacted to these events.

Figure 11.1 shows a spike in optimism and a small drop in pessimism on August 17, 2017. The main event from the news outlook was that Saudi Arabia granted Qatari pilgrims permission to perform Hajj, which indicates a lessening of tension between the two countries. Accordingly, our data showed a spike in **optimism** (from 7% of tweets showing optimistic sentiments to 22%) and a decline in **pessimism** (from 5% to 2%). Note that while the change from 7% to 22% looks bigger than the change from 5% to 2%, they are both roughly threefold changes, which is reasonable given that these two are direct opposites. The spike is very short-lived, with both emotions returning to their baseline levels after a couple of days. The decline in **optimism** is slower than the initial spike, probably reflecting the fact that the initial tweets were retweeted and commented on so that the emotions that they expressed continue to be present even after the significance of the actual event has faded (the **echo chamber** effect):

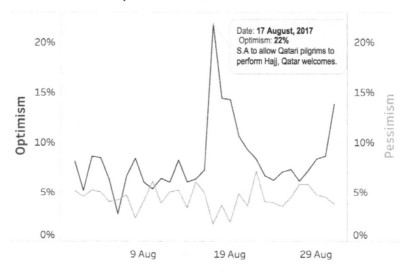

Figure 11.1 – Change of sentiments due to Saudi Arabia allowing pilgrims to perform Hajj

Another example of a radical change in sentiment (July 3) relates to the change of position of the US government concerning Qatar. More specifically, President Trump reviewed his earlier position suggesting that Qatar supports terrorism and said that Qatar is a partner in fighting terrorism and encouraged GCC unity. Harmoniously, the sentiments associated with **joy** spiked from 7% to 20%, while **sadness** declined from 4% to 2% (see *Figure 11.2*). A similar radical change occurred on July 9, when the chief prosecutor of the International Criminal Court praised Qatar and regretted the actions of the Quartet. Simultaneously joyful tweets increased to 14% and sad tweets declined to 2%. Again, the spikes are short-lived and are slightly steeper on the way up than on the way down, and the percentage changes in the upward and downward directions are similar (joy goes up between two- and three-fold, sadness goes down two-fold):

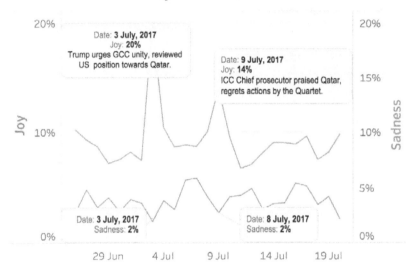

Figure 11.2 – Change of sentiments due to Trump's review of
position and the ICC chief prosecutor's comments

In these cases, the spike in one emotion (**optimism, joy**) was matched by a proportionally similar drop in the opposite emotion (**pessimism, sadness**). This does not always happen. If we look at two days when there is a substantial spike in fear, we will find that there is also a spike in one of the positive emotions:

- **November 1, 2017**: This day was observed to be the most fearful day for the residents of Qatar when 33% of tweets exhibited fearful sentiments (see *Figure 11.3*). It was when Bahrain imposed entry visas on Qatar nationals and residents, which divided many families that had members in both counties.

- **November 4, 2017**: This day was observed to be the third most fearful day for the residents of Qatar when 28% of tweets exhibited fearful sentiments (see *Figures 11.3* and *11.4*). It was when the foreign ministers of Saudi Arabia, Bahrain, UAE, and Egypt met in Abu Dhabi and reiterated freezing the membership of Qatar at the Gulf Cooperation Council.

Figure 11.3 shows that Qatari residents expressed **love** simultaneously with **fear** on November 1 and 4. It is hard to be sure about how to interpret this, especially given the large spike in **love** on October 28, which corresponds to a drop in **fear**. There are several possible explanations: it may be that there was some other significant event around this time that independently led to an increase in tweets expressing **love**; it may be a consequence of the echo-chamber effect, though that seems unlikely since the initial spike on October 28 died away by October 31; or it may be that the rise in tweets expressing **fear** leads directly to a rise in ones expressing **love** (possibly, in fact, to tweets expressing both at the same time) as people contact their loved ones in times of stress. Whatever the underlying reason, this figure shows that conflicting emotions can interact in surprising ways:

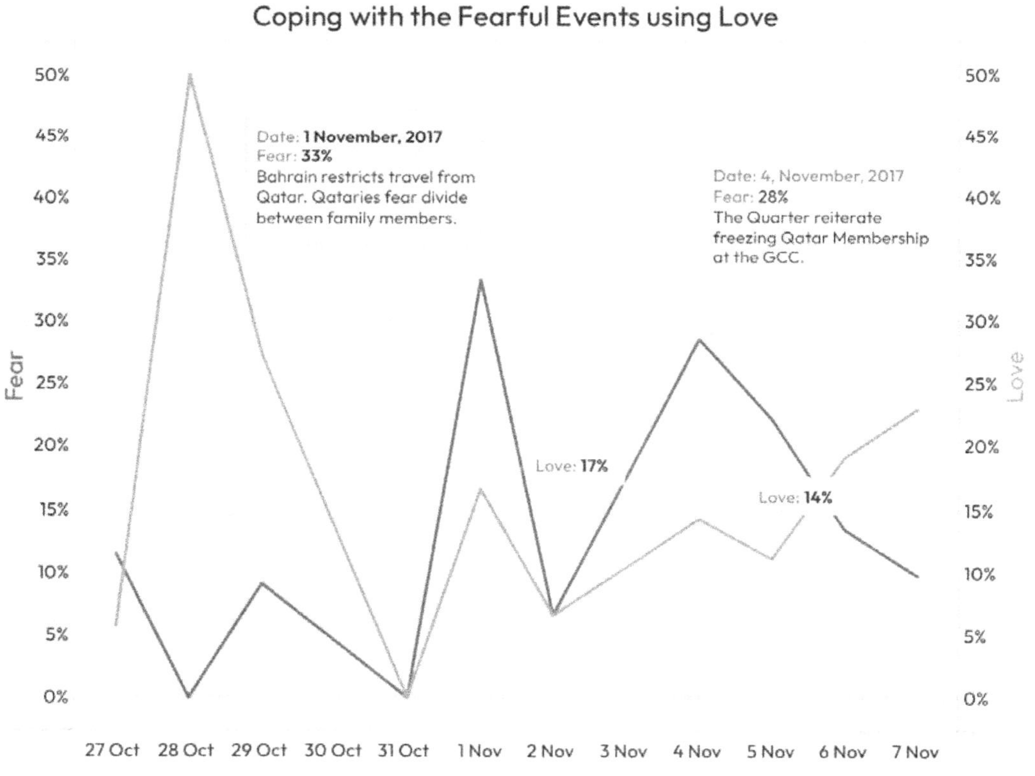

Figure 11.3 – Fear and love cooccurring

In addition to the spikes in tweets expressing **love** over this period, Qatari residents also expressed **joy** at the same time as they expressed the most **fear**:

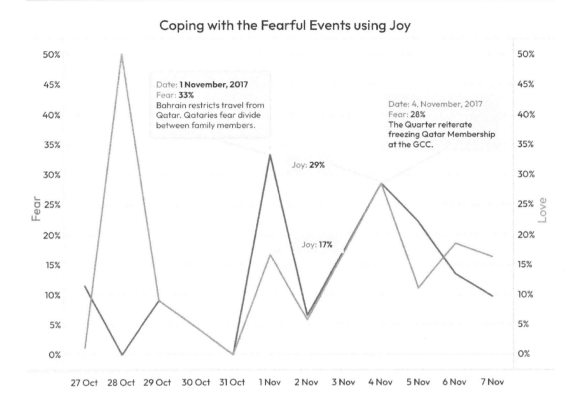

Figure 11.4 – Fear and joy cooccurring

The spikes in **joy** in *Figure 11.4* match those in love from the previous figure, again including spikes in **joy** alongside the spikes in **fear**. **love** continues to increase up to November 7, where **joy** tails off at this point, which may again be an echo-chamber effect. What is clear is that, unsurprisingly, major real-world events are followed very rapidly by spikes in the emotions expressed in tweets, though the emotions that are affected can be more surprising and can occur in surprising combinations. Interpreting exactly what is going on may require detailed analysis (in the same way that gross measures of accuracy such as F1-measure and proportionality may require detailed analysis through finer-grained tools such as confusion matrices), but changes in the distribution of emotions in tweets do indicate changes in public attitudes.

Long-term changes

Significant events, then, produce spikes in the emotions expressed on social media. This is hardly surprising, but it is worth confirming that even quite simple classification algorithms can detect these spikes and that, sometimes, they occur in unexpected combinations. What about long-term trends?

It is harder to interpret these because they do not correspond to easily identifiable changes in the real world. The following figure shows general trends over the nine months of the blockade. Interpreting these is a challenge – do they track the progress of the political situation, or do they reflect a general weary acceptance of a situation that has not changed very much?

These figures show eight of the emotions in matched pairs (**anticipation**, **trust**, and **surprise** tend to have low scores and not to change very much, either in response to specific events or over the long term, so we have omitted them). The given pairs seem reasonable – disgust and fear seem likely to form a matched pair; joy versus sadness, optimism versus pessimism, and anger versus love seem likely to behave as opposites – though as we have seen, opposites can show spikes at the same time, and it may be that pairing them off differently would give us a different overall picture:

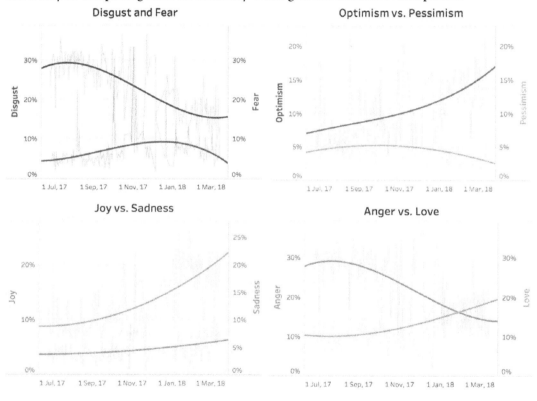

Figure 11.5 – Adaption over an extended period?

The trend lines in these figures are heavily smoothed – the data, as discussed previously, contains very large spikes, and fitting a trend line that obscures these may also obscure other gentler changes. Nonetheless, it is worth trying to see whether any general lessons can be learned from them.

It does seem that there is a general upward trend in the positive emotions – optimism, joy, and love all increase fairly steadily over the period – and a downward trend in the negative ones, with anger and pessimism both falling steadily and disgust and fear both decreasing slightly. Exactly how to interpret this is unclear. It could be that the overall situation was improving over the period covered by the dataset and that these trends are simply a reasonable response to the changes in the political situation. Alternatively, it could reflect the fact that people adjust to whatever situation they find themselves in, so over a period of stress and anxiety, their attitude to the situation becomes more relaxed, and positive emotions simply become more common.

The most surprising thing in this figure is that joy and sadness both show an increase toward the end of the period. It is hard to see why this would be the case – it cannot easily be explained in terms of growing adaptation to an unchanging situation, but at the same time, it is hard to see what changes in the situation could lead to an increase in both joy and sadness. Looking at trends over an extended period can be revealing, but it can also be confusing!

Proportionality revisited

The preceding curves were obtained by running the multi-LEX classifier on the date-stamped tweets about the Qatar blockade. In the previous chapter, we looked at the notion that proportionality might provide a useful measure of how accurately a classifier that assigned a large number of false positives or false negatives might nonetheless provide an accurate general picture, even if its accuracy on individual tweets was flawed. We can approach this question by plotting the outputs of a range of different classifiers on the individual emotions: if these are generally similar, then we can at least hope that the places where they show peaks and troughs are reasonably reliable.

Recall that the F1 and proportionality scores for the various classifiers, when trained and tested using 10-fold cross-validation on the SEM11-AR datasets, were as follows:

	DNN	LEX	MULTI-DNN	MULTI-LEX	MULTI-NB	MULTI-SVM	NB	SVM
SEM11-AR	0.360 (0.742)	0.549 (0.940)	0.415 (0.971)	0.520 (0.869)	0.543 (0.996)	0.321 (0.878)	0.413 (0.770)	0.379 (0.817)

Figure 11.6 – F1 and proportionality for a range of classifiers on SEM11-AR

In the following figure, we have plotted the proportional scores for various emotions obtained by LEX, MULTI-LEX, and MULTI-NB, which are the classifiers with the best F1, scores over the period – that is, what proportion of the tweets at each date were labeled with the given emotion. Some of the data around the end of October 2017 is missing, and the plots are erratic over this period, but in general, there is a close correspondence between the plots for these three classifiers:

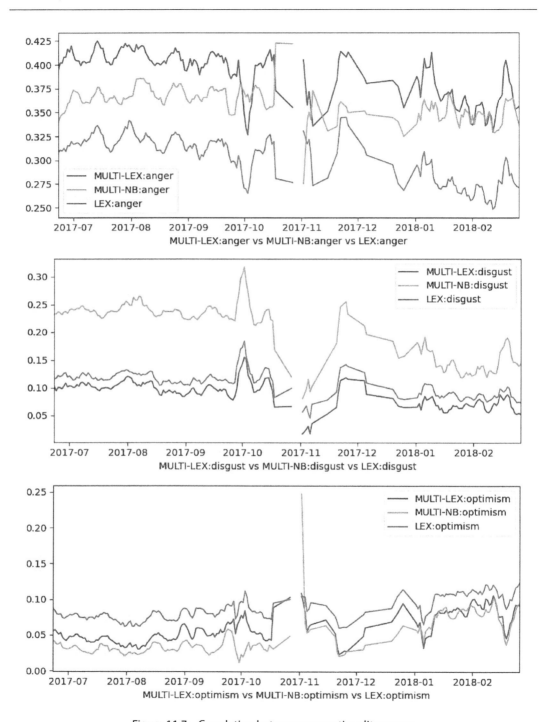

Figure 11.7 – Correlation between proportionality scores

The other plots for these classifiers are similar, with closely matching shapes, albeit sometimes with one lower than the other. It is inevitable that if one classifier assigns a higher proportion of tweets to a specific emotion than the others, then it will assign a lower proportion to another – MULTI-NB assigns more tweets to disgust and pessimism than the other two, and hence it has to assign fewer to the other labels. This also explains why all three have troughs for both joy and sadness around the beginning of October 2017 – they all have large peaks for disgust and pessimism at this point, and there simply is no room for either sadness or joy.

For these classifiers to follow each other as closely as they do, they must be tracking something similar. Are they tracking the proportion of tweets that express each emotion day by day, or are they just tracking the same words? They are all lexicon-based, and LEX and MULTI-LEX collect their lexicons in much the same way, so it seems very likely that they are tracking words. But the fact that we can correlate the major peaks to specific blockade-related events suggests that the words they are paying attention to correspond to emotions – that is, they are tracking emotions. By looking at the words that are most strongly linked to **anger** and **joy** in these classifiers, they do look like words that express these emotions (the translations are taken word by word from Google Translate, so they might be a bit strange).

ANGER

MULTI-LEX

الغضب (anger) الكهرب (electrification) المسلمين (Muslims) 😡 (😡) حسبنا (we counted) ونعم (and yes) استياء (discontent) خيانة (betrayal) الوكيل (agent)

LEX

حقير (intimidation) وترهيب (and yes) ونعم (؎‎) (؎‎) 😡 (😡) (electrification) الكهرب (anger) الغضب (despicable) جاب (gap) نرفزة (willies)

MULTI-NB

(grouchy) حانق (and yes) ونعم (agent) الوكيل (willies) نرفزة (ugliness) قبحهم (😡) 😡 (anger) غضب (😡) 😡 الدول (countries) غضبي (my anger)

JOY

MULTI-LEX

وسعاده (disturb) يعكرها (💗) 💗 (💗) 💗 (🥰) (😊) (😊) 😊 (advertisement) اعلان (🙆) 🙆 (happy) مبسوط(happiness)

LEX

السعادة# (#the_wind_of_madam) ريح_المدام# (joy) الفرحه (🐝) (🐝) joy_of_hope# (#joy_of_hope) بهجة_أمل# (🐝) (🐝) مبسوط (happy) ( ) (#happiness) happiness#

MULTI-NB

سعيد (advertisement) اعلان (💚) (💚) happiness# (#happiness) السعادة# joy_of_hope# (#joy_of_hope) بهجة_أمل# (general) عام (happy) يعكرها (disturb) 💔 (💔) 💔 (💔)

There are several things to note here:

- Emojis appear quite high on the list of emotion markers. This really should not be surprising since that is exactly what emojis are for, but it is at least interesting to note that they do appear in the top 10 words for both sentiments for all the classifiers.

- A lot of words are shared by the three classifiers, though they are not always ranked the same. However, some words are emotion-bearing that are found by one but not the others (استياء (discontent), حانق (grouchy)), so they are not just finding the same sets.

- Some words are not emotion-bearing – المسلمين (Muslims) seems unlikely to be a term for expressing anger, but if there are a large number of angry tweets about the way that Muslims are treated, then this word will come to be associated with anger.

So, we have several independent ways of checking that classifiers are doing what they are supposed to do in addition to re-annotating all the data:

- If several classifiers assign the same peaks and troughs, they are likely to be identifying the same patterns in the text

- If these peaks and troughs can be aligned with external events, then the patterns probably do correspond to emotions

- If the words and emojis that are strongly linked to an emotion include words that would be expected to express that emotion, then the outputs probably do correspond to the given emotions

Not all classifiers behave as nicely as this. If we add, for instance, SVM and simple Naive Bayes to the mix, we get the following:

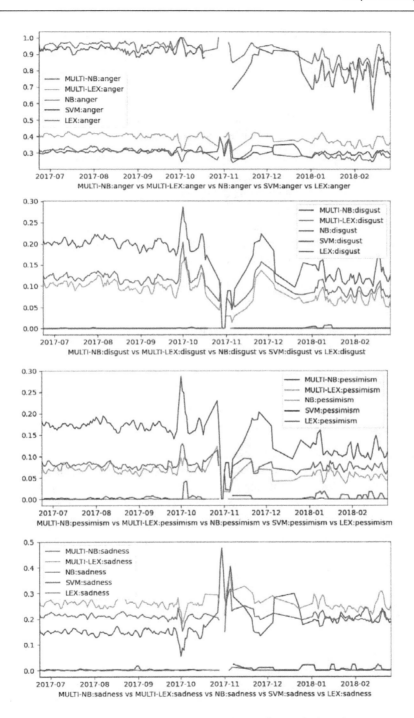

Figure 11.8 – Naive Bayes and SVM don't correlate with the others

What has happened here is that the training of both Naive Bayes and SVM is dominated by the first label that is assigned to each tweet. So, if a tweet is assigned anger and disgust, it is simply treated as an instance of anger since there is no scope for assigning multiple labels **during training** for these classifiers, even if it is possible to assign thresholds to allow multiple labels in the test/application data. So, we get very high scores for **anger** and very low ones for other negative emotions. There are some peaks and troughs in roughly the right places for these classifiers, but they are swamped by the fact that they both assign anger to 90% or more of all tweets and less than 5% to all the other negative emotions.

A number of the other classifiers (DNN, SVM) simply assign everything to neutral, which shows up as a flat line in every plot. This is despite the fact that they score moderately well on the test data (which is drawn from the same source as the training data, though of course the two are kept apart on each fold). This suggests that these classifiers are more easily influenced by properties of the training data that are specific to the way it was obtained and presented, rather than just to the gross distribution of words. In a sense, what makes them perform well in the original experiments – namely that they are sensitive to things other than the raw word counts – is exactly what makes them less robust when applied to new data.

The two main lessons from this case study are as follows:

- Looking at longitudinal data can be extremely revealing. By plotting the proportion of tweets that are assigned different labels and comparing these plots to external events and each other, we can obtain information about their reliability as indicators of emotions in tweets drawn from entirely new sources. This is not easily available if we just look at a single source. When testing with single sources, we obtained very high scores for classifiers that did not transfer well to the new data, despite the care that we took to carry out 10-fold cross-validation with properly separated training and test sets.

- The very high scores that were obtained by the more sophisticated classifiers fell away sharply when they were applied to the new data. It seems likely that these classifiers were responding to characteristics of the original data that are not replicated in the new material. The simple classifiers, which rely very heavily on simple statistics about the probability of a particular word being linked to a particular emotion, are more robust since that is all that they are sensitive to and that is typically carried over into new text types.

Let's summarize everything we've covered so far.

Summary

In the previous chapters, we looked at the performance of a collection of classifiers on a range of datasets, with datasets with varying numbers of emotions, varying sizes, and varying kinds of text and, most importantly, with some datasets that assigned exactly one label to each tweet and some that allowed zero or more labels per tweet. The conclusion at the end of *Chapter 10, Multiclassifier* was that "different tasks require different classifiers." This holds even more strongly now that we have tried our classifiers on data that does not match the data they were trained on, with the DNN and SVM classifiers that performed well on some of the previous datasets doing extremely poorly on the case study data.

These two classifiers seem to have assigned **neutral** to almost all the tweets in this dataset. This seems likely because the clues that these classifiers are sensitive to are missing from, or at any rate rare in, the data, and hence they are not assigning any labels. It looks as though these classifiers assign very strong weights to specific cues, and if those cues are not present in the data that has been collected from different sources or following different guidelines, then the classifiers cannot make use of the information that *is* present.

It is, of course, difficult to assess the performance of data for which you do not have a Gold Standard. It is infeasible to construct a fresh Gold Standard every time you want to try your classifier on a new dataset – the data used in this case study, for instance, contains 160K tweets, and annotating all of these would be an extremely time-consuming task. Given that we do not have a Gold Standard for this data, how can we be sure that DNN and SVM are not correct in deciding that virtually none of the tweets in it express any emotion?

We have two checks on this:

- The fact that the other classifiers shadow each very closely suggests that they are indeed tracking something – it would be beyond coincidence that they all show peaks and troughs at the same points.

- The correlation between the major peaks and troughs and real-world events relating to the blockade further suggests that what they are tracking is public opinion. Again, it would be beyond coincidence that the largest peaks in **fear** occur following events such as the ban on entry visas to Bahrain and the meeting at which Qatar's membership of the Gulf Cooperation Council was frozen, and the largest peaks in **joy** follow events such as permission being granted for pilgrims to perform Hajj.

So, yet again, you can see that you should be wary of assuming that a classifier that performs well on some dataset will perform equally well on another. Always, always, always try out different classifiers, with different settings, and make your own decision about which works best for your task on your data.

The correlation between the scores for the various classifiers does, however, also suggest a further strategy: combine them. There are several ensemble learning strategies for using the results of a combination of classifiers – for example, by assigning a label if the majority of classifiers in the ensemble recommend assigning it, by assigning a label if the sum of the individual scores for that label exceeds some threshold, or even by training a new classifier whose input is the predictions of the members of the ensemble. Just as there is a wide range of classifiers to choose from, there is also a wide range of strategies for combining the results of classifiers. So, again, you should try different ensemble strategies and don't believe what people say about their favorites.

Always, always, always, try out different classifiers, with different settings, and make your own decision about which works best for your task on your data.

Index

Packtpub.com

Subscribe to our online digital library for full access to over 7,000 books and videos, as well as industry leading tools to help you plan your personal development and advance your career. For more information, please visit our website.

Why subscribe?

- Spend less time learning and more time coding with practical eBooks and Videos from over 4,000 industry professionals
- Improve your learning with Skill Plans built especially for you
- Get a free eBook or video every month
- Fully searchable for easy access to vital information
- Copy and paste, print, and bookmark content

Did you know that Packt offers eBook versions of every book published, with PDF and ePub files available? You can upgrade to the eBook version at packtpub.com and as a print book customer, you are entitled to a discount on the eBook copy. Get in touch with us at customercare@packtpub.com for more details.

At www.packtpub.com, you can also read a collection of free technical articles, sign up for a range of free newsletters, and receive exclusive discounts and offers on Packt books and eBooks.

Other Books You May Enjoy

If you enjoyed this book, you may be interested in these other books by Packt:

Machine Learning with R - Fourth Edition

Brett Lantz

ISBN: 978-1-80107-132-1

- Learn the end-to-end process of machine learning from raw data to implementation
- Classify important outcomes using nearest neighbor and Bayesian methods
- Predict future events using decision trees, rules, and support vector machines
- Forecast numeric data and estimate financial values using regression methods
- Model complex processes with artificial neural networks
- Prepare, transform, and clean data using the tidyverse
- Evaluate your models and improve their performance
- Connect R to SQL databases and emerging big data technologies such as Spark, Hadoop, H2O, and TensorFlow

Machine Learning in Microservices

Mohamed Abouahmed, Omar Ahmed

ISBN: 978-1-80461-774-8

- Recognize the importance of MSA and ML and deploy both technologies in enterprise systems
- Explore MSA enterprise systems and their general practical challenges
- Discover how to design and develop microservices architecture
- Understand the different AI algorithms, types, and models and how they can be applied to MSA
- Identify and overcome common MSA deployment challenges using AI and ML algorithms
- Explore general open source and commercial tools commonly used in MSA enterprise systems

Packt is searching for authors like you

If you're interested in becoming an author for Packt, please visit `authors.packtpub.com` and apply today. We have worked with thousands of developers and tech professionals, just like you, to help them share their insight with the global tech community. You can make a general application, apply for a specific hot topic that we are recruiting an author for, or submit your own idea.

Share Your Thoughts

Now you've finished *Machine Learning for Emotion Analysis in Python*, we'd love to hear your thoughts! Scan the QR code below to go straight to the Amazon review page for this book and share your feedback or leave a review on the site that you purchased it from.

`https://packt.link/r/1-803-24068-7`

Your review is important to us and the tech community and will help us make sure we're delivering excellent quality content.

Download a free PDF copy of this book

Thanks for purchasing this book!

Do you like to read on the go but are unable to carry your print books everywhere?

Is your eBook purchase not compatible with the device of your choice?

Don't worry, now with every Packt book you get a DRM-free PDF version of that book at no cost.

Read anywhere, any place, on any device. Search, copy, and paste code from your favorite technical books directly into your application.

The perks don't stop there, you can get exclusive access to discounts, newsletters, and great free content in your inbox daily

Follow these simple steps to get the benefits:

1. Scan the QR code or visit the link below

https://packt.link/free-ebook/9781803240688

2. Submit your proof of purchase
3. That's it! We'll send your free PDF and other benefits to your email directly

www.ingramcontent.com/pod-product-compliance
Lightning Source LLC
Chambersburg PA
CBHW080622060326
40690CB00021B/4779